An OPUS book

THE ENGLISH LANGUAGE

OPUS General Editors

Keith Thomas
Alan Ryan
Peter Medawar

The
English Language

ROBERT BURCHFIELD

Oxford   New York
OXFORD UNIVERSITY PRESS
1985

Oxford University Press, Walton Street, Oxford OX2 6DP

London New York Toronto
Delhi Bombay Calcutta Madras Karachi
Kuala Lumpur Singapore Hong Kong Tokyo
Nairobi Dar es Salaam Cape Town
Melbourne Auckland
and associated companies in
Beirut Berlin Ibadan Mexico City Nicosia

Oxford is a trade mark of Oxford University Press

British Library Cataloguing in Publication Data
Burchfield, Robert W.
The English language.—(OPUS)
1. English language
I. Title II. Series
420 PE1072
ISBN 0-19-219173-X

Library of Congress Cataloging in Publication Data
Burchfield, R. W.
The English language.
(An Opus book)
Bibliography: p. 187
Includes index.
1. English language. I. Title. II. Series: OPUS.
PE1072.B79 1985 420'.9 84-9677
ISBN 0-19-219173-X

Printed in Great Britain
at the University Press, Oxford
by David Stanford
Printer to the University

For Margaret Knight

Preface

In 1937 I acquired a copy of Logan Pearsall Smith's book *The English Language* (first published in 1912) and the fly-leaf shows that I was then in Form G4 at Wanganui Technical College in New Zealand. I was 14, and it was the first book on the history and nature of the English language that I had encountered. I could scarcely have known that it would turn out, after an interval of nearly half a century, that I would write a book on the same subject myself.

Logan Pearsall Smith's work became an OPUS book in 1966. It was still a valuable introduction to the subject. But the time has now come to give a more up-to-date account of the nature, origin, and development of the language.

The English language remains a central subject in schools and universities. Despite the fact that it seems to be less conscientiously taught and less successfully mastered by many people than once was the case, its inner power remains undisturbed. In its spoken form, in a variety of regional accents, it remains an effective instrument for the communication of ideas, for the conduct of business and of ceremonies, and for the small civilities of life. In its written form it retains the power, in the hands of our best writers, to reach standards as high as those set by the great writers of the past—Ælfric, Chaucer, Shakespeare, Donne, Milton, Johnson, Jane Austen, Macaulay, Ruskin, and so many others.

This book is offered to the new generation of students at schools and universities, and to people in other walks of life, who wish to acquire a knowledge of the pedigree and credentials of their own language. It is not a textbook—it is too short to be that. Here and there it departs from received opinions, but there was not space to argue these departures if the book was to remain in proportion. These are revolutionary times and we are passing into an age in which the printed word on paper is threatened by the summoning of dismembered segments of printed texts on to screens. It is also a time when the views and techniques of post-structuralists, transformational grammarians, and reductivists of one type or another are knocking the humanity out of one of our greatest national heritages. Time will show how the everlasting contest between the old techniques and the new will resolve itself. The passage of time will also doubtless reveal which new parcels of the language are about to become subject to slow but irreversible change while the core remains substantially intact.

Debts accumulate as one writes a book: to colleagues many years ago in Wellington, especially Professor P. S. Ardern, and in Oxford, especially Dr C. T. Onions; to many of my lexicographical colleagues in the Oxford English Dictionary Department, especially Mrs L. S. Burnett, Ms K. H. Emms, Miss E. M. Knowles, J. A. Simpson, and E. S. C. Weiner; to my secretary, Miss K. C. E. Vines; and to my wife, Elizabeth Knight. Valuable comments on the typescript were made by Keith Thomas, one of the General Editors of OPUS books, and by two OUP editors, Henry Hardy and David Attwooll. The typescript was copy-edited by D. J. Edmonds. The book is the better for their attention and I am grateful to them all. For the weaknesses that remain I must of course accept full responsibility.

R. W. B.

Sutton Courtenay, Oxfordshire
December 1983

Contents

List of Illustrations

The publishers wish to express their gratitude to the following for permission to reproduce material: Messrs E. J. Brill for the illustration on p. 102; and The Athlone Press for that on p. 129.

Abbreviations

a.	*ante* (before)
Anglo-Lat.	Anglo-Latin
c.	*circa* (about)
ELT	English Language Teaching
L., Lat.	Latin
ME.	Middle English
medL.	medieval Latin
modE.	modern English
modF.	modern French
OE.	Old English
OED	*Oxford English Dictionary*
OF.	Old French
ON.	Old Norse
pa.t.	past tense
RP	Received Pronunciation
*	used in etymologies to indicate a form not recorded but merely inferred. Also used to indicate unacceptable constructions in modern English.
†	obsolete

Phonetic Symbols

Symbols of the International Phonetic Alphabet used in this book

Consonants

b	*as in* bat		ŋg	*as in* finger
tʃ	chin		p	pet
d	dog		r	rat
ð	then		s	sip
f	fat		ʃ	ship
g	go		t	tip
h	hat		θ	thin
dʒ	jam		v	van
k	kit		w	win
l	lot		j	yet
m	mat		z	zip
n	net		ʒ	vision
ŋ	sing		x	loch

Vowels

eɪ	*as in* fate		ɑɪə(r)	*as in* fire
æ	fat		əʊ	goat
ə	*a*go, tok*e*n		ɒ	got
ɑː	bah		ɔɪ	boil
eə(r)	fare		uː	boot
ɑ(r)	far		ʊ	book
ɔː	paw		ʊə(r)	poor
iː	meet		ɔ(r)	port
ɛ	met		aʊ	brow
ɪə(r)	fear		aʊə(r)	sour
ɜː(r)	fur		ju	due
ɑɪ	bite		ʌ	dug
ɪ	bit		jʊə(r)	pure

In the IPA system the symbol : denotes length.

The primary stress of a word is shown by the symbol ' placed before the stressed syllable, e.g. /'əʊtkeɪk/ oatcake. Slashes are conventionally printed at the beginning and end of IPA pronunciations.

Language is a labyrinth of paths. You approach from *one* side and know your way about; you approach the same place from another side and no longer know your way about.

Ludwig Wittgenstein, *Philosophical Investigations* (1953), para. 203

Language . . . is the instrument of all our distinctively human development, of everything in which we go beyond the other animals.

I. A. Richards, *The Philosophy of Rhetoric* (1936), p. 131

Chaucer, Henry James and, very humbly, myself are practising the same art. Miss Stein is not. She is outside the world-order in which words have a precise and ascertainable meaning and sentences a logical structure.

Evelyn Waugh, letter of 27 December 1945, in *Letters*, edited by Mark Amory (1980), p. 215

Language, eight-armed, problematic, demiurgic, infinitely entrailed, must be honoured. Its riddling, jokey, mischievous, metaphoric, flawed, lapsible, parapraxic life must not be repressed, but tolerated, pleasured, submitted to, enjoyed, and so revealed for what it is.

Galen Strawson in *Quarto*, March 1982, p. 17

Which words
Will come through air unbent,
Saying, so to say, only what
they mean?

Peter Porter in *Times Literary Supplement*, 16 July 1982, p. 771

1

Some Preliminary Considerations

A man that seeketh precise truth, had need to remember
what every name he uses stands for; and to place it
accordingly; or else he will find himselfe entangled in
words, as a bird in lime-twiggs; the more he struggles, the
more belimed.

Thomas Hobbes, *Leviathan* (1651), I. iv. 15

Hobbes pointed out that in Geometry 'men begin at settling the
significations of their words . . . and place them at the beginning of
their reckoning'. What is necessary in Geometry is just as necessary in a book about the English language. I shall therefore begin
this book by setting down some of the general propositions that
govern the mode and manner of the later chapters.

Hobbes's view (ibid. 12) that 'the generall use of Speech, is to
transferre our Mentall Discourse, into Verbal; or the Trayne of
our Thoughts, into a Trayne of Words' is a useful starting-point
for any discussion about the nature of language. History shows
that men have endeavoured, with extraordinary unevenness and
sometimes at great intervals of time, to represent 'trains of words'
in a written form for greater convenience, instruction, or imaginative enjoyment.

Systems of words have been established in societies throughout
the world, all of them infinitely complex even when seemingly
simple. No tribe, however primitive in its social arrangements,
lacks a distinct and distinguishable language of great complexity
and subtlety. Some of these systems of words can be shown to be
closely related, others more distantly, but the great majority stand
at such remove, one from another, that it is impossible to
establish links.

The ability to acquire a system of words and to use it as a means
of communication is restricted to human beings. Animals of the
same kind communicate with one another but not by means of
words.

Most societies in the world have devised complicated sets of signs to set down the words and sentences they use in speech. The written systems display various degrees of formalization and artificiality. These graphic systems are themselves subject to intermittent change, and there are many detailed substitutions as time goes by.

These linguistic systems are each so complex that they cannot be completely analysed even by the greatest grammarians, lexicographers, and philosophers. We must necessarily accept as working hypotheses the incomplete analyses that exist already or that come into being during our lifetimes.

The members of a given society, even those who are competent and fluent speakers of their language, paradoxically have little formal ability to analyse their own language without instruction. The pursuit of learning in itself, unless it is focused on linguistic analysis and on the history of the language in question, leaves a person poorly equipped to make any but prejudiced judgements about the nature and importance of developments in the language in his own time.

The origin of language is unknown and all theories about this problem are spurious. No languageless human society has ever been discovered on the earth. The faculty of speech therefore precedes recorded history and it is unhelpful to speculate about the circumstances of its origin. The doctrine of Hobbes, and of many Christians, that 'all this language gotten, and augmented by Adam and his posterity, was again lost at the tower of Babel, when by the hand of God, every man was stricken for his rebellion, with an oblivion of his former language' (ibid. 12) is an engaging but unacceptable myth.

A primary cause of language change lies in the imprecision of individual sounds. Identifiable sounds, approximately equal in tone, nature, and volume, are perceived by members of a given society as being identical though they are not. Geographical separation of societies, necessarily involving a physical distancing of systems of sound, produces further dissimilarities and dislocations in the whole system. The permanent migration of the speakers of a given language abroad is always the first step in the establishment in due course of a new mode of speech, increasingly dissimilar from that of the home country, and in due course unintelligible.

Other primary causes of language change lie deeply embedded in the social and political development of each society. Social distinctions and political power are of primary importance in language.

Literary forms of English show degrees of nobility, competence, and inventiveness unmatched by everyday speech and by most academic and journalistic writing. Modern linguistic scholars, particularly those who attempt to describe English grammar and vocabulary mainly from their own intuitions and from recorded everyday speech, without reference to the work of poets and novelists, and with sparse reference to the past, are describing an amputated and artificial system. Such scholars are reacting, understandably, against older, somewhat discredited, methods. Dr Johnson was wrong when he said that the diction of 'the laborious and mercantile part of the people, . . . which is always in a state of increase or decay, cannot be regarded as any part of the durable materials of a language, and therefore must be suffered to perish with other things unworthy of preservation'. Colin McCabe was right—or partially right—to assert that 'the eighteenth-century grammars, and more importantly the views of language and class which underpinned them, continue to terrorize English speech'.[1] The influence of eighteenth-century grammars has indeed been pernicious in many respects. But if McCabe's post-structuralist views were to prevail, some new and even more unacceptable views of language and class would place grave restrictions on (that is, terrorize) English speech.

The work of Ludwig Wittgenstein (in philosophy) and of Ferdinand de Saussure (in linguistics) has been of fundamental importance. Other scholars, for example M. Bréal,[2] Leonard Bloomfield, and A. Martinet, have made signal contributions at a more practical level. But since 1945 linguistics as a subject has been riven and dismembered by disastrous civil wars between eminent scholars, most of them still unresolved, and the theoretical outlook is gloomy.

*

These are general propositions about language and about linguistic evolution. It seems desirable to set down a set of similar propositions about the English language and its evolution before moving on to the main task.

The English language, in its earliest period, was spoken by a few thousand people, most of them illiterate, who crossed the English Channel from Angeln in Schleswig and from the Cimbric peninsula in (modern) Holstein in primitive ships from the fifth century onward and gradually wrested political power from the earlier Celtic inhabitants of the British Isles. The subjugation of the Celtic inhabitants released very few words from their languages into Anglo-Saxon, and no new sounds or grammatical constructions. But the Anglo-Saxons adopted a great many of their place-names.

The formal language of the Anglo-Saxons was fairly amply recorded by their priests and poets, and we know, by comparing it with continental records of the earliest period, that it was a richly endowed language of the Germanic family. Old English (as the language up to 1066 is usually called)[3] possessed a set of inflexions more complicated by far than our own, but less complicated than those of Greek or Latin. Its grammatical system enabled Old English writers to construct sentences of great power and diversity, but with the emphasis on different elements from those of the present day, especially in the way verbs and prepositions were used.

The scholars and priests who adapted the roman alphabet to their own modes of speech did not regard it as part of their duty to set down the everyday spoken form of the language, except, for example, the reduced forms of the third person present indicative of verbs (e.g. *bint* as well as *bindeþ* 'he binds'). We can only assume, from later developments, that the spoken language was much more fluid and variegated than the surviving written records show.

Conventional views about the pronunciation of Old English are based on reasonable assumptions from the way words were spelt. In the nature of things they are not verifiable by any other means, though it seems desirable to posit the existence of a type of speech called Vulgar Old English just as Romance etymologists posit the existence of Vulgar Latin as a 'debased' or informal variety of Classical Latin. This Vulgar Old English, an unrecorded species of ancient spoken English, must have been substantially different from the language recorded by the scribes, just as transcripts of unscripted and unrehearsed modern spoken English differ quite radically from rule-governed modern written English.

For convenience, and often coincidentally for reasons of political power, a form of English has in most centuries (but not always) been regarded as being the 'received' form. The majority of Anglo-Saxon manuscripts, especially the later ones, were written in a *Schriftsprache* (standardized written variety) representing the dialect of a school of scribes in Winchester and thereabouts. In later centuries the dominant written forms of English were spelt in the regional form of English of the educated classes of London and surrounding counties. This London-based form of educated English is now the normal variety used by the media throughout Great Britain (except for variations on local broadcasting channels) and by teachers of English to foreigners.

When considering a word set down in print it is desirable first to consider whether in fact it is an English word: for example, that *pain* is the English word meaning 'suffering or distress of the body, etc.' and not the French word for 'bread', and that *mutter* is the English verb meaning 'to speak in a barely audible manner' and not the German word for 'mother'. This may seem an extravagantly obvious remark but not when one recalls that the English language has many words with the same spelling but with a different etymology. For example, *boil* 'an inflamed swelling' is a native word, but *boil* 'to bubble up' is French. There are six distinct nouns and four separate verbs written as *sound*, as well as the adjective and the adverb. *Excise* (duty on commodities) is an entirely distinct word from *excise* (to cut out), and so on. The establishment of the separate origin of such words is perhaps the main contribution of the twelve-volume *Oxford English Dictionary* and its Supplements. Dictionaries before the *OED*, including Dr Johnson's, are extremely vulnerable in this respect, and some modern dictionaries unwisely dismiss such distinctions as being irrelevant to their purpose.[4]

Since the Old English period remarkable and irreversible changes have come upon the English language and change continues. These changes have at most periods occurred without the expression by contemporaries of any degree of hostility, and even without comment of any kind. There have been exceptions. Scholars and gentlemen objected to the introduction of 'inkhorn' (learned and bookish) terminology in the sixteenth century; and many writers, not only grammarians, from the eighteenth century onward have expressed prescriptive views. But the dissolution of many of the elements of English that once linked it in one degree or another with the major Germanic languages of Europe occurred largely without comment. English writers of the Middle Ages seemed unaware of the implications of the loss of grammatical gender, the abandonment of the perfective prefix *ge-* and also of the dual forms of English pronouns, the great vowel shift of the fifteenth century, the loss of final *-e* as a pronounced syllable at the end of the fourteenth century, the decay of the subjunctive mood and of impersonal constructions, and many other such matters.

By contrast, beginning in the 1970s, there has occurred a kind of middle-class revolt, not yet resolved, in which a great many people seem to believe that the English language is entering a period of decline.[5] This battle between linguistic radicals and linguistic conservatives continues unabated. To me it is axiomatic that the language 'far from bleeding to death from past crudities and past wounds . . . can be used [at the present time as in the past] with majesty and power, free of all fault, by our greatest writers'.[6]

2

From Runes to Printing

The powers of the letters, when they were applied to a
new language, must have been vague and unsettled, and
therefore different hands would exhibit the same sound by
different combinations.

Samuel Johnson, Preface to the *Dictionary* (1755)

The English language arrived in these islands, with much tribula-
tion and darkness of deed, in the speech of tribesmen from Frisia
and neighbouring territories in the fifth century AD. Britain was
not empty and many battles followed, mournfully celebrated by
the newcomers in lugubrious alliterative poems, and used as
admonitory *exempla* by homiletic prose-writers like Archbishop
Wulfstan. The Celtic-speaking Britons, who had already accommodated, and had absorbed or expelled, an earlier set of invaders,
the Romans, retreated before the Germanic tribes. They consolidated themselves in Cornwall, 'North Wales' (that is, Wales),
Scotland, and Ireland, leaving most of the rest of the large island
to the soldiers, farmers, poets, and others from the longitudinal
western edges of Europe.

Most of the newcomers were illiterate but their rune-masters
brought with them an alphabet, widely distributed throughout
Europe, called the runic alphabet (p. 8), which they scratched or
carved on many objects as indications of ownership or of fabrica-
tion, or for some other purpose. The runes had many practical
and ornamental purposes but were also inwardly powerful,
symbolically representing simple concepts, in that each character
was also a word: thus *ash* (Old English *æsc*, as a letter written *æ*)
meant 'ash-tree; a ship made from the ash', and *wynn* (as a letter
written ᚹ, closely resembling the Roman p) meant 'joy'. Many
objects survive with English runes marked on them, the most
famous being the inscription on the Ruthwell Cross near Dumfries
and that on the Franks Casket, both in a Northumbrian dialect
of the early eighth century. Another, discovered in Hartlepool

1	2	3	4	5	6	7	8 :		9	10	11	12	13	14	15	16:
ᚠ	ᚢ	ᚦ	ᚩ	ᚱ	ᚳ	ᚷ	ᚹ	:	ᚻ	ᚾ	ᛁ	ᛄ	ᛋ	ᛤ	ᛡ	ᚻ
f	u	þ	o	r	c	g	w	:	h	n	i	j	ȝ	p	(x)	s :

17	18	19	20	21	22	23	24 :		25	26	27	28	29	30	31:
ᛏ	ᛒ	ᛖ	ᛗ	ᛚ	ᛝ	ᛟ	ᛞ	:	ᚪ	ᚫ	ᚣ	ᛠ	ᛣ	ᛤ	ᛥ
t	b	e	m	l	ŋ	œ	d	:	a	æ	y	êa	k	k̄	ḡ.

The 'Fuþorc' used in Old English inscriptions. Most scholars adopt this transliteration, suggested by Bruce Dickins in *Leeds Studies in English*, 1932, p. 4

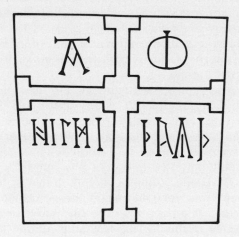

A name-stone bearing the name *Hildiþryþ* in runic letters (after that in St Hilda's Church, Hartlepool).

in 1833 and now in St Hilda's Church, Hartlepool, bears the name *Hildiþryþ* (p. 8).

The main orthographic feature of the alphabet—called a *futhorc* after the names of the first six characters, *feoh* wealth, *ur* aurochs, *th* thorn, *os* ?month, *rad* riding, and *cen* torch—is that it consists of symbols formed with straight lines which were easy to carve on stone, wood, metal, or bone. Altogether thirty-one distinct runic characters appear in the surviving Anglo-Saxon inscriptions.

The surviving runes are fragments of a lost and forgotten art. They were sufficiently numerous to represent all the separate speech sounds of the spoken form of the languages of the various Germanic tribes. In practice they were reserved for special purposes, but could have been more widely used if a tradition had established itself. Instead the tribes encountered a new alphabet, ultimately derived from the Romans, when Christian missionaries arrived at the end of the sixth century, and they forced their language into a new set of symbols, retaining only the thorn, wynn, and ash of their own alphabet.[1]

Our language, in the newly acquired Latin alphabet in insular script, first appears in writing in the early eighth century in the age of the Venerable Bede. The earliest recorded passages happen to be written in a northern variety of Old English, or 'Northumbrian' in the terminology of scholars.

One of them, Cædmon's *Hymn, c.* AD 737, preserved in Cambridge University Library, begins as follows:

> Nu scylun hergan   hefaenricaes uard
> metudæs maecti   end his modgidanc
> uerc uuldurfadur,   sue he uundra gihuaes,
> eci dryctin,   or astelidæ.

Now we must praise the guardian of the heavenly kingdom, the power of the Creator, and his understanding, the work of the father of glory, even as He, the eternal Lord, ordained the beginning of every wonderful thing.

The agrarian newcomers, soon to call themselves 'English', had made their mark. They had separated themselves in nationality and language from their European counterparts—even from members of their own tribes—for ever, though it could not have been evident to them at the time. Trading and seafaring linked them with their homeland for a time. But the first great severance of the English language had occurred, and the phonetic systems of the newly settled tribes began to differentiate themselves from those of the linguistically related tribes they had left behind. They had also acquired an alphabet which in later centuries helped to make it possible for the language to spread throughout the world.

The number of tribes that came to Britain is not known, nor their composition, except in broad terms. What is known is that they fell into four main linguistic groups, and the varieties of English spoken by these groups came to be called Northumbrian, Mercian, West Saxon, and Kentish by later scholars. They warred among themselves. They intermarried, both among the tribes and also with the subjugated Celts. Cultural rivalry and political animosity marked the whole of the Anglo-Saxon period, that is from the mid-fifth century until 1066.

Old English does not look particularly like modern English and in many respects it must be regarded as a foreign language:

Ic Ælfric wolde þas lytlan boc awendan to Engliscum gereorde of þæm stæf-cræfte þe is gehaten grammatica, siþþan ic þa twa bec awende on hundeahtatigum spellum, for þæm þe stæf cræft is seo cæg þe þara boca andgiet unlycþ.

I Ælfric wished to translate this little book [Priscian's grammar] into the English language from the grammar that is called *grammatica*, after I had rendered two books into eighty stories [his own two series of 'Catholic Homilies'], because grammar is the key that unlocks the meaning of the books.

It is faithful to its origins in that its vocabulary is almost entirely Germanic. Nouns, which fell clearly into numerous demonstrably different declensions, also possessed grammatical gender (masculine, feminine, or neuter) and were inflected according to case (nominative, accusative, genitive, and dative) and number. Nouns in the dative case were sometimes, but not always, preceded by a preposition. Verbs, then as now, fell into three main classes, called by modern grammarians strong (in which the past tense is formed by a change of internal vowel, for example, OE. *rīdan*, *rād*, modE. *ride*, *rode*); weak (in which the past tense is formed in modE. by the addition of *-ed*, for example, OE. *cyssan*, *cyssede*, modE. *kiss*, *kissed*); and irregular (OE. *bēon*, *gān*, etc., modE. *be*, *go*, etc.). Adjectives and most of the numbers were inflected according to certain obligatory rules. The numbering system changed after the number 60 (*þrītig* 30, *fēowertig* 40, *fīftig* 50, *siextig* 60, but *hundseofontig* 70, *hundeahtatig* 80). The subjunctive mood and impersonal constructions were obligatory in many more circumstances than they are now. There was no future tense.[2] Periphrastic verbal forms of the type 'he was coming' were exceedingly rare. Dialectal variation was cruelly complicated. Nearly all of the written work that has survived is literary (especially alliterative poetry), documentary (charters, wills, etc.), or religious (homilies): in other words formal in content and elevated in style. The daily chatter of Anglo-Saxons has not survived except in a piece of stilted conversation of just over 300 lines between a schoolmaster and his pupils:

Hæfst þu hafoc?
Habes accipitrem?
Do you have a hawk?

Ic hæbbe.
Habeo.
I have.

Canst þu temian hig?
Scis domitare eos?
Do you know how to tame them?

Gea, ic cann. Hwæt sceoldon hig me buton ic cuþe temian hig?
Etiam, scio. Quid deberent mihi nisi scirem domitare eos?
Yes, I do. What use would they be to me if I could not tame them?

And even this work, Ælfric's *Colloquy*, was written as a means of teaching pupils Latin (as the interlinear gloss indicates), not as a deliberate record of the English language itself.

Historical events usually have linguistic as well as political and social results, and the Anglo-Saxon period was no exception.

First, especially after the arrival of St Augustine in Canterbury in AD 597, and the gradual adoption of Christianity in most parts of the country, the language began to absorb some Latin words. A few Latin words had even made their way into the tribal homelands of the Germanic peoples before our ancestors moved to Britain, among them *mint* (OE. *mynet* coin), *pound* (OE. *pund*), *sack* (OE. *sacc*), and *street* (OE. *strǣt*). In the Christian period a much larger group of Latin words appeared in the language for the first time, among them *cook* (OE. *cōc*), *font* (OE. *font*), the word *Latin* itself,[3] *pope* (OE. *pāpa*), and *school* (OE. *scōl*, from medL. *scōla*, L. *schola*). For the most part these were thoroughly naturalized to the point even that some of them acquired native English suffixes, for example *pāpdōm* 'papacy' (OE. *-dōm* as in *kingdom*) and *sacerdhād* 'priesthood' (L. *sacerdōs* priest). Hybrid formations consisting of two nouns were also acceptable, for example *sealmscop* 'psalmist' (from L. *psalma* and OE. *scop* 'poet').

It is interesting to observe how Anglo-Saxon writers, under the influence of Latin, the language of the books they read most, regarded it as entirely natural to admit Latin words into their own language. The principle of absorption was accepted from the beginning and the new words were made to conform to the existing patterns of the language. In *Beowulf*, for example, the only epic poem from the Anglo-Saxon period, the word *draca* 'dragon' coexists with the native word *wyrm*, probably introduced into the poet's vocabulary because of the needs of the alliterative metre. For this poet a sword was *giganta weorc* 'the work of giants' (L. *gigās*, *gigantem*) and the men drank wine (*druncon win weras*) (L. *vīnum*) as well as beer and mead (both native words).

Secondly, starting in the late eighth century, marauding bands of Scandinavian warriors raided coastal settlements, especially in the north-east. By AD 900 they were established in the area known as the Danelaw, which included the East Midlands, stretching as far north as the Tees, as far west as the Pennines, Nottingham, and Bedford, and as far south as the Thames. Animosities came and went and further battles were fought until Canute became king of England in 1016. During this period of some two and a quarter centuries the language received many new elements from the Scandinavians. Most of the expressions must have entered the popular areas of the language at an early stage but a good many of them are not recorded in written form until much later. The poems and chronicles of the Anglo-Saxon period show words of Scandinavian origin like *dreng* 'warrior', *niðing* 'villain', *cnearr* 'a small ship', and *scegð* 'a light ship', words doubtless tinged with fear and hostility like the words *storm-trooper* and *Exocet* in the present century. The settling down of the Danes is reflected in other loanwords—*husbonda* 'householder, husband', *feolaga* 'fellow',[4] *griþ* 'peace', and, perhaps most important of all, *lagu* 'law'.[5] Three of the commonest Old English verbs were gradually superseded by their Scandinavian equivalents: as time went on *call* (late OE. *ceallian*, ON. *kalla*) slowly displaced OE. *hātan* and *clipian*; *take* (late OE. *tacan*, ON. *taka*) superseded OE. *niman* in its main senses, leaving *nim* only in the restricted sense 'steal'; and *cast* (early ME. *casten*, ON. *kasta*) slowly displaced OE. *weorpan* in the sense 'throw'. Vocabulary and constructions of the Scandinavian newcomers are embedded in the surviving literary and historical works of the period *c.*1000–*c.*1300, especially in works written in the East Midlands like the *Ormulum* (*c.*1200) and *Havelok* (*c.*1300), and in the northern and western parts of England, for example the *Cursor Mundi* (*c.*1300) and *Sir Gawain and the Green Knight* (*c.*1380). Thus (with the words of Scandinavian origin in italics):

> & *trigg* & trowwe *gripþ* & friþþ
> Reʒʒsepþ betwenenn lede.
> (*Ormulum*, Pref. 60–1)

(Who) brings about true peace between people [*trigg* and *trowwe* both mean 'true' and *gripþ* and *friþþ* both mean 'peace'].

> Your *gryndellayk* and your *greme*, and your grete words
> (*Sir Gawain* 312)

Your fierceness and your wrath and your great words

Their presence in these works places a barrier between these poems and modern readers of them because most of the incoming Scandinavian words did not survive the medieval period and drifted into the area of the language needing scholarly interpretation in glossaries and commentaries.

In passing I should mention that some scholars have inclined to the view that the mixing of the Scandinavian dialects and those of the Anglo-Saxons produced a kind of creolized (flexionless) English as the two sets of people sought to understand each other by ignoring inflexions, and that this mutilated kind of discourse led to the loss of grammatical gender and the emergence of new patterns of accidence in the post-Conquest period. This view, which supposes a period, however temporary, of creolized and virtually illiterate speech, cannot be sustained. It is much more likely that the linguistic changes of the period 900 to 1200 result from an increasing social acceptance of informal and unrecorded types of English, which, for convenience, I have called Vulgar Old English. These informal types of English emerged because of the instability of the Old English declensional system itself—it seems to have had too few clearly distinguishable case endings to bring out the necessary relationships between words. Moreover, lying ready at hand was a set of powerful but insufficiently exploited prepositions.

Thirdly, the early ascendancy of the northern tribal kings meant that many of our earliest records in English were written in a northern variety of the language; and the political decline of these kings was accompanied by a sharp increase in the number of West Saxon documents in the later part of the Anglo-Saxon period. Had the Normans never come we might well have seen the ascendancy of a Winchester type of English.

*

In 1066 the Normans came and more or less transformed English vocabulary and also the way it was written down. From then for nearly three hundred years the official language was French, though English remained the ordinary language of the majority of the population.

It should be borne in mind that Old French was a mixture of many dialects just as Old English had been, and also that, chronologically, the period called Old French corresponds more closely to Middle English than to Old English. In broad terms the influence of Norman French in this period of bilingualism was moderate in grammar though it was strong enough to bring an ordinal numeral into English (*second*) to replace the traditional Old English one (*other*, OE. *ōþer*). The phonetic contribution was somewhat more substantial. For example, numerous words came into English with the diphthong *-oi-* (or *-oy*), a very rare combination in the system developed from native Old English words.[6] Many such words, for example *choice, cloister, coy, employ, exploit, joy, loyal, noise, poise, royal*, and *voyage*, came into English then.

But the main development was the replacement of a large number of outmoded Old English words by more or less synonymous French words. The old patterns of behaviour and of social codification of the Anglo-Saxons were replaced by new Gallic ones, and in consequence new vocabulary drove out the old. In the space of two or three hundred years English vocabulary was revolutionized by the acquisition of such words.

Obsolete OE. words	*Replaced by OF. words*
æþeling	prince
ēam	uncle
fulluht	baptism
hǣlend	saviour
milts	mercy
rǣdbora	counsellor
sige	victory
stōw	place
wuldor	glory

The radical nature of the change is underlined by the fact that whereas the words *king* and *queen* are English, *advise, command, commons, country, court, govern, parliament, peer, people, Privy Council, realm, reign, royalty, rule,* and *sovereign* are all French. As with the terms for government and power, so too with the old concepts for poor and poverty. Thus OE. *earm* miserable, *þearfa* destitute, *wǣdl* poverty, and *wǣdla* pauper gave way to *miserable, poor, destitute, poverty, pauper, mendicant,* etc. And most of the Old English words for war (*gūþ, wīg, tohte,* etc.) were replaced by *battle, conflict, strife,* and *war,* etc., all of French derivation.

Some Romance words, borrowed at different periods, produced doublets in English:

cadence/chance both ultimately descended from Lat. cadere 'to fall'
compute/count	computāre
dignity/dainty	dignitās
ounce/inch	uncia
secure/sure	sēcūrus

In most of these the longer form came more or less directly from Latin, and the shorter one from a reduced form produced by phonetic change in France.

Some of these early loanwords show features subsequently changed or abandoned in the French language itself. English retains, for example, the *s* that the French have abandoned in such words as *beast* and *feast* (*bête* and *fête* in modern French). Similarly the initial *ch-* in many French loanwords came to be pronounced like native words that in Anglo-Saxon were spelt *c-* but pronounced /tʃ/: so *chain, charity* (from French, cf. Latin *catēna, cāritās*) were anglicized with initial /tʃ/ to accord with the initial sound of the native words *chaff* (OE. *cæf, ceaf*), *chalk* (OE.

cælc, cealc).[7] In other cases words which had /k/ in Norman French but /ʃ/ in Parisian French came to us in their Norman French form, for example *caitiff* (cf. modF. *chétif*), *catch* (cf. modF. *chasser*), and *carrion* (cf. modF. *charogne*). Anyone considering the nature of the indebtedness of English to French must always keep in mind that most of the loanwords did not come from the central repository of received or standard French but from that variety which happened to be spoken by the Norman conquerors.

From the Conquest until the fourteenth century a French dialect, or 'Anglo-French' as scholars call it, was the official language of this country. It was the accredited language of the Court and of the Law. As a result, many legal terms which came into English from Norman French during this period still remain as part of the central terminology of English law, for example *embezzle, judge* (Lat. *jūdex, jūdicem* as noun, *jūdicāre* as verb), *jury, larceny, lease* (related to modF. *laisser* and modE. *lax*), *perjury*.

At the same time French literature was dominant in Western Europe, and hundreds of literary terms became fashionable, and then permanent, in this country. One way of showing the development is to compare passages from literary works of the medieval period. The abandonment of ancient Germanic concepts and their replacement by the feudal and courtly ones of the French can be observed in the following passages:

hwæþre hē gemunde	mægenes strenge	No French
ginfæste gife,	ðe him God sealde,	loanwords
and him tō Anwaldum	āre gelȳfde,	
frōfre and fultum.		

(*Beowulf* 1270-3; eighth century)

Yet he remembered the power of his might
The ample gift which God had granted him,
And trusted himself to the Lord for grace,
Help and support.

Ich *granti* wel þat he us deme	The beginning of
vor þeȝ he were wile breme.	French influence

(*The Owl and the Nightingale* 201-2; twelfth century)

I readily grant that he should judge us
For though he was spirited (OE. *brēme*) at one time . . .

Singest with *vois memorial* in the shade,   Marked French
Under the *laurer* which that may not *fade*.   influence
(Chaucer's *Anelida and Arcite* 18–19; fourteenth century)

Singest with memorial voice in the shade,
Under the laurel which may not fade.

The contrast between English of the eighth century and that of the fourteenth can be glimpsed in these passages. Old English seems, and remains, irretrievably distant; the early Middle English of *The Owl and the Nightingale* more recognizable but hazardously obscure without a glossary; the Middle English of Chaucer just a suburb or two away.

Orthographical changes brought to the language by Norman scribes were very remarkable. The scribes assessed the language they found before them and in general respelt it to accord with their own conventions. They also, in a quite straightforward way, set down the language as it was *used*, without the embellishments and anachronisms employed and preserved by the Anglo-Saxon scribes during the reigns of Edward the Confessor and of Harold.

Among their adventurous innovations was the adoption of the spelling *qu*, especially familiar to them from Latin pronouns, as a replacement for the 'foreign-looking' *cw* of the Anglo-Saxons.

  OE. cwealm   →   qualm (modE. qualm)
        cwellan   →   quelen (modE. quell)
        cwēn   →   queen (modE. queen)
        cweþan   →   quethen (cf. archaic modE. quoth 'said')
        cwic   →   quik (modE. quick)

At a stroke this change caused English to take on the outward appearance of a Romance language: *queen* and *quest*, *quick* and *quit*, *quell* and *quiet* were made to look like members of the same linguistic family by the scholarly clerks as they copied their manuscripts.

In passing it is worthy of note that the temptation to treat all words of French origin as if once adopted they had the same history should be resisted. Many became thoroughly acclimatized as time went on, and in particular those adopted before the middle of the seventeenth century. French words that have come into English since the Restoration have often retained at any rate some of the phonetic or intonational features of the original language.

Thus, for example, old borrowings like *baron* (XIII, i.e. thirteenth century), *button* (XIII), and *mutton* (XIII) have fallen into the English dominant pattern, and are always stressed on the first syllable; by contrast the later loanwords *balloon* (XVIII), *bassoon* (XVIII), *cartoon* (XIX), and *platoon* (XVII) are invariably stressed on the second syllable. Similarly *baggage* (XV), *cabbage* (XIV), *homage* (XIII), and *language* (XIII) show the primary accent on the first syllable, and a fully anglicized /dʒ/ in the unstressed second syllable; whereas *badinage* (XVII), *camouflage* (XX), *entourage* (XIX), and *sabotage* (XX) remain at a kind of half-way house with the main stress on the first syllable but with the last syllable pronounced /ɑːʒ/.

One enduring myth about French loanwords of the medieval period needs to be discounted. It is sometimes said that the Normans brought many culinary and gastronomic terms with them and, in particular, that they brought the terms for the flesh of animals eaten as food. This is no more than a half-truth. The culinary revolution, and the importation of French vocabulary into English society, scarcely preceded the eighteenth century, and consolidated itself in the nineteenth. The words *veal, beef, venison, pork*, and *mutton*, all of French origin, entered the English language in the early Middle Ages, and would all have been known to Chaucer. But they meant not only the flesh of a calf, of an ox, of a deer, etc., but also the animals themselves. Thus Samuel Johnson refers to 'a beef' being killed for the house in his *Journey to the Western Isles* (1775); and William Cowper used the word *mutton* to mean 'a sheep' in 1795:

> A mutton, statelier than the rest,
> A ram, the ewes and wethers, sad, address'd.[8]

The *restriction* of these French words to the sense 'flesh of an animal eaten as food' did not become general before the eighteenth century. Expressed another way, a farmer could graze *muttons* (which he sometimes called *sheep*), and eat mutton, until about the eighteenth century. Thereafter he grazed sheep and ate mutton.

The more exotic terminology of French cookery made its way into English menus only from the beginning of the nineteenth century onwards: for example *Béarnaise sauce* (1877), *coq au vin* (1938), *crème brûlée* (1886), *œuf en cocotte* (1900), and *pâté maison* (1947). The lateness of arrival of such terminology is underlined by the history of the word *profiterole*. It is defined vaguely in the *OED* as 'some kind of cooked food', with examples of 1515 and 1727. The modern familiar confections have not been found in print in an English context before 1884.

This great period of older English, set down by the rune-masters and then by medieval scribes using the roman alphabet, came to an end with the invention of printing in the late fifteenth century. No standard language existed except for the highly formalized written variety of the late West Saxon scribes. The Saxons in their villages and settlements maintained and extended their ancient linguistic differences, but the scribes and scholars of the time kept a tight rein on the way they set the language down. The Scandinavian and French invaders left valuable linguistic legacies of permanent value but by the 1470s the main penetration of English by these two sets of languages was at an end. The Norman scribes had respelt the language, and in broad terms had moved with the times, changing spellings as sound changes made the old conjunctions of letters untenable. Provincial scribes in Lincolnshire, Shropshire, and elsewhere kept regional sounds and symbols together as best they could.

The English language remained a recognizable branch of the Germanic family—but by the 1470s firmly severed from its western European analogues. Its unstandardized varieties were about to be subjected to a new regularizing procedure. The invention of printing ended the old flexibility. Spoken English went on diversifying but the typesetters, wherever they worked, soon began to set down the language in a London way. Immobility came to the printed word while the spoken word continued to change.[9]

3

From William Caxton to
George Washington: 1476 to 1776

> Our English tongue of all languages most swarmeth with
> the single money of monasillables which are the onely
> scandall of it. Bookes written in them and no other, seeme
> like Shop-keepers boxes, that containe nothing else, saue
> halfepence, three-farthings and two pences.
>
> Thomas Nashe, *Christs teares ouer Ierusalem*
> (1594), p. 2^v

A period of three hundred years, in conditions of social and
political stability, could presumably leave a language largely
unchanged. For the English language the period 1476 to 1776 is
one of radical change, and it is no accident that these three
centuries witnessed striking developments in the social, religious,
political, and industrial bases of English society. The French
religious wars, unrest in the Netherlands, and the beliefs of Luther
and Calvin, caused disruptive European ideas to be brought from
Geneva, Leiden, La Rochelle, and elsewhere to the shores, and
then to the shires, of the British Isles. The rediscovery of the
classical past, and in particular of the literary and philosophical
works of Greece and Rome, brought in its wake many new stylistic
models and much new vocabulary. No longer was it possible to
regard writing as an art belonging to the special few—conservative writers whose works were recorded in small clusters of manuscripts, most of them initiated by clerical groups, or at court, or
in baronial halls. Pens came into the hands of merchants, artisans,
yeomen, and scientists, and they all brought their own linguistic
patterns with them, and a stern preference for the vernacular.
The intellectuals 'despaired and anatomized'.[1] Gentlemen and
scholars took sides and waged battles about Latin neologisms,
'inkhorn' terms, and 'indenture' English—Edward Hall, Sir
Thomas Elyot, and others were on the side of the new learning,
while Sir Thomas More, Sir John Cheke, and others sang the

praises of 'our own tung . . . cleane and pure, unmixt and unmangeled with borowing of other tunges'.[2] And as they fought their paper wars, the Latin tongue retreated, except as an admired model for certain kinds of writing. The vernacular advanced and triumphed.

Written English came to be set down everywhere in a standard form—in general terms that of people writing in London or within a reasonable distance of London. Spoken English remained as diverse and frustratingly just out of reach as ever. During this period too the ceremonial language of Parliament and the Law, and of the Bible and the Book of Common Prayer, settled into a form resembling permanence—forms of language tinged with Latinity and other elements of antiquity, but firmly and finally presented in or rendered into the vernacular. The triumph of the vernacular, and its presentation in a fairly standardized printed form, are the main linguistic results of a period marked here, as in European countries, by the rise of capitalism and of urbanization, the emergence of a national church and (in some countries) the retreat of Roman Catholicism, and an unparalleled diversification of types of writing. Sheer practical needs led to the preparation first of dictionaries and grammars of English for foreigners seeking refuge in this country from religious oppression in Europe, and then of lexicons and grammatical works for the use of native speakers themselves. These developments will be looked at in more detail in chapter 6.

As was the case in the medieval period it is normally impossible to link particular linguistic changes with specific social, religious, political, or industrial developments, though there are exceptions. Nevertheless there is no reason to doubt that they are closely connected and interrelated. In this period, as at an earlier stage, language change is not so much a matter of gradual and imperceptible development within a given social group as of the perpetual mobility, upwards or downwards, of modes and conventions of speech as the fortunes and way of life of social groups continued to change. The whole system of vowels of a given social or regional group does not change in any radical way within a generation or even within a century by the ordinary laws of physics. Nor can a particular group absorb layers of new vocabulary or complex new syntactic arrangements in a short period. But social mobility can bring about rapid linguistic change, and this is just what happened as people left the countryside and the provinces to populate London. In 1500 the population of London was 75,000. By 1600 it had increased to 220,000, and by 1650 to 450,000.

With these general considerations in mind, it is time to turn to some of the more important detailed linguistic changes of the period. Necessarily many linguistic disturbances and dislocations must be left uncatalogued here. The account that follows is also restricted to the changes that occurred in the standard written language. I shall deal in turn with spelling, punctuation, pronunciation, vocabulary, and grammar.

Caxton and the early printers in England broadly accepted the spelling patterns of the late Middle English period and rendered them relatively immobile, though they tolerated more, fairly trivial, variation in detail than is allowed today. For example:

There was a *damoyselle* that had a pye in a cage.
This *damoysell* was after moche scorned.

And it happed that the lord of the *hows* . . .
And in the *hous* therfore was grete sorowe.

But . . . yf ony man cam in to that hows/that was *balled* or pylled . . .
The pye . . . so ofte remembryd it to suche as cam thyder so *ballyd* or pylled.[3]

In the same passage, words like *a, and, cam* (came), *ele* (eel), *eten* (eaten), *good, grete* (great), *had, hede* (head), *his, hym* (him), *in, it, lady, lord, moche* (much), *my, not, of, ponde* (pond), *pye* (magpie), *she, so, that, the, they, when, yf* (if), are systematically spelt as shown with no variation. The scribes in slightly earlier manuscripts had been much less thorough in the avoidance of casual variation.[4]

Similarly, the spelling of Shakespeare's words in the First Folio (1623) is less rigidly fixed than in modernized systems but somewhat more flexible than that of medieval manuscripts:

> LEO. Her naturall Posture.
> Chide me (deare Stone) that I may say indeed
> Thou art *Hermione*; or rather, thou art she,
> In thy not chiding: for she was as tender
> As Infancie, and Grace. But yet (*Paulina*)
> *Hermione* was not so much wrinckled, nothing
> So aged as this seemes.
>
> (*The Winter's Tale*, Act v)

Some of the detailed spelling changes of the period stand like milestones between distant cities. This is the time when initial *fn* (ME. *fnēsen*, modE. *sneeze*) and *wl* (ME. *wlatsom* loathsome) disappeared from the language; when *gh* or *f* took the place of earlier *h* or *ȝ* (yogh), pronounced /x/ in final position or before another consonant, as in *cough* (ME. *coȝe*), *enough* (OE. *genōh*), *fight* (OE. *feoht*), and *plight* (OE. *pliht*).[5] The old runic letter *thorn* (þ) drifted in the way it was written until it so resembled the letter *y* that it had to be abandoned in favour of *th*.[6] Final *s* and *f* after a short vowel passed through periods of great uncertainty (*blis*/*bliss*, *witnes*/*witness*; *bailif*/*bailiff*, *mastif*/*mastiff*) but finally settled down in doubled form. The spelling *-ick* (for earlier *-ic* or *-ik(e)*), as in *academick*, *authentick*, *musick*, *publick*, *stoick*, and so on, adorned the great literary works of the period, and remained as the spelling preferred by Dr Johnson in his *Dictionary* (1755) but not much beyond. The letters *u* and *v*, largely interchangeable or used as mere positional variants in such words as *vnder* (under), *vse* (use), *saue* (save), and *vniuersal* (universal) for much of the period, had divided themselves into their present-day functions by about 1630. So too had *i* and *j* (and *g*): the earlier consonantal use of *i* in words like *ientyl* (gentle), *Iob* (Job), *iudge* (judge), and *reioyce* (rejoice) was abandoned in the early part of the seventeenth century, as was the earlier occasional vocalic use of *j*, as in *jn* (in), and *jngeniously* (ingeniously).[7] Despite the differentiation of *I* and *J*, however, the impression that they were merely forms of the same letter remained. *J*, and also *V*, are still normally omitted by printers from the signatures of sheets of books; and Dr Johnson, as well as some later lexicographers, listed *I* and *J* words in a single alphabetical series (thus JAM, JAMB, IAMBIC, JANGLE, etc.).

Changes in pronunciation during this period are no less important. The 'Great Vowel Shift' was mostly at an end before Caxton's first book came off the press, but its reverberations are central to an understanding of what happened later. There is not room here to give full details of the transformations brought about by this great process.[8] Suffice it to say that it affected nearly all the long vowel sounds in the standard language. It is self-evident that the whole phonetic basis of the language was changed when, for example, *mood*, which before 1400 was pronounced in the manner of modern English *mode*, gained its present-day pronunciation, as did *house* (before 1400 pronounced with the main vowel sound of modE. *loose*).

Some other changes in pronunciation in the standard language during this period follow in listed form, with indications of the approximate date of their occurrence:

1. The voicing of *s* (i.e. pronouncing it as /z/) after an unstressed syllable, as in *desist, dessert, discern, possess, resist*, believed to have started first (?in the Elizabethan period) in popular speech (and later overturned in some cases because of the spelling).

2. The voicing of the final syllable in such words as *knowledge* (ME. *knowleche*), *partridge* (ME. *partrich*), *sausage* (OF. *saussiche*), *Greenwich* (old pronunciation /ˈgrɪnɪdʒ/), and *Norwich* (/ˈnɔrɪdʒ/). ?Seventeenth century. Here too spelling pronunciation has in some cases reversed the change.

3. The silencing of *t* in *chestnut, Christmas, mortgage*, and *often*; of *d* in *handsome, handkerchief*; and of *p* in *consumption, temptation*. ?Elizabethan period.

4. In the eighteenth century, the silencing or dropping of *r* before a consonant or standing by itself in final position. The effects of this change were quite dramatic:

beard	scared	part	north	horse	gourd	near	fair	better
bɪərd	skeərd	pɑːrt	nɔːrθ	hɔərs	guərd	nɪər	fɛər	ˈbɛtər

became

| bɪəd | skeəd | pɑːt | nɔːθ | hɔəs | guəd | nɪə | fɛə | ˈbɛtə. |

This radical change divided RP speakers from speakers in Scotland and some other areas in the British Isles. Since most North American speakers have retained the *r* (or a glottal variety of *r*) in such positions, this feature is also one of the major distinctions between RP and spoken varieties of North American English. Types of English which have dropped the *r* in such positions are often called 'non-rhotic', and those which have retained it 'rhotic'. The presence or absence of rhoticity usually provides an instant first indication of the regional speech of a given speaker.[9]

*

The period 1476 to 1776 witnessed the establishment of the modern system of punctuation. Because most modern editions of texts of this period are punctuated in a modern way there is no widespread public knowledge of the conventions of earlier periods. Anglo-Saxon scribes used a system of light punctuation that was developed from the marking of liturgical chants and was

designed to help with the public reading of a text.[10] They wrote
their verse in a continuous manner (that is, not divided in lines),
just as they did their prose. This system was modified somewhat
in the Middle English period but when printing was introduced
marks of punctuation were still very sparse. Caxton punctuated
his texts with full-length and short oblique strokes, and with stops.
The stops are normally lozenge-shaped, and they can occur in a
low, mid, or high position relative to the base of words in the text.
In Shakespeare's works the punctuation remained light and vari-
able with much overlapping of the role of the full stop, the colon,
and the semicolon. In eighteenth-century books, proper names
were normally printed in italic type and many nouns were printed
(in the modern German manner) with a capital initial letter. Until
the late seventeenth century the apostrophe was not used to
indicate the possessive case but rather to guide the reader to the
simplex or basic form of a possibly unfamiliar word (*Siloa's brook*
in Milton to show that the simplex was *Siloa*, not *Siloas*). It was
introduced as a sign of the possessive case in the singular after the
death of Milton; and not until the eighteenth century as a sign of
the possessive case in the plural.

The prevalence of incorrect instances of the use of the apostrophe at the present time, even in the work of otherwise reasonably well-educated people (e.g. *it's wings*, *apple's for sale*, *this is
your's*), together with the abandonment of it by many business
firms (*Barclays Bank*, *Lloyds Bank*), suggest that the time is close
at hand when this moderately useful device should be abandoned.

*

When one turns to vocabulary one cannot but be impressed by the
amazing hospitality of the English language. Wave after wave of
words entered the language from French, Latin, and Italian, and
were for the most part made to conform to the vernacular patterns
of spelling and pronunciation. The Renaissance, with its renewed
interest in antiquity, also brought a solid vein of Greek words into
the language. Smaller clusters of words were adopted from other
European countries, especially the Netherlands, and also from
much further afield—from Japan, China, and the Dutch East
Indies (now Malaysia, Singapore, and Indonesia). Not all the
loanwords entered the general language: many of them eked out
a temporary existence in literary or scientific works and were then

abandoned. Others came to stay and became so thoroughly acclimatized that their original foreignness is no longer evident.

The extent of the French element can be gauged from the following tables, which show the period of first record in each case:

1476-1576   abeyance, battery, colonel, compatible, entertain, gauze, grotesque, minion, passport, pioneer, portrait, trophy, vase, vogue

1577-1676   adroit, bayonet, chocolate, fanfare, minuet, moustache, portmanteau, reveille, tube, vehicle, version

1677-1776   boulevard, brochure, cohesion, envelope, glacier, meringue, précis, salon, vaudeville

In a great many cases it cannot be determined whether a particular word entered English from French or directly from Latin, for example *conclusion* (OF. *conclusion*, L. *conclūsiōnem*) and *genitive* (OF. *génitif*, fem. *-ive*, L. *genetīvus*).

Italian loanwords of the period include *balcony, ballot, carnival, cupola, lottery, macaroni,* and *squadron,* as well as numerous musical words, for example *cantata, concerto, impresario, oratorio, solo, soprano,* and *violoncello.*

Words from the Netherlands mainly reflect the trade and shipping contacts of the two countries, for example *cruise, freebooter, hawker, hustle, keelhaul, knapsack,* and *yacht.*

Words adopted from more distant countries are self-evidently exotic, and many reached English by an indirect route, transmitted through French, Spanish, or medieval Latin. A few examples: *harem, hashish, mufti* (Arabic); *mikado, soy* (Japanese); *kapok, sago* (Malay); *bazaar, shawl* (Persian); and *caviare, kiosk* (Turkish).

By far the most enlivening aspect of the vocabulary of this period, however, is the adoption of Latin or latinate words as part of a process of filling real or fancied cavities in the literary language and the language of business. Young men from good families, drawn into trade or other forms of private administration, or seeking a post in the Church, the civil service, or the diplomatic service needed to acquire a working knowledge of the Latin language and of Latin literature at school and university, and also, though to a lesser extent, of Greek. The indebtedness to these ancient languages did not end with the adoption of words: the fabric and nature of English sentences of the period, particularly in the sixteenth century, display a startling resemblance to their classical exemplars. Long Ciceronian sentences abound, subordinate clauses are neatly tucked in, and the meaning is subtly brought out by every kind of rhetorical device.

Thomas Wilson attacked the adoption of 'inkhorn' (latinate) words—or 'to catche an ynke horne terme by the taile', as he expressed it—by describing how a 'Lincolnshire man' applied for a benefice:

I doubt not but you will adiuuate such poore adnichilate orphanes, as whilome ware condisciples with you, and of antique familiaritie in Lincolneshire. Among whom I being a Scholasticall panion, obtestate your Sublimitie, to extoll mine infirmitie. There is a sacerdotall dignitie in my natiue Countrey contiguate to me, where I now contemplate.[11]

The whole passage is a parody, but some of the 'hard' words that he used, for example *contiguate* (from medL. *contiguātus* touching together), were neither invented for the occasion nor even particularly rare in the sixteenth century.

The all-pervading influence of Latin syntax and of handbooks of rhetoric is observable in the works of writers like Sir Thomas Elyot (?1499-1546), author of the 'Boke named the Governour' (1531) and Sir Thomas North (?1535-?1601), the translator of many works including Plutarch's 'Lives'. Thus, for example:

Who when he was returned unto his campe, his souldiers came in great companies unto him, and were very sory, that he mistrusted he was not able with them alone to overcome his enemies, but would put his person in daunger, to goe fetch them that were absent, putting no trust in them that were present.[12]

A century later John Milton occasionally wrote in the same heavily ornate style:

Julius Caesar (of whom, and of the Roman Free State, more than what appertains, it is not here to be discours'd) having subdu'd most parts of Gallia, which by a potent faction, he had obtain'd of the Senat as his province for many years, stirr'd up with a desire of adding still more glory to his name, and the whole Roman Empire to his ambition, som say, with a farr meaner and ignobler, the desire of Brittish Pearls, whose bigness he delighted to balance in his hand, determins, and that upon no unjust pretended occasion, to trie his Force in the conquest also of Britain.[13]

These, especially the example from Milton, are extreme types. They show writers too close to the desk and to the ancient language they revered. But it was not always an unequal contest with the awkwardnesses of a half-conquered language. In the sixteenth and seventeenth centuries the best English prose-writers mastered the techniques of rhetoric and manufactured new sentence-structures of a kind that commended themselves later to many of our greatest writers of prose, including Edward Gibbon, Dr Johnson, and Macaulay. 'Periodic sentences', nobly constructed utterances subtly joined together in a classical manner, balanced antithetical clauses, rhetorical contrarieties and 'exornations', metaphors, 'similitudes', a whole world of tropes, and many other resplendent decorations, adorn the work of the best prose-writers of the seventeenth century. It would be easy to cite passages from the works of Bacon, Ralegh, Sir Thomas Browne, Jeremy Taylor, John Milton, and others to show the power of the language that lay to hand. One, from Donne, must needs suffice:

It comes equally to us all, and makes us all equall when it comes. The ashes of an Oak in the Chimney, are no Epitaph of that Oak, to tell me how high or how large that was: It tels me not what flocks it sheltered while it stood, nor what men it hurt when it fell. The dust of great persons graves is speechlesse too, it sayes nothing, it distinguishes nothing . . . and when a whirle-winde hath blowne the dust of the Church-yard into the Church, and the man sweeps out the dust of the Church into the Church-yard, who will undertake to sift those dusts again, and to pronounce. This is the Patrician, this is the noble flowre, and this the yeomanly, this the Plebeian bran.[14, 15]

*

Changes in accidence and syntax in the received standard language during the period 1476 to 1776 are somewhat easier to map. The main changes are at first sight less numerous, though no less important, than those in spelling, punctuation, and vocabulary. It is necessary to bear in mind, though, that their timing is important in that some occurred before British settlers began to colonize North America, and others occurred at a later date. Those who travelled to Cape Cod, Massachusetts, in the *Mayflower* in 1620 very probably all *said* 'he runs' and 'he lives in London' but their parents and grandparents would have said and written 'he runneth' and 'he liveth in London', and they probably continued to use the *-eth* forms themselves in formal correspondence. They would also all have been using the forms *got* and *gotten* more or less in a modern American way, whereas those who never left England gradually came to abandon *gotten* (but not *forgotten*) as the normal past participle of the verb *got* in the course of the seventeenth century.

Before 1476 many nouns still had plurals in *-en* (*eyen*, *hosen*, *housen*, *shoon*, etc.). By 1776 they had dwindled to the few that still remain in the language: *brethren*, *children*, *oxen*, and the archaic *kine*. The normal sign of plurality, then as now, was *-s* (*ships*, *wars*), and so much so that a number of words that naturally ended in *-s* were apprehended as plural formations and gave way to 'erroneous' (and then standard) forms without this *-s*, for example *burial* (from OE. *byrgels*); *cherry* (cf. OF. and modF. *cerise*); *pea* (from *pease*, surviving only in *pease-pudding* and *pease-brose*, from OE. *pise*, pl. *pisan*); and *sherry* (sixteenth-century *sherris*, from Spanish *Xeres*).

The pronominal system developed in various ways. By 1476 the main modern English pronouns existed (*I*, *he*, *she*, *it*, *we*, *us*, *they*, etc.) in the standard language, though some of them were relative newcomers (*she*, *they*, *their*, *them*), and many of them had various restrictions placed upon their use. *It* lacked a possessive form of its own: *his* (the traditional genitive of (*h*)*it*) or *her* were called on as the context required, as well as such devices as *thereof*:

Salt is good but yf salt have loste hyr saltnes what shall be seasoned ther with?[16]
Euery batayle had his vawarde [vanguard].[17]
Vnto the riuer of Egypt and the great sea and the border thereof.[18]

The most striking development, perhaps, occurred in the second-person pronouns. In 1476 *thou* was the regular singular form and *ye* the normal plural one; *ye* was the normal subject of a sentence and *you* was used in the objective case. Tyndale's use of each of these second-person pronouns in his translation of the New Testament in 1525 reflected the normal standard usage of the period. Towards the end of the sixteenth century a marked shift in usage occurred, and from about 1600 the normal custom was to use *you* when addressing a single person and *thou* only in special uses. In particular *thou* was used in the French *tutoyer* manner, that is to close friends, children, and servants; and, significantly, when addressing God. By 1776 *thou* had irrevocably disappeared except in religious language, in the speech of Quakers, and in dialectal speech. The pre-1600 case-distinction between *ye* and *you* was also given up, and *ye* disappeared from standard speech altogether.

Its as the genitive of the pronoun *it* is not recorded until the late 1590s. In Shakespeare the normal genitive is *his*, but examples of both *it* ('The innocent milke in it most innocent mouth', *Winter's Tale* III. ii. 101) and *its* (or *it's*) are also found ('Heaven grant us its peace', *Measure for Measure* I. ii. 4; 'How sometimes nature will betray it's folly', *Winter's Tale* I. ii. 152). The same general patterning persisted for much of the seventeenth century:

The Earth . . . and the principall causes of her Barrenness.[19]
The Sun | Had first his precept so to move.[20]

In 1476 *my/mine* and *thy/thine* were mainly phonological variants: the first form in each case was normally used before a consonant (*my book*) and the second before a word beginning with a vowel or *h* (*mine arm, mine heart*). Between 1476 and 1776 this convention receded, and new ones became established. *My* became an all-purpose possessive adjective before nouns (and also *thy* before it began to drop out altogether). *Mine* was the normal form elsewhere in a sentence (*O Father myne* 1567; *my doctryne is not myne, but* . . . 1535; *as mine is set on hers, so hers is set on mine* 1592).

Related to this rearrangement of functions was the gradual restriction of *our* and *your* to the position immediately before the governed noun (*our children, your grief*), and the establishment of *ours* and *yours* in other parts of the sentence (*He and al his is owris* 1533; *this weak and feeble fortress of ours* 1578; *all this Netherworld Is yours* 1625).

The main relative pronoun in 1476 was *that*, though *which* was used, and increasingly so throughout the sixteenth and seventeenth centuries:

1485   Eche took an hors . . . which ranne at al aduenture.[21]
1590   A springing well, From which fast trickled forth a siluer flood.[22]
1650   The Hebrews measuring their land by a bow-shot . . . which . . . admits of variation.[23]
1526   [with a personal antecedent] Thankes be vnto God, whych hath geven vs victory.[24]
1693   He had nine Wives, all which he cast off successively.[25]

Easily the most striking changes of the period, however, are found in the development of the verbs. The so-called 'strong' verbs—those which changed their stem vowels when used in the past tense, like *ride/rode* (OE. *rīdan, rād*)—receded sharply. Many now became established as 'weak': *reap/*pa.t. *rope* (OE. *rīpan/rāp*) became *reap/reaped*; *bow/*pa.t. *beh* (OE. *būgan/bēag*) became *bow/bowed*. Others fell out of use altogether or retreated into dialectal use: the Middle English descendants of OE. *hrīnan* touch, *snīpan* cut, *stīgan* ascend, *brēotan* break, and many others. The weak verbs became the dominant class, those which for the most part form their past tense in *-ed*. Nearly all new verbs, whether formed within English or directly adopted from other languages (*contend, elect, fuse, insert, postulate, suggest*) were fashioned in the mould of the old 'weak' class. There were a few exceptions, for example *strive* (OF. *estriver*), taken over at an earlier date into the native conjugation of *drive*, etc.; and *dig*, originally conjugated weak (*digged*), as always in Shakespeare, the Authorized Version, and Milton, but drawn into the class of strong verbs in the seventeenth century under the influence of verbs like *stick/stuck*. But these were rare.

The third class of older verbs, the irregular or anomalous ones, moved about improvidently as new needs arose, especially the ones traditionally known as 'preterite-present' verbs, the descendants of OE. *witan* to know (*wāt* knows, pa.t. *wiste*), *āgan* to own (*āh* owns, pa.t. *āhte*), *cunnan* to know (*cann* knows, pa.t. *cūpe*); (without infinitive) *mæg* be able (pa.t. *mihte*), *sceal* be obliged (pa.t. *scolde*), *dearr* dares (pa.t. *dorste*), *mōt* may (pa.t. *mōste*); and also the descendants of the OE. verbs *wesan, bēon* to be, *willan* to be willing, *dōn* to do, and *gān* to go.

From this group the language acquired a range of ways of forming the future tense. Wyclif rendered the Latin future tense of verbs in the Bible by *shall* and the present tense of Latin *volo* by *will*. Throughout the period, and in the standard language in Britain to this day, this distinction remained, though it is now fast falling away.

May, might, can, could, ought, and *do* spread their wings and had an extraordinarily complex history between the Old English period and about 1700, by which time most of their present-day functions had been established. For example, *may* started out (in Anglo-Saxon) as a verb of complete predication: OE. *ic mæg wel*

I am in good health; ME. (1398) *Shepe that haue longe taylles may worse* (are less hardy) *wyth wynter than those that haue brode taylles.* It was also a mere, but yet very powerful, auxiliary of predication: *No man may separate me from thee* (1582); *when thou comest there . . . thou maist see to the Gate* (Bunyan, 1678). The first use disappeared before 1476. Meanwhile *may* acquired the power to express permission or sanction: *Justice did but (if I may so speak) play and sport together in the businesse* (1653). The intermediate steps, and other uses of *may* before 1776, cannot be briefly described. And so it is with the other auxiliaries.

The old anomalous verbs branched out to enable the language to express periphrastic tenses of commanding usefulness and naturalness to the native speaker, and of equally striking difficulty for foreigners learning the language, expressions of the type, *is beaten, is being beaten, will be beaten, has been beaten; am eating, will be eating, have been eating; will have been shown; are you reading?; do you believe?; I do not believe*, and so on. The virtual absence of such constructions is a striking feature of the language at an earlier stage, and particularly of Old English, and inevitably suggests that early speakers of the language suffered from an intolerable degree of grammatical deprivation. Nevertheless one should resist the temptation to think of Old English as a deficient form of English. The patterns of accidence and syntax of a language wax and wane from generation to generation, and seem always to meet the daily needs of the tribes, families, or groups using them.

Two other features of the period call for brief mention. As in Old and Middle English, negation continued to be cumulative and not self-cancelling, at least until late in the seventeenth century:

1154 þe erthe ne bar nan corn.
1411 He knoweth wel that . . . he ne hath noght born hym as he sholde hav doon.
1471 Take heede . . . that they be not in noon place wher that sykenesse is regnyng.
1568 They should not neede no more to feare him then his shadowe.
1632 Rauenna, which for antiquity will not bow her top to none in Italy.

Finally, the particle *to* followed by an infinitive continued to appear in all the customary circumstances,[26] the so-called 'split' infinitive among them. The construction shades off into antiquity:

*c.*1400   To enserche sciences, and to perfitly knowe alle manere of
         Naturels þinges.
1606   To quite rid himselfe out of thraldome.
1650   Anniball was advised . . . to not go to Rome.

Just after the secession of the American colonies, Dr Johnson
wrote his 'Lives of the Poets', and in the life of Milton he wrote
'Milton was too busy to much miss his wife'. It seems an appropriate way to end the chapter, at a point when prescriptive
grammarians had not yet emerged to place real as well as false
constraints upon writers.

Between 1476 and 1776 the language had been set down in
writing with every kind of burgeoning ornamental device and
subtle constructive power by some of the greatest of English
writers. A standard language had been established, and it was
admired and imitated in the provinces, that is by writers who did
not happen to live in London. Side by side with the majestical
prose of Bacon, Ralegh, Donne, Milton, Thomas Browne, Jeremy
Taylor, Edward Gibbon, and many other great writers, stood the
undecorated work of the new urban scientific writers, beginning
with the 'mathematical plainness' of the Royal Society's ideal of
prose as defined by Bishop Sprat in 1661.

The informal language of the people, ungoverned by rules laid
down in books, and shaped in its standard form by the customary
social rites and conventions of London and thereabouts, had
taken an established form. But exactly what that form was and
how it differed from the written standard is difficult to determine in
detail except in so far as we can discern something of its nature
from the colloquial language of drama and from letters that
survive from the period.

4

The Disjunctive Period: 1776 to the Present Day

English, no longer an English language, now grows from many roots.

Salman Rushdie, *The Times*, 3 July 1982, p. 8

In 1776 the main body of English speakers still lived in the British Isles. English was indisputably a language with its centre of gravity in London. With its main provincial varieties, it was spoken by more people in the British Isles than by all those who had moved abroad, whether as explorers or as colonists.

George III had reigned for sixteen years and Lord North was the first minister of the Tory government of the time. Other leading politicians included William Pitt the Elder, who had been the first minister in 1766 and 1767 but was by this date too ill to spend much time in Parliament; Edmund Burke, the great Irish-born orator and writer; the controversial radical John Wilkes; and Charles James Fox, one of the best-known debaters in the House.

Many of the major literary figures of the eighteenth century were already dead, Pope in the 1740s, Jonathan Swift in 1745, Henry Fielding in 1754, Laurence Sterne in 1768, Smollett in 1771, and Oliver Goldsmith in 1774. The Romantic movement of art and literature had scarcely begun. Jane Austen and Charles Lamb were babies of 1, as was the painter J. M. W. Turner; Samuel Taylor Coleridge was 4, Walter Scott 5, and William Wordsworth 6. William Blake was a young man of 19 and Fanny Burney a young woman of 24. Robert Lowth, Professor of Poetry at Oxford 1741–50, and a prescriptive grammarian, was 66. Samuel Johnson was 67 and his friend Mrs Thrale 35.

The language of Johnson and Mrs Thrale, and that of their adult contemporaries, was the stately language of the time, polished, stylish, unordinary, even in the intimate pages of their diaries, and the regime of instruction was severe and practical.

The severity of the private education of the time is underlined by a passage from Hester Thrale's diary of 20 January 1775, describing the education of her sixth child Susanna, then five years old:

Her Improvements more than equal my hopes, my Wishes, nay my very Fancies. She reads even elegantly & with an Emphasis, says her Catechism both in French & English: is got into Joyn hand [cursive script] with her pen, & works at her Needle so neatly, that She has made her Sister a Shift all herself. She knows the Map of Europe as well as I do, with the Capital Cities, Forms of Govt. &c. the Lines Circles & general Geography of the Globe She is Mistress of; & has a Knowledge of the Parts of Speech that She cannot be ensnared by any Question.[1]

The picture that emerges from the books and dictionaries of the eighteenth century is of an orderly language. Almost everyone had absolutist views of linguistic correctness, and such views were buttressed by grammarians like Robert Lowth and Lindley Murray.

From the early eighteenth century, and especially in Swift's *Proposal for Correcting, Improving and Ascertaining the English Tongue* (1712), the rallying cry was for a linguistic standard. The main outlines of the argument are well documented and are well known. Inherent in Swift's *Proposal* is a cyclical theory of language—that, however language first descended to Man, whether as a gift from God, or as a spontaneous creation of a group of men at a particular point in time, or for whatever reason, a given language slowly made its way to a fine point of perfection, as it had in ancient Greece and Rome, from which it would gradually become subject to debilitating influences and become weakened. Swift was hopeful that the cyclical movement of English might be arrested at the point of perfection:

The English Tongue is not arrived to such a Degree of Perfection, as to make us apprehend any Thoughts of its Decay; and if it were once refined to a certain Standard, perhaps there might be Ways found to fix it for ever.[2]

The debilitating influences, he thought, as others also did, were far more potentially dangerous in the spoken language than in the written form, and were present especially in regional and provincial forms of English. In the coffee houses and picture galleries of London, the language of the literary élite, that is of Johnson and his circle, was proclaimed to be the form of English to which others should aspire. Out there in the provinces, and in the colonies, the death-watch beetles of language lurked.[3]

Dr Johnson, like the other English lexicographers and grammarians of the time, did not visit America, and his comments on America, and on the English used in North America, fell far short of the subtlety with which he applied his mind to many other subjects that he knew from personal experience. Another great lexicographer of the eighteenth century, Nathan Bailey, in his *Universal Etymological English Dictionary* (1721) did give some attention to American words. For example he defined the exotic bird *loon* as

A bird, in New-England, like a Cormorant, that can scarce go, much less fly; and makes a noise like a Sowgelder's Horn.

Dr Johnson would have none of this: there is no entry for *loon* in his *Dictionary*, nor entries for any of the American Indian words like *skunk*, *squaw*, and *moccasin*, that we know now were well established in American written English long before Johnson's dictionary was published in 1755. In his review of Lewis Evans's *General Map and Account of the Middle British Colonies in America* (1756) Johnson remarked:

This treatise [is] written with such elegance as the subject admits tho' not without some mixture of the American dialect, a tract of corruption to which every language widely diffused must always be exposed.[4]

In 1776, at the point of political severance between Great Britain and the United States, except for a small infusion of words from east coast Indian languages, the English language of North America was not in any radical way dissimilar from that of the land the American settlers called the mother country. George Washington and Lord North would not have detected any more than trivial differences in the other's vocabulary and mode of speaking. The soldiers of the opposing armies were recognizably different in their uniforms but not in their speech, except in minor particularities.

Such differences as there were have yielded themselves up to the busy research of modern scholars but they could not have been commandingly obvious to people at the time. For example, the word *body* used to mean 'a person', as in 'a body should be very cautious in admitting a stranger to her family', had been taken to North America by regional speakers of English, and was not a home-grown Americanism nor a standard meaning in the British Isles. Further evidence of minor deviations from standard English usage is to be found in the works of English reviewers who complained about the presence of distinctive American words and senses in publications emanating from North America. For example, a reviewer in the *Critical Review*, writing of Charles Chauncy's *The Benevolence of the Deity* (1784):

The style of this treatise is, in general, clear and unaffected, though not elegant. We meet with some uncouth words; such as *bestowment, exertment, lengthy, enlargedness, preparedness*; which we cannot account for on any other supposition than that of their being current in America.[5]

But the same reviewers made very similar remarks about works written in Britain outside the literary groups of London. For example, the *Monthly Review* reviewer of a book by 'Peter Pennyless' called *Sentimental Lucubrations* (1770), believing that 'Peter Pennyless' was either a Scotsman, or a Scotsman living in America, objected to such 'unspiritual and carnal words' as *perlimanory, facilitously, positiviously,* and *concentricated.* It was the start of a long period, not yet over, of assuming that unfamiliar words or constructions were very likely of provincial or uneducated origin, or, much more disastrously, of American origin. In 1776, however, the American cloud was no bigger than a man's hand. There were only three million people in the American colonies, and no one saw American English as posing any more than a minor and containable threat to the English of the British Isles.

By 1776 speakers of English had caught glimpses of territories in other parts of the globe and some of them had settled, but mostly in small communities and not yet with any kind of local linguistic sovereignty, whatever the political circumstances. For example, Warren Hastings, the first Governor-General of British India, went to India in 1750 and was appointed governor of Bengal in 1772. But the main period of adoption of Indian words into English came later, and later still the preservation of now discarded English words and meanings by the Indians themselves. James Cook rounded the Cape of Good Hope and 'discovered' Australia and New Zealand in his voyages of 1768-71, 1772-5, and 1776–9, but the main groups of English settlers did not arrive in South Africa and in Australia and New Zealand until the early nineteenth century. Canada was a battlefield between the English and the French, and the first adumbrations of Canadian bilingualism were discernible. But here too Canadian Indians and the unique geographical features of this vast country had produced only the faint outline of a new variety of English. The West Indies was a territory for economic exploitation; nearly two centuries were to pass before the speech of West Indian immigrants began to draw the attention of the rest of the world to the distinctive forms of English forged in these Caribbean islands.

The dispersal of people from an imperialist country inevitably leads to linguistic change and the last quarter of the eighteenth century witnessed the beginning of a disjunctive process which was just as important as the great linguistic severing processes of earlier centuries, including that of the hiving off of the Angles, Saxons, and Jutes from their European counterparts. Neat bundles of regional forms of English in the British Isles, and also the received standard variety of educated speakers in London and the Home Counties, were physically transported abroad where they began, at first slowly, and then dramatically, to break up into new bundles or parcels, all of them wrenched and twisted from their original shape by the new circumstances in which the settlers found themselves. Political independence came to the new territories at different rates, none so quickly as that of the United States. Linguistic independence—a plain recognition by the new communities abroad that their own form of English was at the same time different from that of the mother country yet not inferior to it—came much later. Meanwhile the English language continued to change, but in different ways, in the British Isles themselves.

*

The rest of this chapter will be devoted to the main changes that have affected the home variety of English—British English—since 1776. Some of them are shared by Englishes abroad: others are not.

Paradoxically, authorities find it more difficult to analyse the changes in pronunciation of the last two hundred years than of any similar period at any earlier date. As Barbara Strang remarked,

'Some short histories of English give the impression that change in pronunciation stopped dead in the 18c.'[6] But she went on to say:

It is true that the sweeping systematic changes we can detect in earlier periods are missing, but the amount of change is no less. Rather, its location has changed; in the last two hundred years changes in pronunciation are predominantly due, not, as in the past, to evolution of the system, but to what, in a very broad sense, we may call the interplay of different varieties, and to the complex analogical relationship between different parts of the language. These tendencies are old, but are not until recently predominant.[7]

H. C. Wyld, at a somewhat earlier date, argued that before the late eighteenth century 'the natural tendencies were allowed more or less unrestricted play, and this among speakers of the Received Standard of the period no less than among the more uneducated. Purists . . . existed, who protested against this or that usage, but few listened to them.'[8] From the third quarter of the eighteenth century onward, he said, new attitudes towards correctness became established:

It was assuredly not the Verneys and Wentworths, the Lady Hobarts, or 'my sister Carburer' who first adopted the new-fangled English . . . It was the new men and their families, who were winning a place in the great world and in public affairs, who would be attracted by the refinements offered by the new and 'correct' system of pronunciation which they learnt from their masters of rhetoric, or from their University tutors. That this new, wealthy, and often highly cultivated class should gradually have imposed upon society at large the gentilities of the academy of deportment, and have been able to insist with success upon *gown* instead of '*gownd*', *strict* instead of '*strick*', *vermin* instead of '*varmint*', *richest* instead of '*richis*', and so on, would have seemed incredible to Lady Wentworth and her friends. But so it has come about.[9]

It cannot be gainsaid that from the time of the eighteenth-century grammarians onward broad views about linguistic correctness established themselves in this country and in English-speaking countries abroad. The printers of books and of newspapers were governed by generally agreed rules of spelling and punctuation. House-style books abounded, culminating in the current printers' bibles, *Hart's Rules for Compositors and Readers at the University Press, Oxford*, the *Oxford Dictionary for Writers and Editors*, the *Chicago Manual of Style*, and equivalent books in other countries. University teachers and schoolteachers adopted standard grammars and dictionaries and devised prescriptive rules to set before their pupils. Public speakers, actors, and in due course broadcasting authorities followed more or less fixed rules of elocution and pronunciation, the rules being changed at intervals but only in this particular or that. The written language has become imprisoned within walls of rules and nobody seems to mind, least of all authors. The new rune-masters are the desk editors and the sub-editors. By 1936 H. C. Wyld could say:

Though each generation probably sees something of the old usage given up, there are many strongholds of ancient habits which still resist the encroachments of innovation. *'Ed'ard'*, *'husban''*, *'edjikate'*, *'Injun'*, *'ooman'*, *'masty'* (mastiff), *'pagin'* (pageant), and the like have gone, but [grinidž (Greenwich), nɔridž (Norwich), ɔfn (often), litrətʃə (literature), bousən (bosun)], and many others, survive from the wreckage. These natural and historic forms are growing steadily less, and every 'advance' in education sweeps more of them away. It will be interesting to see what fresh pranks the rising generation will play, and with what new refinements they will adorn our language.[10]

Some of the detailed changes that have happened in the period since 1776 may be listed. But it must be emphasized that much more space would be needed if an attempt were made to describe the whole system and its development.

At some time between Middle English and 1776 it had become fashionable to pronounce unstressed examples of /ŋ/ as /n/, for example 'huntin', 'shootin', instead of 'hunting', 'shooting'. Under the influence of spelling this fashion retreated and except in isolated pockets of speech the sound /ŋ/ is now usual in RP in both stressed and unstressed syllables, for example *stinging*. It remains uncertain when this came about, and such changes can rarely be pinned down to periods of less than an century.

Before 1776, as now, /h/ was normally pronounced in native words that began with the letter *h* provided that the main stress fell at the beginning of the word, as in *house, heathen*. It was also commonly, though mistakenly, introduced in such circumstances in words which correctly began with a vowel, for example *able* pronounced /ˈheɪbˈl/, and not only in uneducated speech. In words of French origin like *herb, hospital, hotel, humble*, and *humour*, the initial *h* was normally silent until about 1930, and then changed as the notion of the 'dropping of h' emerged and came under attack. In American English, though, *herb* is still usually pronounced without the initial /h/ as a survival of the older rule.

Other consonants have been reintroduced as a result of the convention of following the spelling. Thus from the mid-nineteenth century the dominance of /w/ was restored in the pronunciation of words like *swore* (cf. *sword*) and *woman* (cf. *ooze* f. OE. *wāse*); and, in unstressed syllables, *Edward*, *Ipswich*, and *upward*, formerly often 'Ed'ard', etc. The silent *w* can still be observed in *towards* when it is pronounced /tɔːdz/ and *untoward* when it is pronounced /ʌnˈtɔːd/. Many other words now show the pronunciation of consonants that before 1776 were often silent, e.g. husban*d*, masti*ff*, so*l*dier, fa*l*con, and pa*v*ement. Similarly the glide /j/, formerly assimilated to a preceding *d* as in *immediate* and *idiot* (thus /dʒ/), reverted to /dj/ in the course of the nineteenth century. In the present century words with initial *wh-* have for the most part lost the initial aspiration in RP, so that, for example, *whine* and *wine, whales* and *Wales* are now usually pronounced identically. Some RP speakers, however, prefer to retain the aspiration, and nearly all speakers in northern counties of England and in Scotland retain it. In practice the difference is hardly noticed unless attention is drawn to it.

In the same period /ɑː/ has been replaced by /ɔː/ in such words as *jaundice, launch, laundry*, and *Maundy*. The final syllable *-ile* reverted to /aɪl/ in words like *fertile* and *missile*, whereas the earlier pronunciation /əl/ has survived in the United States. How typically American /ˈmɪsəl/ sounds and yet how British it once was! In words like *leisure, pleasure*, and *treasure* the stressed vowel was pronounced either long or short in the eighteenth century. The variant with a long vowel has survived as the normal form in the United States in the word *leisure* /ˈliːʒər/ but not in the others. In fairly recent times, and especially since the 1914-18 war, words of the type *cloth, cross, lost, off* have normally acquired a short vowel—thus /ɒ/ instead of /ɔː/—though many speakers of the Nancy Mitford type still say 'clorth', 'crors', 'lorst', etc.

Readers will all be able to draw on their own experience for instances of most of the above changes and variations. It is the same when one turns to the positioning of the stress in words of two or more syllables. Rightly or wrongly, delicate judgements are made about a person's social acceptability or his level of education by the way in which the stress is placed in such words as *centrifugal, controversy, dispute* (noun), *exquisite, formidable,* and *kilometre.* Few speakers know how often the pendulum swings in such matters and at what rate. Judgements tend to be made subjectively ('it has always been so', 'I was brought up to say'), doubtless because of the existence of a bewildering and difficult array of conflicting models and analogies. Thus, for example, four-syllabled words have two main models, represented by Type 1 *matrimony* (stressed on the first syllable) and Type 2 *monotony* (stressed on the second). The positioning of the stress in these two words never varies. But numerous other four-syllabled words are unstable, and have moved from their once traditional pattern to another. Thus, within living memory, Type 2 has steadily overtaken Type 1 in *accessory, applicable, controversy, despicable, formidable, hospitable,* and *metallurgy.* Within the same period a second type, with secondary stress on the first syllable and main stress on the third, has tended to replace an earlier Type 2 pattern in *centrifugal* and *centripetal.*

Similar shiftings of stress have occurred in words of three syllables. Thus *balcony* (until *c.*1825) and *remonstrate* were normally pronounced with the main stress on the second syllable in the nineteenth century; in the case of *sonorous* and *subsidence* the stress is now commonly being brought forward to the first syllable; words ending in *-ein,* like *casein* and *protein,* were pronounced as three syllables (like 'racy in', 'moaty inn') earlier in the present century, as was *rabies* (like 'baby ease'). The word *syndrome,* now invariably pronounced as two syllables, was regularly pronounced with three (like 'syncope') as late as 1920.

*

Lexical changes in the period from 1776 to the present day are very numerous. To some extent the sheer number of accessions to the language reflects the increasing industry of lexicographers since 1857 when Dean Trench set in motion the greatest trawling of English words ever undertaken; that is, when he took the first steps towards the compilation of the twelve-volume *Oxford English Dictionary.* By the time the dictionary was completed in 1928 a permanent record of more than 414,000 words had been set down in alphabetical order. The total and the rate of accession of words can be analysed in various ways but it would be unwise to draw any but very cautious conclusions from the results. For example, it is of some interest to observe that in the period of the language recorded in the *OED*, namely *c.*740 to 1928, a period of approximately 1200 years, a total of 414,000 words would appear to work out at an average annual intake of some 350 new words. But it naturally does not follow that, after allowing for additions (new formations, loanwords, etc.) and losses (by obsolescence etc.), we could identify 350 words that came into the language in a particular year.

Dr Johnson's *Dictionary of the English Language* (1755) contains about the same number of items as the *Concise Oxford Dictionary* (1982). But the entries are physically presented in such a way that Dr Johnson's dictionary looks much longer than the *COD*. This is partly because of Johnson's numerous illustrative examples, but also because of the layout and typography. Tall pages and large type are great disguisers of true dimensions.

As in the three earlier periods, the new vocabulary of the modern period since 1776 can be classified into two main groups, those formed within the language by one means or another, and loanwords.

Almost all the normal methods of word-formation have been drawn on generously in the modern period. The prefixes *a-*, *de-*, *meta-*, *micro-*, *mini-*, *multi-*, *neo-*, *non-*, *retro-*, and *ultra-* (as well as many others) have been especially prolific, as in *apolitical* (1952), *decaffeinate* (1934), *metastable* (1897), *microcosmic* (1783), *minibus* (1845), *multistorey* (1918), *neo-grammarian* (1885), *non-event* (1962), *retroflexion* (1845), and *ultrasonic*.[11]

Similarly old suffixes like *-ish*, *-ize*, *-less*, *-like*, *-ness*, *-some*, and *-y* have lost none of their formative power, for example *voguish*, *privatize* (1969), *carless* (1927), *pianola-like* (1945), *pushiness* (1920), *chillsome* (1927), and *jazzy* (1919).

Somewhat more complicated formations, though still containing familiar elements, are commonplace, for example *demythologize* (1950), *denazify* (1944), *paraphrasability* (1965), *post-doctoral* (1939), *prepsychotically* (1941), *renormalization* (1948), and *rubbernecker* (1934).

New suffixes of the nineteenth and twentieth centuries include *-burger*, as in *beefburger* (1940) and *cheeseburger* (1938); *-ette*, denoting a female, as in *majorette* (1941), *suffragette*, and *usherette*; *-in*, signifying a large gathering, as in *love-in* (1967), *sit-in*, and *teach-in*; and *-nik* (from Russian or Yiddish), as in *beatnik* (1958), *peacenik* (1965), and *sputnik* (1957).

Back-formations are very numerous, as *reminisce* (verb) (1829) from *reminiscence*, and *window-shop* (verb) from *window-shopping*. So too are shortened or clipped formations like *exam* (1877), *gym* (1871), and *lab* (1895).

Blended words abound, for example *brunch* (breakfast + lunch, 1896), *chortle* (chuckle + snort, 1872), *octopush* (octopus + push, 1970, a kind of underwater hockey), *rurban* (rural + urban, 1918), *savagerous* (savage + dangerous, 1832), Joyce's *scribbledehobble* (scribble + hobbledehoy, 1922), *smaze* (smoke + haze, 1953), and *smog* (smoke + fog, 1903). Closely related are humorous perversions of similarly sounding words, for example *screwmatics* (after *rheumatics*, 1895) and *slimnastics* (after *gymnastics*, 1970).

Rhyming slang has a produced a crop of interesting expressions, for example *apple(s) and pears* (= stairs, 1857), *half-inch* (= to 'pinch', steal, 1925), and *butcher's* (short for *butcher's hook* = look, 1936).[12] Rhyming combinations like *brain-drain* (1963), *fuddy-duddy* (1904), *hanky-panky* (1841), and *walkie-talkie* continue an old tradition,[13] as do near-rhyming combinations like *pingpong* (1900).[14]

Newly coined words as such are comparatively rare in the modern period (see the table on p. 45), apart from acronyms. It is almost as if the ancient minting processes have become exhausted, to judge from the fact that most of the new vocabulary is built up from combinations of old elements or is drawn from foreign (ancient or modern) languages.

Primary additions to the wordhoard tend to come from commercial sources (e.g. *Kodak*, *nylon*); from academic writers drawing on traditional and newly delved-out ancient elements, e.g. *oligopsony* (from the prefix *oligo-*, Greek ὀλίγος 'small', in plural 'few', and ὀψωνεῖν 'to buy provisions') first recorded in 1943 in the sense 'in marketing, a situation in which only a small number of buyers exists for a product'; and from literary writers. Those of the third type have little life outside bookish circles and most of them, though delightful in themselves, are likely to remain only in the minds and arguments of literary scholars. Examples abound:

Then I scoff at the floridity and absurdity of some *scrolloping* [heavily ornamented] tomb. (Virginia Woolf, *The Waves* (1931), p. 308)[15]

I loathe and always have loathed Indian art. . . . *Obnubilated* [obscure], short curves, muddle, jungle. (E. Pound, letter of 7 Nov. 1939 (edited by D. D. Paige, 1971), p. 330)

Brand-new words in the letter O

Brand-new words coming into general public use are now comparatively rare. Some typical examples of new words in the letter O are given below as an indication of the way in which such words emerge. Excluded from the list are abbreviations, loanwords, acronyms, technical and scientific words only in specialized use, and derivatives of existing words.

Word	Subject, etc.	Meaning	Etymology	Date of first recorded use
Obie	US theatre	a theatrical award	represents pronunciation of *OB* 'Off-Broadway'	1967
ocker	Australian slang	boorish person	name of character in a TV series	1971
Oerlikon	gunnery	light anti-aircraft cannon	suburb of Zurich where first made	1944
oick, oik	school slang	a disliked pupil	unknown	1933
olde, oldie	general colloquial	supposedly archaic way of saying 'old'	affected form of 'old'	1927
Olivetti	industry	trade name of a range of typewriters	name of business firm in Turin	1949
oomph	slang (orig. US)	sex appeal	invented (imitative)	1937
oops	interjection	exclamation expressing apology etc.	a natural exclamation	1933
oracy	linguistics	fluency in speech	L. *ōs, ōr-* mouth, after 'literacy'	1965
Oreo	US slang	an American Black (derogatory use)	commercial name of a chocolate wafer	1968
Oscar	US cinema, etc.	a motion-picture award	arbitrary use of the Christian name of a person	1936
Ozalid	printing	trade name of a kind of photographic proof	*diazo-* reversed with *l* inserted	1924

It happened that you were *peloothered* [drunk], Tom. (James Joyce, *Dubliners* (1914), p. 197)

Will the sea be *polyphloisbic* [boisterous] and wine dark and unvintageable? (Rupert Brooke, a letter of 1915 (edited by G. Keynes, 1968), p. 662)

Words signifying 'the collecting of ———' are particularly common in our acquisitive age. The class of such words is typified by *scripophily* 'the collecting of old bond and share certificates as a pursuit', which was coined in 1978.

Various factors cause local and regional words to make their way from villages and hamlets into the central wordstock. This is a perpetual process, and it has possibly been speeded up somewhat by modern conditions. In quite a short time such words, at one time buried deep in the obscurity of a remote region, stride into the central language with their rural origins forgotten. Among modern words of this kind one can cite *gormless*, a respelling of older *gaumless*, and not common in general English before the 1930s; *scrounge* (noun and verb), apparently popularized by servicemen in the 1914-18 war; and *seep* 'to ooze, drip, trickle', a verb that did not come into general English use before the present century.

Among the more questionable methods of word-formation at the present time is that which gives us acronyms, that is words formed from the initial letters of (usually) separate words. This technique of word-formation seems to be political and military in origin, to judge from the types *Ogpu* (Russ. *Ob"edinënnoe Gosudárstvennoe Politícheskoe Upravlénie*, United State Political Directorate), first recorded in 1923, and *Anzac* (Australian and New Zealand Army Corps), first recorded in 1915. In more recent times they have become more numerous than crows, especially in the period since 1945, and are now admitted to general dictionaries only on a very selective basis. Well-known acronyms include *Nato* (*N*orth *A*tlantic *T*reaty *O*rganization, set up in 1949) and *radar* (*ra*dio *d*etection *a*nd *r*anging, 1941). But organizations of every kind cast around for a set of initials pronounceable as a word: typical examples of trade-union acronyms, for example, are *Aslef* (*A*ssociated *S*ociety of *L*ocomotive *E*ngineers and *F*iremen), *COHSE* /ˈkəʊzɪ/ (*C*onfederation *o*f *H*ealth *S*ervice *E*mployees), and *SOGAT* /ˈsəʊɡæt/ (*S*ociety *o*f *G*raphical and *A*llied *T*rades). The great majority of them have no other meaning than the name

of the organization itself, and there are no derivatives. Thus
*Aslefer does not exist in the sense 'a member of Aslef', nor is there
a verb *to* *aslef, 'to become a member of Aslef, to act in the manner
of members of Aslef', though it seems likely that such derivatives
will in due course occur. Many acronyms are so skilfully contrived
that they seem to presuppose the existence of genuine Latin,
Greek, or Old English words: thus *Nato* has distant echoes of L.
natāre to swim; *thalidomide* (a near relation of an acronym in that
it is formed from ph*thali*mi*do*glutari*mide*) misleadingly suggests
some kind of connection with Greek θάλαμος, Latin *thalamus*, an
inner chamber; and *rurp* (realized *u*ltimate *r*eality *p*iton), first
recorded in 1968, sounds like an imitative word of native origin
(cf. *burp*, *slurp*). Others are made as homonyms of ordinary
English words, for example *DARE* (*D*ictionary of *A*merican
*R*egional *E*nglish), *Sarah* (*s*earch *a*nd *r*escue *a*nd *h*oming), the
name of a portable radio transmitter, and *OWLS*, the *O*xford
*W*ord and *L*anguage *S*ervice (launched 1983).

*

The period since 1776 has witnessed a slowing-down of the rate
of absorption of loanwords from foreign languages, though such
words are still common enough in all conscience. By contrast
there has been an enormous increase in the outflow of English
words to foreign languages—hence the phenomena of *franglais*,
Japlish, etc.

The adoption of foreign loanwords is a direct result of culture
contact, whether by imperialist conquest, by tourism, or by the
receiving of new fashions of food, clothing, entertainment, or the
like, in one's own country from abroad. French expressions of
varying degree of naturalization (*blasé*, *femme de chambre*, *jeune
fille*, *pendule*, *porte-cochère*, etc.) abound in nineteenth-century
novels. But modern writers tend to look further afield. Travel,
war, and politics have brought into our language a great many
expressions from all the major languages of the world, many of
them awkwardly pronounced and only half understood. A few
examples must suffice: from Arabic, *Hadith* (body of traditions
relating to Muhammad), *naskhi* (cursive script), *qasida* (elegiac
poem), and *rafik* (companion); Chinese, *Lapsang Souchong*, *Mah
Jong*, *Pinyin* (alphabet), *putonghua* (standard spoken language),
qi (life-force), and loan-translations like *capitalist roader*, *running*

dog, and *scorched earth*; German, *Bildungsroman, Gestalt, Gestapo, gesundheit* (expression to wish good health), *hausfrau*, and *langlauf* (cross-country skiing); Hebrew, *mazel tov* (good luck!), *Mizpah* (expression of association), *Mizrach* (Judaic practice of turning towards Israel in prayer), *pilpul* (rabbinical argumentation), and *Sabra* (Israeli Jew); Japanese, *happi(coat)*, *Noh*, *origami* (paper-folding), *pachinko* (kind of pin-ball), and *sashimi* (strips of raw fish); Malay, *langsat* (edible fruit), *merdeka* (freedom), *nasi* (cooked rice), *ronggeng* (popular dance), and *satay* (skewered meat); Russian, *nekulturny* (boorish person), *samizdat, sastruga*, and *sputnik*; and Yiddish, *lox, mazuma, pastrami, schlemiel* (blunderer), and *schmuck* (idiot).

*

In grammar and syntax the period since 1776 has been characterized, as in earlier periods, by innovation, by new freedoms from traditional constraints, and by losses or forgettings.

Incursions have been made into the traditional territory of the adjective by the noun modifier. First, though, it is important to remember that the adjective itself has never been a clearly distinguishable part of speech with predictable and permanent functions applicable in all cases. From earliest times most adjectives could be used both before the nouns they qualified (OE. *strang rāp*, modE. *strong rope*) and after, in what is usually called the predicative position (OE. *sē rāp is strang*, modE. *the rope is strong*). Most of them could also be used in comparative and superlative forms (OE. *strengra, strengest*, modE. *stronger, strongest*). Most of them could also be modified by the intensifier *very* (or in OE. *sōplice* 'truly' or similar adverb): *very strong*.

In the predicative position adjectives could be used after many other verbs than the verb *to be*. Thus *the problem seemed insoluble* (where the subject is modified by the adjective) and (less commonly) *he thought the problem insoluble* (where the object is modified by the adjective). For the comparative and superlative forms of longer adjectives it has long been customary to use the positive form preceded by *more* or *most* (*these problems are more intractable than you think; the most beautiful woman I have ever seen*).

Some adjectives, however, have been more restricted in their use or have overlapped with other parts of speech, especially adverbs.

Thus the adjective *tantamount* can now only be used predicatively (*her reply was tantamount to a flat refusal*), and *utter* can only be used attributively (*the utter absurdity of his views*).

The overlapping of adjectives and adverbs is evident in cases like the following:

The boy was asleep (but not **the asleep boy*).[16]
He spoke loud and clear or *He spoke loudly and clearly.*
They arrived late (the meaning changes in *They arrived lately*).

Such restrictions and overlappings of adjectives and adverbs have always been important in English. But the complications have been increased enormously in the last two hundred years, and particularly in the present century, by a seemingly ungovernable growth in the use of attributive nouns, that is of nouns (frequently more than one) used where speakers had formerly, for the most part, expected only adjectives to appear. A typical example is *Greenham Common peace women*, where the word *women* is preceded by three nouns; and it would be possible to construct even longer strings of nouns without wrecking intelligibility.

This power to join nouns together without the use of the possessive apostrophe and without the use of *of* is now firmly established. Not unexpectedly it has a long history. From earliest times it was possible to place a noun like *silver* before other nouns:

1032 OE.: þritig seolfor sticca   thirty pieces of silver
*c.*1366 Chaucer: a sylvre nedle   a silver needle
*c.*1407 Lydgate: the colde siluer stremes   the cold silver streams

Other noun modifiers lay ready to hand, for example *head* (OE. *hēafod*):

*c.*1000 Ælfric: ðæra Iudeiscra heafod biscop   chief bishop of the Jews
1357 *Lay Folk's Catech.*: the seuen heued synnes   the seven deadly sins

The decay of inflexions and the loss of final *-e* (pronounced in Middle English as /ə/) also produced a great many noun + noun combinations by 1400:

Old English	*Middle English*	*By 1400*
healle duru	halle dore	hall-door
door of a hall	/ˈhalə/	
fully genitival	semi-genitival	no trace of genitive

By such means, and by later imitation, the language acquired a very large class of compound nouns of the *hall-door* type, for example *handbook, love-song, sackcloth, sunbeam, weekday*, and *woodland*. Some of these, indeed, had fossilized as single words in the Anglo-Saxon period itself.

As time went on this method of combining nouns accelerated, and all memory of the possessive nature of the first noun passed into oblivion. English speakers were free to combine any noun with another, without regard to its etymology or to its original grammatical gender, provided that the combination made sense. Examples:

c.1350	cherry-stone	1663	cannon-ball
1590	sandbag	1748	farm-yard
1650	trade-wind	1849	sea-power

Such two-unit expressions themselves then became attached to other nouns, and noun phrases like *coffeehouse conversation* (Hume, 1752) and *fellow-workman* (Coverdale, 1535) became common enough. From these it was an easy step to the formation of more complex assemblages like *whoreson malt-house drudge* (*Taming of the Shrew*, 1596), *tortoise-shell memorandum book* (*Humphry Clinker*, 1771) and *shellfish supper-house* (Trollope's *The Warden*, 1855). And then, as a matter of course, but much more frequently, we find modern writers (especially journalists and civil servants) using phrases like *university block grant arrangements* and *rate support grant settlement* all the time.

An important development in the modern period, shared by all varieties of English, is a substantial increase in the use of the word *one* as what Henry Sweet called a 'prop-word'.

Another way of using the adjective without its noun in English is to substitute the unmeaning noun-pronoun *one* for the noun, the inflection of the noun being transferred to the prop-word, as we may call it.[17]

Examples: He rents a house, but I own one.
          Two checked shirts and a blue one.

As the *OED* points out (*One* pron. 22), 'Formerly, *one* at the end of a clause or sentence was pleonastic or emphatic'.[18]

The word *one* has been subjected to a number of other functional changes as in:

He's one dexterous handler of words. (= a very)
I will see you or send word, one. (US dialectal, = one or the other)
A one-in-three hill. (= a gradient of)
It took a long time to count the notes as they were mostly in ones. (= a one-pound or one-dollar note)
He is not one to boast. (= a sort of person who would)

Such 'silent' changes, as is pointed out elsewhere in this book, are part of the acceptable face of language change, and are far more numerous than changes which are regarded as regressive.

There is little doubt that expressions of the type *Greenham Common peace protest group*, and extensions of the use of *one* as a prop-word, would have startled Swift, Johnson, and other writers in the eighteenth century. Similarly startling developments by the standards of the eighteenth century have come about in the way in which verbs are used, especially in the emergence of new periphrastic forms and in the use of the passive. An analysis of the various new types lies outside the scope of this book, but the new freedoms can be observed in the following examples—none of them available before 1800:

We were having a nice time before you arrived.
He is having to give up smoking.
Irrigation schemes *had been being developed* in Thailand long before modern techniques arrived.
With a view to preventing waste.
He has been known to be rude to his neighbours.

These are matters for professional investigation and disputation. The din of battle about them hardly extends beyond the seminar and conference room, and the mass of English speakers simply regard them as belonging to the undifferentiated and undisputed mass of constructions that form part of their linguistic heritage.

Since the eighteenth century, however, deep-seated concern has been expressed in many quarters about some other grammatical matters, and a chasm has opened up between prescriptive and descriptive grammarians. The battle between linguistic conservatives and linguistic radicals continues unabated.

One way to discover some of the differences between the two sets of strategies is to examine the sketch called 'A Grammar of the English Tongue' which forms part of the prefatory matter to Dr Johnson's *Dictionary* (1755). I have selected some of the more revealing of Johnson's statements and added a comment of my own (preceded by ●) afterwards.

Present Tense.

Sing. I have, *thou* hast, *he* hath *or* has . . . *Has* is a termination corrupted from *hath*, but now more frequently used both in verse and prose.

● Note that J. does not comment on the distribution of *thou* and *you*. In 1755, although it was very much on the way out, it was still possible to use the pronoun *thou* in spoken and written English with varying degrees of formality, apart altogether from the special use of *Thou* and *Thee* in the Bible and in the Book of Common Prayer. J. also regards the distribution of *has* and *hath* as merely a matter of frequency not of rule.

––––––––

Future.

Sing. I shall have, *thou* shalt have, *he* shall have . . .

Second Future.

Sing. I will have, *thou* wilt have, *he* will have . . . By reading these future tenses may be observed the variations of *shall* and *will.*

● J. makes no comment on the circumstances in which *shall* and *will* were to be differentiated. As an indicator of the first person future tense *shall* (and *should*) is still usual in most regions of England; elsewhere it has almost entirely been supplanted by *will* or *'ll.*

––––––––

I do is sometimes used superfluously, as, *I* do *love*, *I* did *love*; simply for *I love*, or *I loved*; but this is considered as a vitious [J.'s spelling of 'vicious'] mode of speech.

● Emphatic and unemphatic uses of *do/did* as auxiliaries are now commonplace.

––––––––

Its chief use [*sc*. the use of *do*] is in interrogative forms of speech, in which it is used through all the persons; as, Do *I live?* Dost *thou strike me?* Do *they rebel?* Did *I complain?* Didst *thou love her?* Did *she die?* So likewise in negative interrogations; Do *I not yet grieve?* Did *she not die?*

● After allowing for the loss of *dost* and *didst* and for the formality of 'Did she not die?' these statements about the use of *do* in interrogative expressions are still broadly true.

––––––––

In like manner we commonly express the present tense, as, I am going, *eo*.
I am grieving, *doleo*. She is dying, *illa moritur*. The tempest is raging, *furit
procella* . . .

There is another manner of using the active participle, which gives it
a passive signification; as, The grammar is now printing, *grammatica jam
nunc chartis imprimitur*. The brass is forging, *æra excuduntur*. This is, in
my opinion, a vitious expression, probably corrupted from a phrase more
pure, but now somewhat obsolete: *The book is a printing*, *The brass is a
forging*; *a* being properly *at*, and *printing* and *forging* verbal nouns
signifying action, according to the analogy of this language.

● J., like most of his contemporaries, explains English tenses by reference
to Latin, a practice not without merit but now long since abandoned. Of
course, we no longer regard the type *The grammar is now printing* as
'a vicious expression'.

The indicative and conjunctive [subjunctive] moods are by modern writers
frequently confounded, or rather the conjunctive is wholly neglected,
when some convenience of versification does not invite its revival. It is
used among the purer writers after *if*, *though*, *ere*, *before*, *whether*, *except*,
unless, *whatsoever*, *whomsoever*, and words of wishing; as, *Doubtless thou
art our father*, though *Abraham* be *ignorant of us, and Israel* acknowledge
us not.

● The sense of desolation at the widespread disuse of the subjunctive
mood in the mid-eighteenth century is self-evident. By contrast Randolph
Quirk remarked in 1972: 'The subjunctive is not an important category in
contemporary English and is normally replaced by other constructions.'[19]

Quirk says (correctly) that the use of the mandative subjunctive (that
is, the subjunctive in *that*-clauses when the main clause contains an
expression of recommendation, resolution, demand, surprise, and so on)
occurs chiefly in formal style (and in American English), but is avoided by
most writers and speakers. Thus

We ask that the individual citizen *watch* closely any developments in this
matter.

can be re-expressed as:

We ask the individual citizen to watch closely any developments in this
matter.[20]

In present-day English the subjunctive is most commonly used in
formulaic expressions (*come what may*, *suffice it to say*, *be that as it may*,
etc.) and in an optional use of *were* instead of *was* in expressions like *I wish
I were/was dead*.[21]

And so time has moved on. *Thee* and *thou* have been relegated to seldom-opened drawers; *shall* and *will* vie with each other unevenly in different English-speaking areas; Latin has ceased to be a source of self-evident support in matters of grammar; and the subjunctive has retreated to a point of virtual extinction. The prescriptivists (who would have included all the great writers of the Victorian period as well as those of the eighteenth century) had no power to prevent such changes. Nor did the greatest prescriptivist of all, Henry Watson Fowler.

Fowler's *Dictionary of Modern English Usage* (1926), firmly based on tenets of classical grammar and on the English of great writers like Ruskin and less distinguished ones in the columns of the *Pall Mall Gazette* and the *Westminster Review*, is a brilliant summary of the views of a linguistic conservative in the early part of the present century. But radical views have emerged since then, expressed by people who are scornful of cherished myths and sternly insistent on the need to *describe* rather than *prescribe*. Paradoxically such radicals, most of them followers at various real or fancied removes of the Swiss scholar Ferdinand de Saussure (1857–1913), insist on *not* criticizing controversial and even plainly erroneous uses (when a word is, *through ignorance*, used erroneously) while avoiding such uses themselves in their own written work.

The contest between descriptive and prescriptive views of language reached its climax towards the end of the 1970s. My own role in the debate was (*a*) to ensure that in *A Supplement to the OED* all forms of modern English, throughout the world, were set down in so far as they are recorded in print, with suitable usage labels and elucidatory notes, (*b*) to prepare a booklet, *The Spoken Word: a BBC Guide* (BBC, 1981), which focused on the most controversial areas in spoken English. In *The Spoken Word* I argued that debatable features of spoken English grammar could be usefully divided into three groups:

1. *Unacceptable uses in any circumstances*
These included examples of *false concord*:
   The nature of his injuries *are* not known. (*Correctly: The nature* of his injuries *is* not known.)
   The jury hasn't been able to reach *their* verdict. (*Correctly: The jury hasn't* been able to reach *its* verdict, or *The jury haven't* been able to reach *their* verdict.)

Classical plurals construed as singulars:
The media often display (*not* displays) a sensational approach to events.
A phenomenon (*not* phenomena) of considerable importance.

Failure to use the oblique case of pronouns:
He will give another chance to you and I (*correctly* me).
The message was intended for we broadcasters (*correctly* us broadcasters).

Hanging or unattached participles:
Calling upon him last summer, he kindly offered to give me his copy.
(*Correctly*: When I called)

Confusion of 'less' and 'fewer':
The word *less* is correctly used of things that are measured by amount
(e.g. *to eat less butter, to use less fuel*). Its use of things measured by
number is incorrect (e.g. *we need less workers*; correct usage is *fewer
workers*).

Wrong participles:
He was *sat* there (*correctly* sitting).
This needs *changed* (*correctly* this needs changing).

2. *Uses resisted by listeners but permissible in informal English*

Preposition at end:
There are numerous circumstances in which a sentence may and even
must end with a preposition:
   i. *Relative clauses*. You can't imagine the kind of horrors (that) he
      saved us *from*.
  ii. *Wh*-questions.[22] Which hotel is he staying *at*? Who are you voting
      for?
 iii. *Wh*-clauses. What I am certain *of* is that the 1980s will be more
      dangerous than the 1970s.
  iv. *Exclamations*. What a shocking state you are *in*!
   v. *Passives*. The doctor was sent *for*.
  vi. *Infinitive clauses*. He is a nice person to work *for*.

Use of 'like' as a conjunction:
Modern writers regularly use this construction, especially when the
verb is repeated in the same sentence.
   Some girls change their lovers like they change their winter clothes
   (Graham Greene).
   They didn't talk like other people talk (Martin Amis).

Other categories included under this heading were verbless sentences
(*Another sunny day. Still no letters.*); use of the present tense for the
future tense (*At 8.30 Richard Stilgoe hunts through the BBC Sound
Archives for the voices of those who have made history*); and emphasis on

minor words, especially the indefinite and definite article (*a* 16-year-old boy; *the* campaign will be launched; trying to do the best *for* the country). All three are major new features of twentieth-century spoken English: they can be heard all the time in unscripted contexts on the radio and TV, and in all forms of public speaking, in Parliament, the Law Courts, public debates, and elsewhere. Some kind of 'spouters' law' is causing the traditional structures, tenses, and emphases to move in the spoken word. Anyone who doesn't believe it should have their own public utterances tape-recorded and analysed.

3. *Debatable features where considerable variety is found in the usage of educated people*

Use of 'who' and 'whom':
The formal distinction, *who* nominative and *whom* oblique, is breaking up but should be maintained where possible:
It is you *who* are at fault.
My grandfather, *whom* I disliked.
I never met the person from *whom* I bought it.
But in informal speech the nominative form tends to predominate:
Who do they think we are?
If it doesn't matter *who* anyone marries, then it doesn't matter *who* I marry.

Different from/to/than:
The usual construction in Britain is now with *from* ('my policy is in no way different *from* yours'), but that with *to* (after *dissimilar to*) is found in writers of all periods. The construction with *than* (after *other than*) is found in Addison, Steele, Carlyle, and Thackeray, among others, and is now very common in American English.

Split infinitive:
Infinitives have been 'split' (i.e. a word or phrase is inserted between *to* and following infinitive) in English since at least the fourteenth century, and will continue to be split as time goes on, either for humorous effect (Ross wants you *to* for God's sake *stop* attributing human behaviour to dogs—James Thurber), or because of the awkwardness that can result from writing such sentences with unsevered infinitives.

Other widely debated matters include the misplacing of *only*; the use of meaningless fillers (*actually, and um, I mean to say, sort of, see what I mean, you know*, etc.); wrong sequence of tenses; the use of *will/would* for *shall/should* as the simple 1st person future tense; confusion of *may* and *might*; and *none* followed by a plural verb (e.g. *none of us are blameless*).

When current standard English is carefully sifted these are the elements that are in the process of change. They are the present-day equivalent of the major changes described in chapters 2 and 3. There is little doubt that most of the new features that are intensely disliked by linguistic conservatives will triumph in the end. But the language will not bleed to death. Nor will it seem in any way distorted once the old observances have been forgotten.

5

Literature, Ritualistic Works, and Language

Wheresoe'er I turn my View
All is strange, yet nothing new . . .
Uncouth Words in Disarray:
Trickt in Antique Ruff and Bonnet,
Ode and Elegy and Sonnet.

Dr Johnson, poem of 1777 in *Poems*
(2nd edn., 1974), p. 206

This chapter will be concerned not so much with the ordinary elements of language as a means of communication as with enlivened and exceptional versions of it used for special purposes—English literature, and the three religious or ritualistic works that govern the spiritual life of millions of people, namely the Bible, the Book of Common Prayer, and the hymn-book.

Within the complex systems of ordinary day-to-day language lie the structured patterns and models that must be sought out and analysed if we are to understand how our language has evolved and what its nature is now. Declensional and conjugational arrangements, the gluing together of words in acceptably idiomatic order, the power of prepositions and adverbs, the ebb and flow of the meanings of the primary vocabulary of English—these are matters requiring persistent study.

From sheer necessity, however, because of the absence of continuous and unimpeachable evidence about the everyday language of people in the past, scholars have turned to the most extravagantly adorned monuments of all—Anglo-Saxon poetry, the battered beauty of Laȝamon's *Brut* and the resonance of Malory's *Morte Darthur*, Chaucer's tales, the ascetic rhetorical prose of scholars and divines from Ælfric to Cardinal Newman, the unparalleled artistry and potency of Shakespeare, Euphuism, metaphysical poetry, and all the other processes and devices of literature, down through the ages—and have tended to present these highly polished works of art to us as normal records of the language of the British Isles.

It is self-evident that highly polished language is still language, and that our cultural heritage would be devastatingly inadequate without the legacy bequeathed to us by our greatest writers. Let us not forget, however, that language used for special purposes tends to exhibit untypical qualities—features not necessarily present in everyday language—and in doing so often partially conceals the normal verbal and grammatical tendencies of the time.

In the Anglo-Saxon period the *scops* (minstrels) could not lift their harps without breaking into a formalized kind of alliterative verse—arresting, memorable, deeply embedded in tradition. In the moors and fens there inevitably lurk demons and the threat of terror:

> Wæs se grimma gæst   Grendel haten,
> mære mearc-stapa,   se þe moras heold,
> fen ond fæsten.   (*Beowulf* 102–4)

That grim spirit was called Grendel, the renowned traverser of the marches, who held the moors, the fen and fastness.

Outlaws, monsters, revenge, the fleetingness of time, decay, fame—these were the reiterated themes of the verse. Ancient traditional tellings of such matters were made crudely equatable with new Christian virtues. And the semi-Christian poets retold the old legends in ritualized language, with the normal order of words considerably disturbed, and with a range of rhetorical and metrical devices as complicated as those of ancient Greece and Rome:

> Hwær cwom mearg, hwær cwom mago? Hwær cwom maþþumgyfa?
> Hwær cwom symbla gesetu? Hwær sindon seledreamas?
>
> (*The Wanderer* 92–3)

Where has the horse gone and the kinsman? Where has the treasure-giver gone? Where are the feasting places now? Where are the joys of the hall?

The Anglo-Saxon poets obeyed a tradition buried deeply in Germanic antiquity. Their continental coevals inherited and continued with the same traditions, give or take a scaldic device or two. The themes and metrical devices of Old High German, Old Norse, and Old Saxon poetry are not easily distinguishable from those of the Anglo-Saxons—hardly more than those of an

American poet like Wallace Stevens on the one hand and an English one like Philip Larkin on the other. Compare the Anglo-Saxon:

> Hwæt, þu, Eue hæfst yfele gemearcod
> uncer sylfra sið.
>
> (*Later Genesis* 791–2)

Lo! thou, Eve, hast marked the fate of us both with evil.

and the equivalent lines in the Old Saxon poem *Heliand*:

> Uuela that thu nu Eua habas, quað Aðam, ubilo gimarakot
> unkaro selbaro sið.
>
> (*Heliand* (ed. Sievers), p. 8)

The language of Anglo-Saxon poetry, and the similarly elevated language of Anglo-Saxon prose, have both been subjected to minute scrutiny. Grammars, dictionaries, and concordances have been prepared. But one must constantly bear in mind that the noble effusions of the poems and sermons, and the formulaic language of the chronicles, charters, wills, and other documents, provide us with only a selective knowledge of the language—as removed from that of day-to-day Anglo-Saxon as the special language of modern Welsh poets at the Eisteddfods is from the daily language of Welsh speakers.

The *ubi sunt* formula illustrated above is an example of the poetical devices available to the *scops*. There were many others and in particular 'variation', an interlacing of broadly synonymous phrases:

> Swa fela fyrena   feond man-cynnes,
> atol angengea,   oft gefremede,
> heardra hynða;   Heorot eardode,
> sincfage sel   sweartum nihtum.
>
> (*Beowulf* 164–7)

Thus the enemy of mankind [Grendel], the fearsome solitary, often performed many dreadful deeds, unacceptable crimes; he dwelt in Heorot, the treasure-decorated hall, in the dark nights. [*Literally*: Thus many dreadful deeds the enemy of mankind, the fearsome solitary, often performed, unacceptable crimes; Heorot dwelt in, the treasure-decorated hall in dark nights.]

The exigencies of alliteration also brought into being a wide range of poetical near-synonyms, especially for concepts that occur frequently like valour, warrior, sea, exile, and weapon. Thus a warrior is called *æsc-wiga* (spear-warrior), *æþeling*, *beado-rinc* (battle-man), *beorn*, *byrn-wiga* (warrior in his corslet), *cempa*, *eorl*, *freca*, *gar-wiga* (spear-warrior), *guð-beorn* (war-warrior), *guð-rinc* (war-man), *here-rinc* (battle-man), and many other martial names in *Beowulf* alone. Similarly, for alliterative reasons, the Danes in *Beowulf* are called *Gar-Dene* (literally, spear-Danes), *East-Dene*, *Beorht-Dene* (glorious Danes), *Hring-Dene* (ring-Danes), *Norþ-Dene*, *Suþ-Dene*, and *West-Dene*, where the defining word in each case has no demonstrable contextual significance, though the associations are never forced or unpleasing. The poets, like their equivalents in Scandinavia, also employed a wide range of compounds called 'kennings', imaginative disguised metaphors for relatively simple concepts. For example a sword becomes *fela laf* 'what the files have left' or *homera laf* 'what the hammers have left'; similarly *bronda laf* 'what the flames have left' means 'ashes', and *yð-laf* 'what the ocean has left' means 'sand on the shore'.

This highly charged language cannot be contrasted with the ordinary ruminative prose, far less the speech, of a reasonably educated Anglo-Saxon (even less of a churl or peasant) because no ordinary discourse of the period has survived.[1] King Alfred's prefaces to his translations of famous Latin works of his age are the nearest we can get:

Ða gemunde ic hu sio æ wæs ærost on Ebriscgeðiode funden, ond eft, ða ða hie Creacas geliornodon, ða wendon hie hie on heora agen geðiode ealle, ond eac ealle oðre bec.[2]

Then I recalled how the law [of God] was first found in Hebrew, and later, when the Greeks learned it, they translated it into their own tongue, and also all other books.

Something of the spirit of informal Anglo-Saxon resides, perhaps, in a note that C. S. Lewis wrote to me in 1953 when I asked him if he had seen some lines of Anglo-Saxon verse printed in the personal column of *The Times* (9 March) to celebrate the publication of C. L. Wrenn's edition of *Beowulf*:

Giese. Onions me wisade. God wat þæt ic ne wrat þas word. To heanlic me þinceþ þæt Beowulfes leoþ sie on swincstapole gefæstnod.

Yes. Onions told me. God knows I did not write these words. It seems to me too shameful that the poem about Beowulf should have been placed in the 'agony column'.[3]

The distinctive features of Anglo-Saxon literary, religious, and legalistic works represent the leavings and last remnants of a lost culture. As time went on the style and manner of English literature became increasingly diverse, and every kind and level of language was used. *Scops*, English-style troubadours, court poets, balladists, mystical writers, dramatists, essayists, playwrights, belle-lettrists, philosophers, novelists, scientists, and every other kind of author, wrote their works as the centuries passed. The language of a pastoral and marauding people became that of a great mercantile and imperialistic power.

All that I can attempt here is to give fragmentary indications of some of the main types of writing in so far as these gave indications of the development of the language.

Informal dialogue forms part of the general pattern from the early Middle English period onward. For example, from the thirteenth-century poem *The Fox and the Wolf*:

> 'Gossip,' quod þe wolf, 'wat nou?
> Wat hauest þou imunt—weder wolt þou?'
> 'Weder Ich wille?' þe vox sede,
> 'Ich wille oup, so God me rede!'[4]

> *imunt*: in mind.   *oup*: up

Private letters began to be preserved in large numbers from the fifteenth century onwards, for example those of the Paston family:[5]

And I seyd to hym I stoppyd no wey butt myn owyn, and askyd hym why he had sold my lond to John Ball; and he sore [swore] he was nevyr acordyd wyth your fadyr. And I told hym if hys fadyr had do as he dede, he wold a be achamyd to a seyd as he seyd. (Agnes Paston to John Paston I, 1451)

These for the most part were down-to-earth accounts of business transactions, but they were not without literary embellishments of one kind or another, similes, proverbs, balancing of sentences, and reminiscences of literary or religious texts:

This worlde is but a thorughfare, and ful of woo; and whan we departe therfro, righth noughght bere wyth us but oure good dedys and ylle. And ther knoweth no man how soon God woll clepe hym, and therfor it is good for every creature to be ready. (Agnes Paston to John Paston I, ?1465)

Alliterative poetry (*with lel lettres loken* 'locked in true (alliterative) letters')[6] continued to flourish in the provinces and drew into its fold vocabulary and constructions from France and Scandinavia not often found in the courtly poets of the south:

> The throstills full throly they threped to-gedire;
> Hipped vp heghwalles fro heselis tyll othyre;
> Bernacles with thayre billes one barkes þay roungen.
>
> > (*Winner and Waster* 37-9)
>
> The thrushes full keenly argued together;
> Woodpeckers hopped from one hazel to another;
> Wild geese with their beaks sounded loudly on bark.

Throstill, threped, hipped, hesel, bill native words; *throly, they, tyll, thayre, bark* Old Norse; *bernacle* Old French.

But southerners like Chaucer's Parson in the *Canterbury Tales* abandoned the traditional alliterative measures:

> But trusteth wel, I am a Southren man,
> I kan nat geeste 'rum, ram, ruf', by lettre.
>
> > (Parson's Prologue 42-3)

and chose the courtly style instead, a style marked by extensive use of ancient and more recent poetical adornments, the 'colours' of rhetoric. The great themes of the Arthurian court, the life of man, the fall of princes, the dance of death, courtly love, and numberless discourses on purification, martyrdom, courtesy, cuckoldry, virtue, and many other themes, were all bedecked in varying degrees with English imitations of literary devices derived ultimately from Quintilian and more immediately from medieval Latin writers like Geoffrey of Vinsauf.

Discussion of such matters is to be found in standard works on the history of English literature and in the works of individual authors. It is my concern here to give an account, however brief, of some of the areas in which the special language of literature differs from the ordinary language itself. The differences, of course, are never absolute, but are much more a matter of frequency or degree rather than of kind.

In literary works disturbance of the normal order of words is commonplace. Thus in Surrey:

> The statelye sales; the ladyes bright of hewe;
> The *daunces short*, long tales of great delight.[7]

in Dr Johnson's *London* (1738):

> A transient Calm the happy Scenes *below*.   (31)
> While yet *my steady Steps* no Staff sustains.   (41)
> Let such raise Palaces, and *Manors buy*.   (57)

in Yeats's *When You are Old* (1893):

> And slowly read, and dream of the soft look
> Your eyes had once, and of their *shadows deep*. (3–4)

and in Virginia Woolf's *Orlando* (1928):

How harder than the stones of London Bridge it is, and *than the lips of a cannon more severe*.

There are countless other desirable ways in which the language is stretched and turned in literary works. Parts of speech are pleasingly transposed—a process widely known as 'conversion':

> All is best, though we oft doubt,
> What the unsearchable *dispose*
> Of Highest Wisdom brings about.
>
> > (Milton, *Samson Agonistes* 1746)

Dispose used as noun.

> Tending my flocks hard by i'th hilly crofts,
> That *brow* this bottom glade.
>
> > (Milton, *Comus* 532)

Brow used as a verb.

> 'Tis still a dream, or else such stuff as madmen
> Tongue and *brain* not.
>
> > (*Cymbeline* v. iv. 146)

Brain used as a verb 'to conceive in the brain'.

Poetry yields examples of every kind of formal linguistic novelty. Compound nouns, transparent in meaning and yet richly associative in context, abound, formations of the 'rose-finned' type:

The rose-finned roach and bluish bream. (E. Blunden, 1920)
Then, who knows Rose-footed swan from snow, or girl from rose. (E. Sitwell, 1942)
Flowing beneath her rose-hued zone. (Tennyson, 1830)
Freckled like rose-shot apricots. (R. Campbell, 1957)

Words are used once only, in prose and poetry, shackled to their contexts and having no existence elsewhere in literature, but not therefore in any way to be deprecated:

And she bursts into tears, and, in the middle of her salty howling, nimbly spears a small flatfish and *pelicans* [swallow like a pelican] it whole. (Dylan Thomas, 1953)

> These vile tricks, to pluck you from
> Your nuptial *plightage* [the state of being betrothed]
> (T. Hardy, 1908)

He scratched imprecisely with his left hand, though insensible of *prurition* [itching], various points and surfaces of his partly exposed . . . skin. (James Joyce, 1922)

She mistrusted the past's activity and its *queeringness* [aptness to distort or falsify] (E. Bowen, 1955)[8]

Some modern writers have also searched the *OED* for words recorded only once before in earlier centuries:

That separation seems more *offenseful*. (V. Nabokov, 1970; only otherwise in Shakespeare)

A *pugilant* gang theirs, per Bantry. (James Joyce, 1932; only otherwise in *Fraser's Magazine*, 1882)

It seems likely that Nabokov dredged up *nymphet* in this way — the word was used by Drayton and William Drummond of Hawthornden in the seventeenth century. Other withdrawals from the past are found at every turn in modern literary works:

To *herit* [inherit] the tradition of a proper breeding. (James Joyce, 1922; only otherwise in sixteenth- and seventeenth-century contexts)

There is . . . no light In your *inwit*. (E. Pound, 1955; also in James Joyce and other writers, drawn from the medieval work *Ayenbite of Inwit*)

Many kinds of literary inheritance and modelling are found in the work of Gerard Manley Hopkins: new formations based on old ones, like *leafmeal* (after *piecemeal*), *lovescape* (after *landscape*), *quickgold* (after *quicksilver*), *mealdrift* (after *snowdrift*). For the most part he rejected the casual and convenient archaisms of the Victorian period, like *whenas* and *sithence* (found, for example, in the work of William Morris). He also rejected traditional metre by writing much of his verse in a speech-based rhythm that he called 'sprung rhythm':

> And the séa flínt-flàke, bláck-bàcked in the régular blów.

It is 'sprung', not 'regular', in the sense that it is not normally based on a reckoning of the number of stressed and unstressed syllables but on the way in which the stresses might occur in natural speech. His disjointed syntax reflects the disharmony of the emotions being expressed:

> But how shall I . . . make me room there:
> Reach me a . . . Fancy, come faster—
> Strike you the sight of it? look at it loom there,
> Thing that she . . . there then! the Master,
> *Ipse*, the only one, Christ, King, Head.
>
> ('The Wreck of the Deutschland', stanza 28)

And unusual accidence moulded with rule-breaking syntax constitutes much of the normal strength of his poetry:

> why wouldst thou rude on me
> Thy wring-world right foot rock?   (Poem 64)
>
> Delightfully the bright wind boisterous | ropes, wrestles, beats earth bare
> Of yestertempest's creases; | in pool and rutpeel parches
> Squandering ooze to squeezed | dough, crust, dust; stanches, starches
> Squadroned masks and manmarks | treadmire toil there
> Footfretted in it.   (Poem 72)

None of this responds to the normal analyses of grammarians, whether those of an older order or those of more recent times. Passages like these belong in a higher chamber of language, above the level of the way in which the ordinary language normally operates.

The same is true of English literary prose down through the ages. As a source of intellectual power and entertainment the whole range of prose writing in English is probably unequalled anywhere else in the world. Any given passage is of its own age, and indications of the acceptable range of grammaticality and of vocabulary lie embedded in any that one may cite. But these indications are, as it were, incidental to the main purpose of the authors, which is nearly always primarily something else.

For example, Dr Johnson's Preface to his *Dictionary of the English Language* (1755) is an excellent example of expository prose. But its surging power, partly reflecting its Latinity, takes it far beyond the needs of mere communication of ideas:

When I am animated by this wish, I look with pleasure on my book, however defective, and deliver it to the world with the spirit of a man that has endeavoured well. That it will immediately become popular I have not promised to myself: a few wild blunders, and risible absurdities, from which no work of such multiplicity was ever free, may for a time furnish folly with laughter, and harden ignorance in contempt; but useful diligence will at last prevail, and there never can be wanting some who distinguish desert; who will consider that no dictionary of a living tongue ever can be perfect, since while it is hastening to publication, some words are budding, and some falling away; that a whole life cannot be spent upon syntax and etymology, and that even a whole life would not be sufficient; that he, whose design includes whatever language can express, must often speak of what he does not understand; that a writer will sometimes be hurried by eagerness to the end, and sometimes faint with weariness under a task, which Scaliger compares to the labours of the anvil and the mine; that what is obvious is not always known, and what is known is not always present; that sudden fits of inadvertency will surprize vigilance, slight avocations will seduce attention, and casual eclipses will darken learning; and that the writer shall often in vain trace his memory at the moment of need, for that which yesterday he knew with intuitive readiness, and which will come uncalled into his thoughts to-morrow.

Its clarity is not diminished by its rotundity. The qualities are not those which de Saussure distinguished as *langue* or *parole*, but something at once more profound and more mystifying. So it is with the eloquent clarity of the pamphlets of George Savile, First Marquess of Halifax (1633-95). They record the views and experiences of a practising politician, for the most part without the rhetorical ornamentation and flights of fancy that were available and widely used in his day by other writers:

To see the Laws Mangled, Disguised, Speak quite another Language than their own, to see them thrown from the Dignity of protecting Mankind, to the disgraceful Office of destroying them; and notwithstanding their innocence in themselves, to be made the worst Instruments that the most refined Villany can make use of, will raise Mens Anger above the power of laying it down again, and tempt them to follow the Evil Examples given them of Judging without Hearing, when so provoked by their desire of Revenge. Our *Trimmer* [Halifax himself] therefore, as he thinketh the Laws are Jewels, so he believeth they are nowhere better set, than in the constitution of our *English* Government, if rightly understood, and carefully preserved.[9]

This is orderly English of an eloquent kind at the end of the seventeenth century. But the same century contains not only that 'close, natural, naked way of speaking' which was the expressed ideal of the Royal Society,[10] but also quixotic and ostentatious language like that displayed in John Evelyn's *Fumifugium: or The Inconveniencie of the Aer and Smoak of London Dissipated* (1661):

> For is there under Heaven such *Coughing* and *Snuffing* to be heard, as in the *London* Churches and Assemlies of People, where the Barking and the Spitting is uncessant and most importunate. What shall I say?
>   *Hinc hominum pecudumque Lues.*—
> And what may be the cause of these troublesome effects, but the inspiration of this infernal vapour, accompanying the *Aer*, which first heats and sollicits the *Aspera Arteria*, through one of whose Conduits, partly *Cartilaginous* and partly *membranous*, it enters by several branches into the very *Parenchyma*, and substance of the *Lungs*, violating, in this passage, the *Larynx* and *Epiglottis*, together with those multiform and curious Muscles, the immediate and proper instruments of the *Voyce*, which becoming rough and drye, can neither be contracted, or dilated for the due modulation of the Voyce . . .[11]

It can be argued that technical language has a complex and uncriticizable nature of its own, but once more (as with the work of Gerard Manley Hopkins) the ordinary rules of grammar can be applied only with great difficulty.

Certainly stretchings of the normal rules are exhibited in another work which repeatedly seems to dislocate expectations with intent—Laurence Sterne's *Tristram Shandy* (1759–67), a *jeu d'esprit* of a very high order of eccentricity. The unravelling of technical terms—for example, the terminology of fortifications, *ravelin, curtin, bastion, half-moon, epaulment, double tenaille, sap, mine, blind, gabion, pallisado*, and 'such trumpery',[12] and that of music, *moderato, lentamente, tenutè, grave, adagio, con strepito, alla capella*,[13] shows Sterne using an elusive and bewitching technique. Perhaps he displays idiosyncrasy at its most beguiling when discussing language itself, and in particular when writing about auxiliary verbs. Sterne's father, he declared, was convinced that 'there is a North-west passage to the intellectual world' and that this passage 'entirely depends . . . upon the auxiliary verbs':

> The verbs auxiliary we are concerned in here, continued my father, are, am; was; have; had; do; did; make; made; suffer; shall; should; will; would; can; could; owe; ought; used; or is wont.—And these varied with tenses, present, past, future, and conjugated with the verb see,—or with these questions added to them;—Is it? Was it? Will it be? Would it be? May it be? Might it be? And these again put negatively, Is it not? Was it not?

Ought it not?—Or affirmatively,—It is; It was; It ought to be. Or chronologically,—Has it been always? Lately? How long ago?—Or hypothetically,—If it was? If it was not? What would follow?—If the French should beat the English? If the Sun go out of the Zodiac?[14]

Sterne's father goes on to ask 'Didst thou ever see a white bear?'

> A white bear! Very well. Have I ever seen one? Might I ever have seen one? Am I ever to see one? Ought I ever to have seen one? Or can I ever see one?
> Would I had seen a white bear! (for how can I imagine it?)
> If I should see a white bear, what should I say? If I should never see a white bear, what then?
> If I never have, can, must, or shall see a white bear alive; have I ever seen the skin of one? Did I ever see one painted?—described? Have I ever dreamed of one?
> Did my father, mother, uncle, aunt, brothers or sisters, ever see a white bear? What would they give? How would they behave? How would the white bear have behaved? Is he wild? Tame? Terrible? Rough? Smooth?
> —Is the white bear worth seeing?—
> —Is there no sin in it?—
> Is it better than a black one?[15]

If it displays anything it demonstrates that there is no 'North-West Passage' to the encompassing of literary language. The styles of literature lie in labyrinthine chambers, subtly and enchantingly linguistic, and yet twisting and turning in indescribable and unanalysable cavities and byways. The English language, in its more complex forms, is an unstructurable instrument of immense complexity.[16] If one steps beyond the merely literary into the fantastic world of works like James Joyce's *Finnegans Wake*, bafflement is complete:

As we gang along to gigglehouse, talking of molniacs' manias and missions for mades to scotch the schlang and leathercoats for murty magdies, of course this has blameall in that medeoturanian world to say to blessed by Pointer the Grace's his privates judgements whenso to put it, *dispirato, duspurudo, desterrado, despertieu,* or, saving his presents for his own onefriend Bevradge. (3rd edn., 1964, p. 289)

The ordinary rules of language, and virtually every traditional rule of literary language, have been thrown overboard. It is no use examining *Finnegans Wake* for information about linguistic normality of our own century as it luxuriates away 'everywhencewithersoever among skullhullows and charnelcysts of a weedwastewoldwevild' (p. 613).

*

Enhanced and ennobled language for literary purposes has been bequeathed to us by writers in every century of recorded English. So too each century has yielded expository prose, whether technical, scientific, elucidatory, philosophical, or whatever. Genuine colloquial English is unevenly available before the eighteenth century, and before the present century was always likely to be 'improved' or modified to accord with stereotypes of one kind or another. But there is another kind of language, in its supreme forms exhibited in three main works, that is nearly always marked by its relative antiquity and formality—the ritualized language of the Bible, the Book of Common Prayer, and the hymn-book. These deserve separate treatment, and in particular because each of them has been re-examined and largely rewritten in the present century.

Until recently, for most people in Britain, the Bible meant the Authorized Version of 1611, and the Book of Common Prayer that of 1662. Hymns were usually sung from *Hymns Ancient and Modern* (1861) or the *English Hymnal* (1906).

In a series of revisions, seen by many people as deliberate acts of vandalism, the traditional language of these works was set aside and 'the language of today' used instead. Those who welcomed the new versions expressed relief that some half-understood curiosities of seventeenth-century English—for example *thou* and *thee*, the verbal endings *-est* and *-eth*, and archaic meanings of words like *incomprehensible*[17]—had been abandoned. The rightness or wrongness of meddling with what seemed on the face of it to be three unalterable legacies of the past has proved to be one of the most divisive cultural issues of the present century in the British Isles.

> 'The Book of Common Prayer' we knew
> Was that of 1662:
> Though with-it sermons may be well,
> Liturgical reforms are hell.

Thus W. H. Auden in a poem called 'Doggerel by a Senior Citizen' written in 1969. It is desirable to examine the matter a little more closely.

First, a historical note. English translations of the Holy Scriptures had a long and complicated history, even before 1611. Sections of the Bible existed in the vernacular already in the Anglo-Saxon period: for example, a prose version of Psalms 1-50, possibly translated by King Alfred, and a tenth-century West Saxon version of the four Gospels. From the Middle English period several metrical versions of certain books, especially Genesis and Exodus, have survived. And, in particular, two Wycliffite versions of the whole Bible, both of them fairly close renderings of St Jerome's Latin version (*editio vulgata*), the late fourth-century version known as the Vulgate. These versions came under ecclesiastical censure in the Reformation and were replaced in turn by Tyndale's renderings of the New Testament (1526) and of the Pentateuch (1529-30). In 1535, Miles Coverdale published a complete Bible, much of it based on Tyndale, but also owing much to the German translation of Martin Luther. Further sixteenth-century versions followed, among them 'Cranmer's Bible' (1540; Cranmer contributed an important preface), the 'Geneva Bible'[18] (1560), and the 'Bishops' Bible' (1568), in which phrases which savoured of 'lightness or obscenity' were modified and other passages considered unedifying were marked for omission in public reading. Translations were also prepared for Roman Catholics, especially the Douay–Rheims Bible (1609-10).

At the instigation of James I, fifty-four divines set themselves the task of compiling a new version, and the result, more linguistically felicitous than any other version, notwithstanding the fact that it was prepared by 'a committee', appeared in 1611. It was 'Appointed to be read in churches' (thus the title-page), and it soon superseded all earlier versions. Points of detail— spelling, punctuation, the use of capitals, marginal references, etc.—were altered as time went on but it remained essentially unchallenged, even by the fairly ambitious Revised Version (1881-5), until the 1960s when the New Testament of the New English Bible appeared.

The Book of Common Prayer, until recently the official service book of the Church of England, was compiled originally by Thomas Cranmer and others to replace the Latin services of the medieval Church. It first appeared in 1549. It was much revised in the century that followed—with numerous additions and subtractions reflecting the turbulent religious views of the time—but the process of revision ceased in 1662. The 1662 Book of Common Prayer admitted, among other changes, the Authorized Version of 1611 for the Epistles and Gospels.

Individual hymns in the vernacular have been preserved from the earliest times but, apart from metrical versions of the Psalter, were normally written for private and local use. It was not until the eighteenth century that the practice of hymn singing, at first mainly the concern of the Methodists, especially the *Hymns and Sacred Poems* (1739) of John and Charles Wesley, passed, despite opposition by the authorities, into evangelical sections of the Church of England. By the mid-nineteenth century hymn singing was firmly established in all Anglican churches and the collected edition known as *Hymns Ancient and Modern* was published in 1861.

These three works, the Bible, the Book of Common Prayer, and the hymn-book, exercised a profound influence on the English language and on English literature. It is too early yet to judge whether their replacements will have the same beneficial effect but the omens are not good.[19]

For T. S. Eliot, the New Testament of the New English Bible (1961) was not even a work of distinguished mediocrity.[20] He supported his views with examples, among them pairs of parallel translations, e.g.:

> Neither cast ye your pearls before swine. (Matt. 7: 6, AV)
> Do not feed your pearls to pigs. (NEB)

He dismissed the second sentence on two grounds: 'The substitution of "feed" for "cast" makes the figure of speech ludicrous.' 'I should have thought . . . that the word "swine" would be understood, not only by countryfolk who may have heard of "swine fever", but even by the urban public, since it is still applied, I believe, to human beings as a term of abuse.'

But the main linguistic battle did not depend upon this word or that but on the general dismay felt by those who were dispirited by the speed and potency of the movement for liturgical reform. Their outrage was expressed in a petition signed by a list of names[21] occupying six pages of *PN Review 13* (1979):

We, the undersigned, are deeply concerned by the policies and tendencies which decree the loss of both the Authorised Version of the English Bible and the Book of Common Prayer. This great act of forgetting, now under way, is a tragic loss to our historic memory and an impoverishment of present awareness. For centuries these texts have carried forward the freshness and simplicity of our language in its early modern splendour. Without them the resources of expression are reduced, the stock of shared words depleted, and we ourselves diminished. Moreover, they contain nothing which cannot be easily and profitably explained.

Elsewhere,[22] the liturgiologists were said to have 'disembowelled the language of the Book of Common Prayer and the Bible' and produced in its place 'the bland literalisms of Series 3 and the ASB . . . expunging from the language of worship all that poetry and metaphor by which the soul at prayer sensed the inexpressible'.

Prolonged comparison of parallel passages is necessary for a proper consideration of the differences. The procession of change can be glimpsed in the following versions of Luke 20: 22–5:

Wycliffite (Purvey)

22 Is it leueful to vs to ȝyue tribute to the emperour, or nay? 23 And he biheld the disseit of hem, and seide to hem, 'What tempten ȝe me? 24 Shewe ȝe to me a peny; whos ymage and superscripcioun hath it?' Thei answerden, and seiden to hym, 'The emperouris.' 25 And he seide to hem, 'ȝelde ȝe therfor to the emperour tho thingis that ben the emperours, and the thingis that ben of God, to God.'

Tyndale

22 Ys it laufull for vs to geve Cesar tribute or no? 23 He perceaved their craftynes, and sayde vnto them: why tempt ye me? 24 Shewe me a peny. Whose ymage and superscripcion hath it? They answered and sayde: Cesars. 25 And he sayde vnto them: Geve then vnto Cesar, that which belongeth vnto Cesar: and to God, that which pertayneth to God.

Authorized Version

22 Is it lawfull for vs to giue tribute vnto Cesar, or no? 23 But he perceiued their craftines, and said vnto them, Why tempt ye me? 24 Shew me a peny: whose image and superscription hath it? They answered, and said, Cesars. 25 And he said vnto them, Render therefore vnto Cesar the things which be Cesars, and vnto God the things which be Gods.

New English Bible

22 'Are we or are we not permitted to pay taxes to the Roman Emperor?' 23 He saw through their trick and said, 24 'Show me a silver piece. Whose head does it bear, and whose inscription?' 'Caesar's,' they replied. 25 'Very well then,' he said, 'pay Caesar what is due to Caesar, and pay God what is due to God.'[23]

The removals and changes are pointed up in a shadowy way by the extracts. The loss of *ye*, *hath*, *unto*, and a consuetudinal use of *be*; the introduction of the phrases 'are we or are we not' and 'very well then'; and the replacement of the archaic or obsolete word *superscription* by *inscription*. Such is the mysterious power of familiar religious language that, though the formal losses seem few, the summation of the losses seems hardly bearable.

The needs of younger people and in particular of young unbookish people, not familiar with the ways of sixteenth- and seventeenth-century English, were discerned by those responsible for the preparation of the Alternative Service Book. Between 1965 and 1971, Series 1, 2, and 3 of a revised Prayer Book were issued as experimental forms of service, and the ASB itself was published in 1980. During this period some of the most memorable words and phrases in the Book of Common Prayer were replaced by others, and ancient and venerated points of accidence and syntax were removed:

Our Father, which art in heaven
      became
Our Father in heaven

He ascended into heaven, and sitteth
      became
He ascended into heaven, and is seated

Thereto I plight thee my troth
      became
This is my solemn vow

With all my worldly goods I thee endow
      became
All that I have I share with you

It is true that some of the changes in the NEB (particularly) and the ASB are more accurate renderings of the most ancient texts available. The late Professor Sir Godfrey Driver, for example, cited as an example of such an improvement:

Thy sons have fainted, they lie at the head of all the streets, *as a wild bull in a net.* (Isaiah 51: 20, AV)

Your sons are in stupor, they lie at the head of every street, *like antelopes caught in the net.* (NEB)

But these are relatively few and many of them represent a scholarly weighing of evidence rather than a demonstration of undisputed facts.

The addition or removal of hymns from hymnals, and the revision of words and phrases to accord with social and political developments of the last century, is of less moment. At various times verses of some of the best-known hymns, once thought suitable, have become virtually outmoded and disused. Thus, for example, the verse

> The rich man in his castle,
> The poor man at his gate,
> God made them, high or lowly,
> and order'd their estate.

from the Victorian hymn 'All Things Bright and Beautiful' (by Cecil Frances Alexander) was omitted from the standard edition of *Hymns Ancient and Modern* in 1950. Many other verses have strayed harmlessly away from the canon, and many other laudable new hymns have come into being. But the losses and gains to the language of religion are superficial: the hymnal tradition is too recent for such things to bite deep.

It is quite another matter with the deliberate alteration of the traditional and ceremonial language of the Bible and of the Book of Common Prayer. Words like *vouchsafe*, *prevent* (= come before), *fret* (= to eat), *persecute* (= pursue), *vex* (= afflict), and *incomprehensible* (= unknowable), and the passages in which they were once placed in the AV and the BCP, are in the process of being put away in less-accessible storerooms. They will be brought out and dusted less and less as time goes on except by professional scholars.

As one writer[24] expressed it recently, 'the institution [of the Church] remains rooted in the English landscape'. But 'the statue of the Virgin is no longer the target of the iconoclasts' hammer: it is those two distinctive treasures of the Church of England, which have made so rich a contribution to the quality of the English language, James I's Authorised Version of the Bible, and Cranmer's Book of Common Prayer. Now they are seldom heard in church, having been translated into Sunday Supplement prose. The transfiguration is unforgivable.'

Indeed, when one considers the threading of the traditional

language of the AV and the BCP into English literature through the centuries, and the improbability of *any* enrichment of English literature by the NEB and the ASB in the future, the loss for society as a whole—not so much of particular words as of the way they are put together—is grievous beyond all knowing.

6

The Recording of English
in Dictionaries and Grammars

Words—so innocent and powerless as they are, as
standing in a dictionary, how potent for good and evil
they become, in the hands of one who knows how to
combine them!

Nathaniel Hawthorne, *American Notebooks*
(1841–52) (ed. R. Stewart, 1932), p. 122

Dictionaries and grammars are now so much a part of ordinary
life that it is natural to suppose that in one form or another they
have always existed. The truth is quite otherwise. It can even be
argued that the preparation of such works has been in some
respects inimical to the unimpeded development of the language.
The recording of words in dictionaries has led to the widespread
myth that words not actually recorded in dictionaries do not, or
should not, exist. Restrictions of space, and the need to bring even
huge works like the *OED* to a conclusion, inevitably lead to the
inclusion of some items and the exclusion of others. The battles
along the inclusion/exclusion border, from the beginning, have
been almost as ferocious as any territorial border dispute between
great powers.

It is salutary to recall that the great Anglo-Saxon homilist,
Archbishop Wulfstan, had no English dictionary at his disposal
and, for grammar, only one *of the Latin language* by his
contemporary Ælfric. Langland, Chaucer, and Malory at best had
access to lists of 'hard words' in certain subjects, usually glossed
by Latin words which they were assumed to have learnt at school
or university. Spenser and some other Renaissance writers
appended explanations to some of their works so that readers
would understand the more difficult words: the best-known
example is E.K.'s glossary to Spenser's *Shepherd's Calendar*
(1579). The early plays of Shakespeare were written before the first

English dictionary was published. It is self-evident therefore that English literature can proceed at the highest level of performance without the existence of elaborate lexicons and grammars. The spoken language has always proceeded without recourse to dictionaries.

The same phenomenon can be observed in almost all cultures at all times before the Renaissance. Even today the languages of many people, especially in Africa, lack respectable dictionaries and grammars, but yield oral literature of a high order.

In 1604 Robert Cawdrey,[1] who had taught at 'the Grammer Schoole at Okeham in the County of Rutland', published a small volume called *A Table Alphabeticall*, 'conteyning and teaching the true writing, and vnderstanding of hard vsuall English wordes, borrowed from the Hebrew, Greeke, Latine, or French, &c.' This was the first English dictionary. It contained about 2,500 hard words with brief definitions, or as Cawdrey expressed it:

With the interpretation thereof by plaine English words, gathered for the benefit & helpe of Ladies, Gentlewomen, or any other unskilfull persons. Whereby they may the more easilie and better vnderstand many hard English wordes, which they shall heare or read in Scriptures, Sermons, or elsewhere, and also be made able to vse the same aptly themselues.

The opening page began like this (with words of French origin marked by Cawdrey with the sign §):

A

§ Abandon, cast away, or yeelde vp, to leaue, or forsake.
Abash, blush.
abba, father.
§ abbesse, abbatesse, Mistris of a Nunnerie, comforters of others.
§ abbettors, counsellors.
aberration, a going a stray, or wandering.
abbreuiat,
§ abbridge, } to shorten, or make short.
§ abbut, to lie vnto, or border vpon, as one lands end meets with another.
abecédarie, the order of the Letters, or hee that vseth them.
aberration, a going astray, or wandering.
§ abet, to maintaine.

It will be seen at once that features now considered essential are absent—for example pronunciation—and that casualness about consistency was not regarded as a fault. Some defined words begin with a capital, others do not; *abettors* appears in plural form, the other nouns in the singular; the glosses to *abbut* and *abet* lead with the particle *to*, those for *Abandon* and *Abash* do not. Strict alphabetical order is not maintained, and one definition is made to suffice for *abbreuiat* and *abbridge*. The entry for *aberration* is given twice.

Between 1604 and 1755 numerous other dictionaries were published, paving the way, as it were, for the publication in 1755 of one of the most celebrated dictionaries of all time, that of Dr Johnson.

First, though, some account should be given of the kind of glossarial help provided before 1604. From Anglo-Saxon times onward numerous Latin and French texts were provided with interlinear English glosses. Thus, for example:

dryhten	inlihtnis	mine	7	haelu	min	ðone	ic ondredo
Dominus	*inluminatio*	*mea*	*et*	*salus*	*mea*	*quem*	*timebo*
dryhten	gescildend	lifes		mines	from	dæm	ic forhtiu.
Dominus	*defensor*	*vitae*		*meae*	*a*	*quo*	*trepidabo.*

(*Vespasian Psalter*, Ps. 26, *c.* AD 850)

The correspondences were observed in a quite literal sense (i.e. the word order of the Anglo-Saxon glosses corresponds to that of the Latin text and is not that of idiomatic Anglo-Saxon itself), but no attempt was made to list the Anglo-Saxon words in alphabetical order.

In the same tradition is the *De Utensilibus* of Alexander Neckham (1157-1217), but the interlinear glosses are mostly in Anglo-Norman not in English. The grouped names of implements and furniture in the kitchen are followed by lists of names of weapons, the terminology of weaving and sailing (including the earliest known allusion to the use of a mariner's compass), the vocabulary of the craft of the medieval scribe, and so on.

In one such list of the fifteenth century (reproduced in Thomas Wright's *A Volume of Vocabularies* (1857), I. 244-79), engagingly simple drawings were inserted, for example a heart pierced by an arrow, a dog on a lead, a head severed by a sword (drawn upside-down), a bell, a horse with saddle and stirrup, a dragon, a spade, and a scythe—agreeable additions to an otherwise unnoteworthy assemblage of words.

From the mid-fifteenth century onward a number of bilingual dictionaries and manuals were published, for example Claudius

Holyband's *The Frenche Schoolemaister* (1573), an English–French manual, John Florio's *Firste Fruites* (1578), English–Italian, and William Stepney's *The Spanish Schoolemaster* (1591), English–Spanish. The best-known of these 'English into *X*' bilingual dictionaries is the *Promptorium Parvulorum, sive Clericorum* (circa 1440),[2] a 'storeroom' of terminology for young men training for the ministry, prepared by a Dominican Friar in Norfolk, and consisting of about 12,000 English entries with their Latin equivalents. For example:

Abakke, or bakwarde: *Retro, retrorsum*; aduerbia.
A-bashyd, or aferd: *Territus, -a, -um,* uel *perterritus, -a, -um*; participia sunt.
A-bashment: *Terror, -ris*; *pauor, -ris*; omnia masculi generis et tercie declinacionis; *fformido, -is*; femini generis et 3 declinacionis.
A-batement; or withdrawing of mete or mesure, or oþer thyng: *Subtraccio, -is*; *defalcacio, -is*; omnia feminini generis, tercie declinacionis.
Abbey: *Abbathia, -e*; *Abbatia*, secundum 'catholicon'; omnia feminini generis, prime declinacionis.

In 1483 another English–Latin dictionary appeared, the *Catholicon Anglicum*[3] and there were a good many such English–Latin works in the sixteenth century, the best-known of which, perhaps, is John Withals' *A Shorte Dictionarie for Yonge Begynners* (1553).

It should be emphasized that these works were not organized in ways which most people nowadays would regard as desirable. Withals' dictionary, for example, continues the tradition of placing words in conceptual, not alphabetical, order. Thus, under the general heading *Terra* (Earth) there is a sub-heading 'The earth with that belongeth to it', and in this group are found the names of 'serpentes, woormes & creepyng beastes':

A dragon, draco, conis, & dracunculus, li. . . .
A Scorpion, scorpius, pii, & scorpio, onis.
A serpent, serpens, tis. Bilinguis dicitur, *that hath two tunges as serpents have*.
A water snake, Natrix, cis. Sibilat anguis.
The eddir skinne, pellis anguina.
A water eddir, hydrus, dri, vel hidra, drae . . .
The stynging of serpentes or other, dicistur punctura, rae.
A pricke or styng, aculeus, lei.

(The edition of 1562 in the Bodleian Library)

Numerous '*X* into English' bilingual dictionaries were published in the fifteenth and sixteenth centuries, the earliest a Latin-English one (*c*.1460) which was called *Medulla Grammatice* (still unpublished in a modern edition). In 1500 Wynkyn de Worde printed a Latin-English dictionary called *Ortus Vocabulorum* (Garden of Words). Other bilingual dictionaries of the time included Thomas Cooper's *Thesaurus Linguæ Romanæ et Britannicæ* (1565, Latin-English), John Palsgrave's *Lesclarcissement de la Langue Françoyse* (1530, including a French-English vocabulary), John Florio's *A Worlde of Wordes* (1598, Italian-English), and Randle Cotgrave's *A Dictionarie of the French and English Tongues* (1611, French-English).

Thus English writers in the sixteenth century were clearly not without works of reference, though they could not easily have discovered which authors had used a particular word or words except by direct knowledge of the works of writers who had preceded them.

The Renaissance produced two opposing attitudes towards the English language. Some writers, anxious to inject eloquence into the language and to save it from any threat of 'barbarousness', sought out themes and words from foreign languages and from dialects. One of these was Sir Thomas Elyot (?1499-1546) and there were many other borrowers and coiners like him. A reaction set in and scholars like Sir John Cheke (1514-57) and Thomas Wilson (?1525-81) sternly rejected the linguistic innovations of the followers of Elyot. They urged the abandonment of archaisms and 'inkhorn' terms, and a return to the pure currency of native words. Not all the new words remained in the language but many did, and the need gradually began to be felt for a dictionary of 'hard' English words.

Towards the end of the sixteenth century three schoolmasters, William Bullokar, Richard Mulcaster, and Edmund Coote, turned their attention to the spelling, pronunciation, and meaning of English words. In 1580 William Bullokar published *Bullokars Booke at large, for the Amendment of Orthographie for English speech*, a work designed for 'the easie, speedie, and perfect reading and writing of English'. He and also Mulcaster called for the compilation of an English dictionary. Edmund Coote's *The Englishe Scholemaister* (1596) contained sections on English grammar and vocabulary as well as the catechism and prayers. The style was set for the appearance of the first English dictionary, and Robert Cawdrey obliged in 1604.

In the next 150 years dictionary followed dictionary. Copyright rules did not exist and wholesale lifting of material from one dictionary to another was commonplace. Cawdrey himself set the pattern by adopting much of his material from Coote's *The Englishe Scholemaister* and from Thomas Thomas's *Dictionarium Linguae Latinae et Anglicanae* (?1588). Later lexicographers followed suit.

But gradually new features—those now taken for granted—began to emerge. To begin with the first rule was to admit only 'hard' words—no pronouns, modal verbs, or 'obvious' words like *cat* and *dog*. The compilers were learned men (John Bullokar was a 'Doctor of Physicke', Thomas Blount a barrister of the Inner Temple) and their customers were educated people who were curious about literary, scientific, legal, and philosophical works of the time. The 'hard' words that needed to be explained came from 'the great store of strange words, our speech doth borrow, not only from the Latine, and Greeke, (and from the ancient Hebrew) but also from forraine vulgar Languages round about vs: beside sundry olde words now growne out of vse, and diuers terms of art, proper to the learned in Logicke, Philosophy, Law, Physicke, Astronomie, etc.'[4] In practice this meant words like *alacritie*, *anathema*, *gargarize* ('to wash or scowre the mouth with any Physicall liquor'), *intricate*, and *ruminate*. The dictionaries that resulted were not short-lived—John Bullokar's *English Expositor* (1616), for example, was printed (with varying amounts of revision) at least eleven times before the last printing of 1731.

Henry Cockeram's *The English Dictionarie* (1623) is divided into three parts: one containing 'the choicest words . . . now in vse . . . The second Booke containes the vulgar [popular or unlearned] words . . . The last Booke is a recitall of severall persons, Gods and Goddesses, Giants and Deuils, Monsters and Serpents, Birds and Beasts . . . and the like.' The 'hard' ones include some caught in a lost glacier of literature—for example, *commotrix* ('a maid that makes ready and vnready her Mistris'), *parentate* ('to celebrate ones parents funerals'), and *periclitation* ('Ieopardie, hazard'). *Phylologie*, according to Cockeram, is 'loue of much babling'. The encyclopaedic third part gives a foretaste of a modern Larousse:

Chamelion, the least of all beasts, which breeds egges or spawne, it changeth it selfe into any colour that it sits on, except white & red: therefore inconstant men are sometimes called Chamelions; it is said it onely lives by the ayre.

Thomas Blount entered many more words of Latin origin in his *Glossographia* (1656)—*adumbration, aduncous* (crooked), *acupictor* (embroiderer), etc.—and, for good measure, took most of the definitions for these words from a later edition of Thomas Thomas's *Dictionarium Linguae Latinae et Anglicanae* (1632) and from Francis Holyoke's *Dictionarium Etymologicum* (1633). But he was the first English lexicographer to provide systematic etymologies for the words included, fanciful though many of them were. [5]

Edward Phillips increased the word-count to about 11,000 in his *New World of English Words* (1658), mostly by including many more proper names, including names from mythology. In the fourth edition (1678) of his work Phillips defined *California* as 'a very large part of Northern America, uncertain whether Continent or Island', and thereby revealed the beginning of a concern for the language abroad. He also continued the tradition of marking disapproved-of words with an obelisk, for example *acetologous*, *Hybris* (Lat. and Greek) 'talking in a sharp, and as it were Vinegar strain; huffing', *circumbilivagination* 'a going round, or in a circular motion'.

In 1702 J. Kersey's *A New English Dictionary*, which was 'chiefly designed for the benefit of Young Scholars, Tradesmen, Artificers, and the Female Sex, who would learn to spell truely', moved away from the 'hard word' tradition and included ordinary words of daily language like *about, and, any, arm*, and so on. He did not define them but showed how they were used, e.g. 'And, and if, and not. About, as *about Noon*.' The word-count went up to about 28,000.

It was followed in 1721 by Nathan Bailey's *Universal Etymological English Dictionary*, the most popular English dictionary before Johnson's. William Pitt the Elder is said to have read through the dictionary twice 'from beginning to end'. It contained about 40,000 words, including, as a new feature, some proverbs, and an indication that it was intended 'as well for the Entertainment of the Curious, as the Information of the Ignorant'. He paid much more attention to etymology than his predecessors had done, though with the same eloquent obscuration that marked the etymological work of other scholars of his time. Naturally he often gets things right—*Citizen*, (*Citoyen*, F. of *Civis*, L.)—but there is an amusing (or depressing) amount of guesswork:

To *Fuddle*, (from the Word *Puddle*, q.d. to drown himself in a Puddle of Liquors; or from *Full*, by an interposition of the Letter *d*; and hence the *Scots* use the Word *Full* for one that is Drunk).[6]

Of special interest is his inclusion of numerous dialectal terms, a few slang words (taken from Elisha Coles's *English Dictionary*, 1676), and many old words from Chaucer, Spenser, Shakespeare, and other earlier writers. It is believed that Chatterton turned to Bailey's dictionary for words when he devised the pseudo-archaic vocabulary used in his poems by the imaginary fifteenth-century monk, Thomas Rowley.

Bailey's dictionary was repeatedly revised and reissued: thirty editions are known to have appeared between 1721 and 1802. It was a main source for Johnson. And it must have been a standard work of reference for all the main writers of the eighteenth century.

In 1727 Bailey added a second volume, a kind of supplement to his main work. It was a diverting mixture of words and proper names and it was not clearly differentiated from the main volume in that many words are repeated with identical or only slightly enlarged definitions. But it included one new feature: a stress-mark was added 'to direct to their [the words'] proper Pronunciation'. The volume also included many terms from heraldry—mainly derived from James Coats's *New Dictionary of Heraldry* (1725)—and also some equally derivative heraldic illustrations. Bailey also made use of two prescriptive marks, the 'Asterism' (*) for 'Words of approv'd Authority and imitable by the Illiterate', and an 'Obelisk' (†) for words which should be avoided by 'Persons of a slender acquaintance with Literature'. He was at pains to insist that words marked with an obelisk 'may be most proper, drawn by the Pen of an accomplish'd Writer, intermix'd with an agreeable Stile'.

From these two volumes Bailey compiled a more comprehensive work in 1730, the *Dictionarium Britannicum*. This collaborative work—Bailey himself says it was 'Collected by several Hands', and he names a mathematician called G. Gordon and the botanist

Philip Miller on the title-page—was of particular importance since it proved to be the working base for Johnson's dictionary.

It contained 48,000 words. Rare and eccentric words were not included. Mythological and legendary proper names were placed in the main alphabetical sequence; geographical and historical names, in a thoroughly modern manner, were mostly relegated to a special table of proper names. He drew many encyclopaedic items, dealt with in the form of short essays, from such works as Ephraim Chambers's *Cyclopædia* (1728)—for example the entry for *abbies* (abbeys):

A'bbies, anciently one third of the best Benefices in *England*, were by the Pope's Grant appropriated to Abbies, and other religious Houses, which when they were dissolved by K. *Henry* VIII. and became Lay-Fees, there were 190 dissolved, whose revenues were from 200 to 3500 l. *per Annum*, which at a Medium amounted to 2853000 l. *per Annum*.[7]

From this series of dictionaries, and numerous others, including one by John Wesley (1753), a tradition of lexicography emerged. It was absorbed and built on triumphantly by Dr Johnson in 1755.

Samuel Johnson's *A Dictionary of the English Language*[8] consisted of some 2,300 pages, printed at intervals from 1750 onwards, and contained about 40,000 entries. In the two centuries and more since it appeared it has settled into legend as being one of the greatest works of the language.

As is evident from the above it was not the first English dictionary. Far less was it the first dictionary of a European language. It offered less than Johnson had hoped for in 1747 when he wrote *The Plan of a Dictionary of the English Language*, in which he declared 'The chief intent of it is to preserve the purity and ascertain the meaning of the English idiom' (p. 4). It contributed little to the theory of the compilation of dictionaries, and it derived much of its factual content from earlier ones. It is insular: the developing vocabulary of North America (see p. 36) is excluded. It is also intensely prescriptive. Even if he had wished to do so he could not have delved into the vocabulary of English before the sixteenth century because it mostly lay in unedited and uncollected works in monastic libraries and great private houses.

The qualities he inserted, and they are of immeasurable value, are those that only a man of letters of the highest repute could bring to bear. The central body of his illustrative quotations was drawn from the greatest literary, philosophical, and scientific works of the period from Sidney to the Restoration, that is from the 1580s to 1660. And they were drawn from these works by a writer who knew the originals well, and was not merely setting down context-free sentences in order to fit inherited definitions. The quotations form a kind of concordance to the most memorable utterances of his day. The illustrative examples for theological works were largely derived from Hooker and the Bible; those for the terms of natural history from Bacon; from Ralegh he drew the phrases of politics, war, and navigation; the dialect of poetry and fiction from Spenser and Sidney; and the diction of common life from Shakespeare. These, slightly modified, are his own words, and broadly speaking they are true. Every page brims with them:

To Breathe. *v.n.* [from *breath.*]
1. To draw in and throw out the air by the lungs.
   Safe return'd, the race of glory past,
   New to his friends embrace, had *breath'd* his last. *Pope.*

2. To live.
   Let him *breathe*, between the heav'ns and earth,
   A private man in Athens. *Shakesp. Antony and Cleopatra.*

3. To take breath; to rest.
   He presently followed the victory so hot upon the Scots, that he suffered them not to *breathe*, or gather themselves together again. *Spenser's State of Ireland.*
   . . . When France had *breath'd*, after intestine broils,
   And peace and conquest crown'd her foreign toils. *Roscomm.*

4. To pass by breathing.
   Shall I not then be stifled in the vault,
   To whose foul mouth no healthsome air *breathes* in,
   And there be strangl'd ere my Romeo comes? *Shakesp.*

The personal prejudices built into some of his definitions are, of course, at once reprehensible and delightful—'whimsical and licentious manifestations of his personality', they have been called. He entered a vexatious definition of *oats* because he 'meant to vex [the Scots]'—'A grain, which in England is generally given to horses, but in Scotland supports the people.' The definitions of *dedicator, excise, favourite, Grubstreet, lexicographer, patron, pension,* and *Tory* are all splendidly prejudicial. For example:

Lexicógrapher. n.s. [λεξικὸν and γράφω; *lexicographe*, French.] A writer of dictionaries; a harmless drudge, that busies himself in tracing the original, and detailing the signification of words.

Commentators and *lexicographers* acquainted with the Syriac language, have given these hints in their writings on scripture.
Watts's Improvement of the Mind.

Patron. n.s. [*patron*, Fr. *patronus* Latin.]
1. One who countenances, supports or protects. Commonly a wretch who supports with insolence, and is paid with flattery.
[Examples from Shakespeare and Prior. Also three other meanings.]

The words *leeward* and *windward*, though of opposite meaning, are defined identically. He hated Bolingbroke because he used Gallicisms in profusion. As a result Bolingbroke's name appears, censorially presented, in the entry for *Gallicism*. The definition of *irony* reads: 'a mode of speech in which the meaning is contrary to the words: as, *Bolingbroke was a holy man.*' He frequently quoted from his own works, as, for example, under *dissipate*:

3. To spend a fortune.
The wherry that contains
Of *dissipated* wealth the poor remains. *London.*

And at least once he even attributed a couplet from Pope's *Essay on Man* to himself:[9]

Some safer world in depth of woods embrac'd
Some happier *island* in the wat'ry waste. *Johnson.*

Johnson's dictionary is the only English dictionary ever compiled by a writer of the first rank. In the second half of the eighteenth century and well into the nineteenth, in its various editions and adaptations, it remained a primary work of reference for scholars and writers of the day until it came to be superseded by the great dictionaries of Charles Richardson and (in America) Noah Webster, and in due course by the *Oxford English Dictionary* and its derivatives.

In many respects the climate of dictionary-making has not changed since the eighteenth century. In terms of content, fashion rather than principle has continued to determine the right balance between encyclopaedic items (especially proper names) and lexical ones. Bilingual dictionaries abound now as they did then. Dictionaries of slang and of regional words existed then as now.

Small monolingual dictionaries to suit a given market in price or size are now very numerous, but were relatively common then too. But changes there have been.

Three main new concepts have emerged:

1. The idea of compiling dictionaries on historical principles.
2. The replacement of prescriptive rules by a relatively systematic descriptive approach.
3. The idea of compiling independent national dictionaries as the English language developed in distinctive ways, especially in the United States, Canada, Australia, New Zealand, South Africa, and the West Indies.

A brief account of these developments follows.

The Historical Principle[10]

A *lexicon totius Anglicitatis* is a desirable but impossible target. At the other extreme a lexicon of the words in use in someone's own country—or even in someone's own locality—at a given time is a desirable object but one of limited value since it would need to exclude too much. (I was born in a city in New Zealand called Wanganui. A dictionary tailored to the needs of the citizenry of Wanganui would be an entrancing challenge, but however useful on St. John's Hill, and in Aramoho and Putiki, would be unlikely to commend itself to a wider audience.) It became evident early in the nineteenth century that the systematic assembling of parts and segments of the language, especially the uncollected vocabulary of the centuries before 1700, was a natural desideratum. Old manuscripts needed to be transcribed and printed, and standards of textual reliability established. The earliest words needed to be examined carefully, and compared systematically, with their continental Germanic, Romance, and other Indo-European equivalents. Homonyms needed to be distinguished. The meanings of old words needed to be established, and development of meaning, as new senses proliferated, to be ascertained and set down in some kind of comprehensible sequence. The decisive moment for our language came in 1857 with the publication of Dean Trench's celebrated paper 'On Some Deficiencies in our English Dictionaries'.[11]

He wanted a new English dictionary to be prepared which would, with certain exceptions, contain all words previously unregistered as well as those already present in Victorian dictionaries, and would exhibit each word and each meaning in a historical manner, that is with the senses arranged in chronological order, and with illustrative quotations from verified printed sources as the main confirmatory and elucidatory apparatus. He also wanted the vocabulary presented on descriptive rather than prescriptive principles.

James A. H. Murray, a Scottish schoolmaster and self-taught philologist, accepted the editorship of this *New English Dictionary* in 1879 and the compilation began.

The immortal story of the editing and completion of the *NED* (later called *The Oxford English Dictionary*) has been set down by Elisabeth Murray, J. A. H. Murray's granddaughter,[12] and need not be repeated here. Suffice it to say that it is a supreme example of the discovery and establishment of a new linguistic principle—the historical one—and of its execution and completion on a grand scale.

Any entry chosen at random will suffice to show the richness of the material contained in the *OED*: the linguistic genealogy of a word requires the presentation of:

current pronunciation
part(s) of speech
etymology
earliest printed use
original or primary meaning
later meanings set out in chronological order
all meanings illustrated by printed evidence.

Typical entries from Volume VIII of the *OED* and from Volume 3 (*O-Scz*) of *A Supplement to the OED* (1982) are shown on p. 90. The value of the *OED* as a historical record of the English language is self-evident. Some other European countries have followed suit,[13] but unfortunately some of the major languages of the world, for example Chinese, Japanese, and Russian, lack such a dictionary, and as far as can be determined, will go on lacking one at least until the twenty-first century.

Prescriptivism and Descriptivism

In the present century, starting more or less with the work of Ferdinand de Saussure, emphasis has been placed much more

Rote (rōut), *sb.*[1] Now only *Hist.* [a. OF. *rote* (*rothe, route*), = Prov. and med.L. *rota, rotta*; also MDu. *rote*, MLG. *rotte, rode*, MHG. *rote, rott(e,* OHG. *rota, rotta.* The original form was prob. *hrotta, an early Teutonic adoption of the Celtic word recorded by Venantius Fortunatus (6th cent.) as *chrotta*, on which see CROWD *sb.*[1]] A mediæval musical instrument, probably of the violin class.

a 1300 *Cursor M.* 7408 Dauid cuth on sere-kin rote, Bath he cuth on harpe and rote. 13.. *E. E. Allit. P.* B. 1082 Organes & pypes, & rial ryngande rotes & þe reken fyþel. 1390 GOWER *Conf.* III. 303 He tawhte hir til sche was certein Of Harpe, of Citole and of Rote. *c* 1407 LYDG. *Reson & Sens.* 2394 He kan..Touche be crafte, and nat be rote, Harpe and lute, fythel and Rote. *c* 1450 HOLLAND *Howlat* 759 The rote, and the recordour,..The trumpe, and the talburn. 1590 SPENSER *F. Q.* II. x. 3 Argument worthy of Mæonian quill; Or rather worthy of great Phoebus rote. 1596 *Ibid.* IV. ix. 6 There did he find..The faire Pœana playing on a Rote. 1814 SCOTT *Ld. of Isles* III. xxiii, The lad can deftly touch the lute, And on the rote and viol play. 1823 ROSCOE tr. *Sismondi's Lit. Eur.* (1846) I. v. 128 Psaltry, symphony, and rote, Help to charm the listening throng. 1859 JEPHSON *Brittany* vii. 93 To converse, or sing ancient Breton lays to the rote. 1884 HERON-ALLEN *Violin Making* 62 The only difference between the earliest crwths..and the latest rotes..seems to be the addition of the bow and finger-board.

Rote (rōut), *sb.*[2] Also 4–5 roote, 5–6 root, 5 rot, 5–7 roat(e. [Of obscure origin ; there is no evidence to confirm the suggestions that it is a. OF. *rote, route* route, way, or ad. L. *rota* wheel.]

† 1. a. Custom, habit, practice. *Obs.*

c 1315 SHOREHAM III. 210 Þy wykked rote, Wanne þou ne halst by masseday, As god byt haþ y-hote. 1390 GOWER *Conf.* III. 45 Thilke art which Spatula is hote, And used is of comun rote Among Paiens. *Ibid.* 50 He..broght hem into such a rote, That upon him thei bothe assote. *c* 1440 *Promp. Parv.* 437/2 Root, of vse and custome.

† b. Mechanical practice or performance ; regular procedure ; mere routine. *Obs.* (Cf. sense 2.)

1581 MULCASTER *Positions* xli. (1887) 242 By the meere shadow, and roat of these sciences. 1693 EVELYN *De La Quint. Compl. Gard.* I. 3 A presumptuous Pratling Ignorance, upheld by some wretched Rote. 1712 J. JAMES tr. *Le Blond's Gardening* 80 Experience, Tryal upon the Ground, and a certain Rote,..necessary to this End. 1768 *Woman of Honor* II. 81 His education had proceeded in the common rote through school and college. *Ibid.* II. 189 He took the rote of forms to be the very quintessence of affairs.

† c. A rigmarole. *Obs. rare.*

14.. *Sir Beues* (MS. S) 1191 Men seye in olde roote þat wimmannes bolt is sone schote. 1681 *Peace & Truth* 14 The Church of Rome hath turned Prayer into a meer Rote or Charm of unintelligible Words.

2. *By rote*, in a mechanical manner, by routine, *esp.* by the mere exercise of memory without proper understanding of, or reflection upon, the matter in question ; also, † with precision, by heart.

a. With *say, sing, play*, etc.
The meaning of the first quot. is not clear.

13.. *Gaw. & Gr. Knt.* 2207 Þat gere as I trowe, Is ryched at þe reuerence, me renk to mete, bi rote. *c* 1394 *P. Pl. Crede* 377 A ribaut..þat can nou3t wel reden His rewle ne his respondes, but be pure rote. 1444 *Pol. Poems* (Rolls) II. 217 Suych labourerys synge may be roote, ' Alle goo we stille, the cok hath lowe shoon '. 1526 *Pilgr. Perf.* (W. de W. 1531) 160 Yf it were, than I myght..saye my seruyce by rote and custome. 1577–82 BRETON *Toyes Idle Head* Wks. (Grosart) I. 27/1, I did not sing one noate, except it were by roate. 1628 EARLE *Microcosm., Shop-keeper* (Arb.) 54 Hee tels you lyes by rote. 1662 PLAYFORD *Skill Mus.* II. (1674) 110 To learn to play by rote or ear without Book. 1715 DE FOE *Fam. Instruct.* I. vi. (1841) I. 112 We can all repeat the Commandments by rote. 1773 HAN. MORE *Search after Happiness* II. 141, I talk'd by rote the jargon of the schools. 1832 HT. MARTINEAU *Hill & Valley* vii. 111

rocketee·ring, *vbl. sb.* [f. prec. + -ING[1].] = *ROCKETRY.

1932 D. LASSER *Conquest of Space* vii. 116 The support of a financier of world-wide experience, and of men of science..comes as a revelation to those who viewed the field of 'rocketeering' as a visionary dream. 1938 *Forum* Feb. 96/2 Rocketeering may, in some distant future, take us to the moon or elsewhere in space. 1962 *Times Lit. Suppl.* 2 Feb. 68/5 The race is therefore on, for a greater prize..than any that can be won by rocketeering.

rocketer. Add: † b. *Cricket.* = SKYER. *Obs.*

1886 *Cricket* 25 Feb. 18/1 A good man..is the man to go for a 'pocketer' [*sic*] between the wickets. *Ibid.* 25 Mar. 35/2 In my last letter of course 'Pocketer' ought to read 'Rocketer'. 1887 F. GALE *Game of Cricket* iv. 70 He hit [the ball] too quick, and instead of going out of the field, as it might have done, it went up a tremendous rocketer. 1900 *Badminton Mag.* Oct. 380 The great smiter..hit a ball very high straight to the young blacksmith... But for some reason—whether he was thinking too much of the style of the thing, or was unused to rocketers—..the ball fell with a hollow clank on the top of his head.

ro·cketing, *ppl. a.* (Further examples.)

1952 DYLAN THOMAS *Coll. Poems* 172 He..prays, Who knows the rocketing wind will blow The bones out of the hills. 1959 *Economist* 25 Apr. 318/2 Behind the increase in imports there is cited a 'rocketing' increase in Dutch production. 1964 M. ARGYLE *Psychol. & Social Probl.* xvi. 199 We are astounded however by the rocketing crime rate, [etc.]. 1970 *Daily Tel.* 8 May 17 Doctors, headmasters and health educationists are disturbed by the rocketing numbers of young smokers.

ro·cketing, *vbl. sb.* [f. ROCKET *v.* + -ING[1].] The action or practice of the vb. in various senses.

1928 P. F. NOWLAN in *Amazing Stories* Aug. 427 The favorite American method of propulsion was known as 'rocketing'. 1972 *Guardian* 4 May 15/8 Rocketing of Saigon, plus ground probes near the capital, could shake the politicians..out of their current isolation. 1975 *Church Times* 14 Mar. 1/5 Rocketing and shelling of the airfield was going on as the plane left.

rocketry (rǫ·kėtri). [f. ROCKET *sb.*[3] + -RY.] The science or use of rockets and rocket propulsion. Also *fig.*

1930 G. E. PENDRAY in *Bull. Amer. Interplanetary Soc.* Nov.–Dec. 4 The practical work of getting a liquid-fuel rocket actually into the air was a contribution of America's, as were the three most fundamental achievements of modern rocketry. 1934 *Jrnl. Brit. Interplanetary Soc.* I. i. 3 There you have the nucleus of the British movement in rocketry. 1934 *Astronautics* Mar. 7 'Rocketry' itself is a coined word, first suggested at a meeting of the American Interplanetary Society in 1930 and since widely adopted. 1943 C. S. LEWIS *Perelandra* vi. 91 He was a man obsessed with the idea which is.. circulating all over our planet in obscure works of 'scientifiction', in little Interplanetary Societies and Rocketry Clubs. 1951 'J. WYNDHAM' *Day of Triffids* ii. 30 Sustained research in rocketry had at last succeeded in attaining one of its objectives. It had sent up a missile which stayed up. 1957 *Times* 10 Oct. 10/1 The American programme..called for the launching of small test spheres this year..to check rocketry instrumentation. 1958 *Sunday Times* 14 Sept. 7/4 His [sc. Thomas Wolfe's] absurd rocketry about great America, decadent Europe and so on. 1962 F. I. ORDWAY et al. *Basic Astronautics* ii. 21 A scientific analysis of rocketry applied to high altitude meteorological research. 1968 A. DIMENT *Bang Bang Birds* v. 70 A collection of scientists..who weren't quite bright enough to get into the rocketry racket. 1977 *Daily Tel.* 28 July 1/6 The small spaceport at Kagoshima ..looked more like a station for amateur rocketry than a serious rival to Cape Canaveral.

rocketsonde (rǫ·kėtsǫnd). Also rocket-sonde, rocket sonde. [f. ROCKET *sb.*[3] + *-sonde*, after firmly than hitherto on language as it is used rather than on how experts say that it should be used. There is no clear boundary between the doctrines of prescriptivism and those of descriptivism, much more an attitude of mind. Prescriptivists by and large regard innovation as dangerous or at any rate resistable; descriptivists, whether with resignation or merely with a shrug of the shoulders, quickly identify new linguistic habits and record them in dictionaries and grammars with no indication that they might be unwelcome or at any rate debatable. Prescriptivists frequently use restrictive expressions like *loosely, erroneously, sometimes used to mean, falsely, avoided by careful writers,* and the like. Descriptivists are silent about such matters and simply list new or controversial uses without comment. In descriptive dictionaries old words and disused senses of words are usually omitted, and, as far as possible, senses are arranged in order of commonness (the so-called 'logical' order) not in chronological order. A substantially prescriptive approach is to be found in H. W. Fowler's *A Dictionary of Modern English Usage* (1926, revised by E. Gowers in 1965) and in *The Concise Oxford Dictionary* (7th edn., 1982). Descriptive lexicography is seen at its most potent form in *Webster's Third New International Dictionary* (1961 and later impressions) and descriptive grammar in Randolph Quirk *et al., A Grammar of Contemporary English* (1972).

Readers can easily distinguish between the two approaches by consulting the entries for expressions like *all right/alright, anticipate, decimate, dilemma, disinterested, due to, enormity, hopefully, imply/infer, minuscule,* and *refute* in the two types of reference book.

The battle between the opposing groups is as fierce as that in the sixteenth century between those using, and those opposed to, the use of 'inkhorn' terms (see p. 81). Descriptivists, accustomed to the oddities of old spelling and ancient grammar, might be supposed to look with favour on passages like the following (taken from a letter written in 1982 by a well-brought-up fifteen-year-old family friend and reproduced here in uncorrected form):

Thankyou everso much for the Bangles they are a very plesent contributon for my megar Collection. Christmas here was a bit of a bore (not ment to say that but its' true) We had no family or friends to enjoy it with (I'm telling you this Because it becomes very Boreing telling people what a Lovley Christmas we had when infact it was incredibly boreing)

In practice the obvious inadequacies of such writing are not dealt with in standard dictionaries and grammars of either kind, and could hardly be, given that the patterns (if such they are) of spelling, grammar, and punctuation are not easily predictable. Like the Renaissance battles the quarrel is only at a more sophisticated level.

National Dictionaries

In the seventeenth and eighteenth centuries most English dictionaries were compiled and published in London, but from 1800 onward, at first slowly and with a curious disinclination to cut loose from the standard lexicons, Scotland and the United States were the first to issue dictionaries of their own. Much later, national dictionaries of the English used in other countries were compiled, but at a surprising distance in time from the attainment by those countries of various kinds of political independence. The landmarks were: _

Scotland

J. Jamieson, *An etymological dictionary of the Scottish language* (1808), Supplement (1825).

W. Grant and D. Murison, *The Scottish National Dictionary* (1931-76).

W. A. Craigie, A. J. Aitken *et al.*, *A Dictionary of the Older Scottish Tongue* (1931- . By 1982 *A-pavilion* published).

United States

Noah Webster, *A compendious dictionary of the English language* (1806).

—— *An American dictionary of the English Language* (1828).

Followed by numerous revised editions culminating in *Webster's Third New International Dictionary* (1961, and later printings with Addenda and supplementary material).

W. A. Craigie and J. R. Hulbert, *A Dictionary of American English on Historical Principles* (1938-44).

M. M. Mathews, *A Dictionary of Americanisms on Historical Principles* (1951).

In 1969 dictionaries of distinctively Canadian and Jamaican English words, compiled on historical principles, appeared, and in 1982 one of Newfoundland English. One-volume dictionaries are now in active preparation in South Africa and Australia.

In a small book it is impossible to give more than an outline account of the nature of the linguistic independence lying behind the preparation of these dictionaries. Scotland needed to look no further than the entrenched Celtic elements in their form of English—words like *loch*, *pibroch*, and *plaid*—and the numerous preferences they had in pairs of words like *kirk/church*, *brig/ bridge*, *lugs/ears*, etc. Noah Webster designed a differentiated form of spelling for Americans for whole groups of words:

> *center* (Brit. *centre*), *harbor* (Brit. *harbour*)
> *traveler* (Brit. *traveller*), *marvelous* (Brit. *marvellous*)
> *esophagus* (Brit. *oesophagus*)

and the spellings he preferred have proved to be very durable in the United States. Canadians had no difficulty in identifying distinctive elements in their history and culture—the French language has bitten deeply in Canada, and there are also many distinctive terms to do with lumberjacks, Canadian Indians, trading, fishing, and so on. Australians pour words of Aboriginal origin into their local dictionaries, and display a range of slang not paralleled since the slang dictionaries of Francis Grose and James Hardy Vaux. South Africans, when speaking English, display all the trophies they have taken from the Afrikaans language. The Jamaicans' special language is marked by many terms of popular types of music, relics of old grammar long since abandoned in Britain, exotic foods, and strands of vocabulary and information from Africa. These matters are dealt with in more detail in chapter 10.

*

As with the recording of English in dictionaries, the setting down of English in grammars is a much more complicated matter than is commonly supposed. The landmarks have tended to lie concealed beneath shrouds of mythology. Moreover, no one early grammarian bounded into the popular imagination in the way that Dr Johnson did for lexicography. Several attempts have been made by modern scholars to treat English grammar historically, most of them by continental scholars, in particular Henry Sweet (English, of course), Jespersen, Kruisinga, Poutsma, and Visser.[14] The works they produced are of great value to professional scholars, but far too detailed and too bristlingly difficult to serve the needs of the general public. Older grammars, those of the period before 1900, lie virtually unconsulted in the vaults of only the greatest

libraries in the world. Furthermore, scholarly editors of many
older works have made the historical investigation of grammar
even more difficult by silently 'correcting' old and natural
arrangements of words to make them accord with modern
grammar. Even the standard editions of Shakespeare's works are
marred in this way, though for the most part the Authorized
Version of the Bible lay untampered with in this respect until
comparatively recently.

Modern attempts to set down descriptive accounts of English
grammar have rested on two broad assumptions: first, that older
grammarians were unquestioningly prescriptive; and, secondly,
that eighteenth-century grammarians in particular generated
unacceptable views about case-endings, pronouns, prepositions,
infinitives, and so on that were uncritically handed on from
generation to generation by schoolteachers to the detriment of the
subject and against all common sense. There is something in both
charges but they need to be kept in perspective.

For John Brinsley in 1612[15] the study of grammar was a multi-
lingual exercise, 'to write fayre in Secretary, Romane, Greeke,
Hebrue', and 'to know all the principall and necessary Radicis,
Greeke and Hebrue'. Above all the aim was 'to attaine to the
puritie and perfection of the Latine tongue'.

For Ben Jonson in 1640[16] 'the profit of Grammar is great to
Strangers . . . and . . . honourable to our selves. For, by it we
communicate all our labours, studies, profits, without an Inter-
preter. Wee free our Language from the opinion of Rudenesse,
and Barbarisme, wherewith it is mistaken to be diseas'd.' In this
short book, Jonson dealt fairly systematically with 'the true
notation of words' and 'the right ordering of them', classified into
all the usual sections—parts of speech, comparisons, 'the Accent',
nouns and their declensions, verbs and their conjugations, and so
on. Wrong placing of the main stress would mean that a 'word is
in danger to be mis-tuned'. He carefully distinguished the nouns
cónvert, désert, íncense, óbject, présent, réfuse, tórment, etc., from
the corresponding verbs, *convért, desért,* etc. And he set down
reasonably uncontestable rules about the pronunciation of other
classes of contrasted words (*tolerable/intolerable*) and of compound expressions like *ténnis-court-keeper* and *fóot-ball-plaier.*
The first declension of English nouns, he said, were those forming
their plurals in *-s* or *-es,* like *tree/trees, bush/bushes.* He lumped

mouse/mice, tooth/teeth, and other 'mutated' plurals in with them. The second declension consisted of nouns that form their plural in *-n* or *-en,* like *oxe/oxen* and *hose/hosen.* He recognized that there were exceptional and anomalous members of the group: *man/men, woman/women* ('in stead of *manen* and *womanen*'!), *cow/kine* or *keene, brother/brethren* or *brethern,* and so on. And he reported that *house, eye,* and *shoo* appeared in the plural either as *houses, eyes,* and *shooes,* or as *housen, eyen,* and *shooen.* Jonson's illustrative examples for matters of syntax were drawn from the works of earlier writers, Chaucer, Sir Thomas More, and so on. Thus, to illustrate the placing of *neither* and *nor* he cited More:

Hee can be no Sanctuary-man, that hath neither discretion to desire it, nor malice to deserve it.

And for the relationship of *so* and *as,* when used in comparative statements, he turned to Gower:

> Men wist in thilk time none
> So faire a wight, as she was one.

The grammatical doctrine presented is uncomplicated and un-contentious. It does not, however, match the abundant skills he displayed himself as a major dramatist of the period. Seven-teenth-century English lay sprawling about him, not significantly or sufficiently analysed, not that is by the standards of later grammarians.

A century later, English grammar was no longer being forced into the mould of Latin declensions and conjugations. The aim was 'to reduce our Language, which is naturally very easy, to a few short Rules, by which the Language may be rendered more easy to be learnt by Foreigners; and our Countrymen'.[17] James Greenwood said that he was 'not ignorant that several Persons have undertaken this work before [him]' and he went on:

But none of these have [NB not 'has'], in my Opinion, taken the right Method; for all of them forcing our English Tongue too much to the Latin Method (into which Errour almost all who have wrote Grammars of the modern Languages have fallen) have delivered many useless Precepts concerning the Cases, Genders, and Declensions of Nouns; the Tenses, Moods and Conjugations of Verbs, and other such like Things, which our Language hath nothing at all to do with.[18]

Greenwood plainly saw that English grammar, unlike Latin, depended heavily on its prepositions and, for verbs, on auxiliaries. The breakthrough had occurred and the way was clear for other professional grammarians of the century to reshape the whole subject if they so desired. In fact, deceived by the surface simplicity of English grammar by comparison with that of contemporary continental languages, they let the opportunity go past.

Perhaps the most instructive account of English grammar in the eighteenth century is to be found in the Preface of Robert Lowth's *A Short Introduction to English Grammar* (1762). He began by setting the problem down in a somewhat worrying way:

> The English Language hath been much cultivated during the last two hundred years. It hath been considerably polished and refined; it hath been greatly enlarged in extent and compass; its force and energy, its variety, richness, and elegance, have been tried with good success, in verse and in prose . . . but whatever other improvements it may have received, it hath made no advances in Grammatical accuracy.[19]

He went on:

> Does it mean, that the English Language as it is spoken by the politest part of the nation, and as it stands in the writings of our most approved authors, oftentimes offends against every part of Grammar? Thus far, I am afraid, the charge is true. Or does it further imply, that our Language is in its nature irregular and capricious; not subject, or not easily reduceable, to a System of rules? In this respect, I am persuaded, the charge is wholly without foundation.

Lowth regarded the genitive *'s* in *'God's grace'* as an improper shortening of *-is*, i.e. *'Godis* grace':

> We now very improperly always shorten it with an Apostrophe, even tho' we are obliged to pronounce it fully; as, *'Thomas's* book:' that is, *'Thomasis* book;' not *'Thomas his* book,' as it is commonly supposed.[20]

Prescriptiveness appeared in many parts of the book, and reputable writers were not spared. For example, he condemned the use of the pronoun *ye* in the oblique case, as in Milton's

> His wrath, which one day will destroy *ye* both
> (*PL* II. 734)

Another use of the second-person pronoun was firmly attacked:

> *You was*, the Second Person Plural of the Pronoun placed in agreement with the First or Third Person Singular of the Verb, is an enormous

Solecism: and yet Authors of the first rank have inadvertently fallen into it. 'Knowing that *you was* my old master's good friend.' Addison, Spect. No. 517. 'Would to God *you was* within her reach.' (Lord Bolingbroke to Swift, Letter 46.)

He went on to accuse Alexander Pope of 'great impropriety' in using *touch'd* rather than *touchedst* or *didst touch* in:

> O *Thou* my voice inspire
> Who *touch'd* Isaiah's hallow'd lips with fire!

He recognized, however, that prepositions could properly fall at the end of sentences:

The Preposition is often separated from the Relative which it governs, and is joined to the Verb at the end of the Sentence, or of some member of it: as, 'Horace is an author, *whom* I am much delighted *with*.' 'The world is too well bred to shock authors with a truth, *which* generally their booksellers are the first to inform them *of*.' This is an Idiom which our language is strongly inclined to; it prevails in common conversation, and suits very well with the familiar style in writing; but the placing of the Preposition before the Relative is more graceful, as well as more perspicuous; and agrees much better with the solemn and elevated Style.[21]

It is of interest to observe that he saw that one method of dealing with such prepositional uses was more formal than the other—an early example of the recognition of the concept of grammatical formality.

Other eighteenth-century grammarians reflected and adapted the views of Lowth. Joseph Priestley, for example, in his *The Rudiments of English Grammar* (1768) was 'surprized to see so much of the distribution, and technical terms of the Latin grammar, [still] retained in the grammar of our tongue; where they are exceedingly aukward, and absolutely superfluous.'[22] He continued:

It must be allowed that the custom of speaking, is the original, and only just standard of any language. We see, in all grammars, that this is sufficient to establish a rule, even contrary to the strongest analogies of the language with itself. Must not this custom, therefore, be allowed to have some weight, in favour of those forms of speech, to which our best writers and speakers seem evidently prone.[23]

Priestley deplored the 'very great number of *gallicisms*, which have insinuated themselves into the style of many of our most justly admired writers'; and he is nervous about the prodigious acceleration in 'the progress of every branch of real science'. Above all he believed that a language 'can never be properly fixed, till all the varieties with which it is used, have been held forth to public view, and the general preference of certain forms have been declared, by the general practice afterwards'. The fixing will be done by the users of the language themselves not by an Academy, by 'the decisions of *Time*, which are slow and sure . . . [not] of *Synods*, which are often hasty and injudicious'.

Lindley Murray in his *English Grammar* (5th edn., 1799) followed a similar course. Obsolete and foreign expressions 'should be avoided': '*Quoth he*; *I wist not*; *erewhile*; *behest*; *selfsame*; *delicatesse*, for delicacy; *politesse*, for politeness; *hauteur*, for haughtiness; *incumberment*, *connexity*, *martyrised* for encumbrance, connexion, martyred.'[24] Also to be avoided were *low expressions*: such as, 'Topsy turvy, hurly burly, pellmell; having a month's mind for a thing; currying favour with a person; dancing attendance on the great', etc. Repetition of words in the same sentence, and the injudicious use of technical terms (like *larboard*), were deprecated.

The grammars of Robert Lowth, Joseph Priestley, and Lindley Murray, and the views expressed in them, continued to be used in the nineteenth century. Theirs, or the works of grammarians influenced by them, must have set standards of acceptability for Jane Austen, Sir Walter Scott, Wordsworth, and other writers of the period, though I do not know if records survive of the grammars that stood on the shelves of these great writers. New grammarians appeared. David Booth's *The Principles of English Grammar* (1837) recognized (p. 59) that English, by contrast with Latin, possessed only one oblique case, the possessive case, as in 'Alexander's house', 'God's grace'. He observed that 'In the English language, the juxtaposition of nouns is, of itself, a sufficient indication of the genitive', giving rise to combinations 'without any mark of connexion' like '*Morning Song*', '*London Review*', '*Edinburgh Magazine*', and so on. He pointed out that if Cicero could be brought back to life 'for the purpose of residing amongst us', he would find English syntax hard to follow: 'I say that if any one were to address Cicero thus,—"Illustrious Roman, after your death Augustus conquered Antony," Cicero would understand every one of these words separately, but he

would be unable to distinguish the conqueror from the conquered'
(p. 62). He cited Dr Webster (i.e. Noah Webster) with approval
while defending the use of the adjectival forms in the following
lines:

Let us write *slow* and *exact*. (Guthrie's *Quintilian*)
Drink *deep*, or taste not the Pierian spring. (Pope)

Similar books followed. T. Weedon's *A Practical Grammar of
the English Language* (1848) once more rejected rules of grammar
based upon Latin grammar. William Cobbett, best known for
his *Rural Rides* (1825), followed suit. In his *Grammar of the
English Language* (1823 edition) he went further by appending
'Six lessons, intended to prevent Statesmen from using false
grammar, and from writing in an awkward manner'. For example,
he attacked the use of 'have heard' in 'I thought to have heard the
Noble Lord produce something like proof'. His advice (given in
fact to his son, James Paul Cobbett, to whom the book is
addressed) was as follows:

No! my dear James will never fall into the use of such senseless gabble!
You would think of *hearing* something; you would think of *to hear*, not *to
have heard*. You would be *waiting to hear*, and not, like these men, *be
waiting to have heard*. '*I should have liked to have been informed* of the
amount of the Exchequer Bills.' A phraseology like this can be becoming
only in those Houses, where it was proposed to relieve the distresses of
the nation by setting the labourers to dig holes one day and fill them up
the next. (Letter XIX, p. 135)

All grammars before Richard Morris's *Historical Outlines of
English Accidence* (1872) are at the same time partly persuasive
but in the end wholly inadequate. It took nearly three hundred
years for grammarians to see plainly that the English language
had a grammatical system that was unique to itself and in need
of a descriptive technique that would account for its main operations. Morris observed that the science of grammar is of two
kinds, descriptive and comparative, by which he meant, in
modern terminology, synchronic and diachronic. Descriptive grammar 'classifies, arranges, and describes words as
separate parts of speech, and notes the changes they undergo
under certain conditions'. Morris elected not to attempt such
a grammar. Comparative grammar 'goes beyond the limits of
Descriptive Grammar . . . It analyses words, accounts for the

The verb meaning nonplus (with its noun *poser* unanswerable question) is a different word from that meaning to lay down or place, being shortened from *appose*.

poseur. See FRENCH WORDS.

POSITION OF ADVERBS. The word *adverb* is here to be taken as including adverbial phrases (e.g. *for a time*) & adverbial clauses (e.g. *if possible*), adjectives used predicatively (e.g. *alone*), & adverbial conjunctions (e.g. *then*), as well as simple adverbs such as *soon* & *undoubtedly*. To lay down & illustrate exhaustive rules would not be possible in reasonable compass ; nor is there any need to do so ; the mistakes that occur are almost always due to certain false principles, & these may be isolated for treatment. Many readers may justly feel that they do not require advice on so simple a matter as where their adverbs should go, &, to save them the trouble of reading this long article, here is a string of sentences exhibiting all the types of misplacement to be discussed. Those who perceive that the adverb in each is wrongly placed, & why, can safely neglect the rest ; the bracketed number after each refers to the section in which its type is discussed :—*The people are now returning & trying to* again *get together a home* (1)./*He came to study* personally *the situation* (2)./*He exercised an influence that is still potent & has yet* adequately *to be measured on the education of our younger artists* (3)./*It deals with matters as to which most persons long ago have made up their minds* (4)./*We still are of opinion that the only way of getting rid of ' abuses ' is a root-&-branch alteration of the thing itself* (5)./*The Food Ministry must either take action or defend* effectively *their inactivity* (6)./*To decry the infantry arm for the sake* unduly *of piling up artillery & what not, is the notion of persons who . . .* (7)./*As ' the Monroe doctrine ' of late years has* loomed *so*

largely *in all discussions upon the international policy of the United States, an attempt to trace its growth & development as a popular ' cry ' might prove of some service* (8).

There are certain verb groups about which the question is conceivable— Should they be allowed to be interrupted by adverbs ? Such are the infinitive e.g. *to try* (may we say *to* earnestly *try ?*), the compound verb e.g. *have thought* (may we say *I have* never *thought so ?*), the copula & complement e.g. *was a riddle* (may we say *He was in some ways a riddle ?*), the verb & its object e.g. *passed the time* (may we say *It passed* pleasantly *the time ?*), the gerund & its governing preposition e.g. *by going* (may we say *by often going ?*). The first of these questions is a very familiar one ; almost all who aspire to write English have had the split infinitive forced on their attention, & the avoidance of it has become a fetish ; the other questions are not familiar, but the points here to be made are that they also require consideration, that a universal yes or a universal no is not the right answer either to the split-infinitive question or to any of the others, that the various answers sometimes come into conflict, & that to concentrate on the split-infinitive question & let the others take care of themselves is absurd.

The misplacements to be considered will be taken under the heads :— 1. Split infinitive. 2. Fear of split infinitive. 3. Imaginary split infinitive passive. 4. Splitting of the compound verb. 5. Separation of copulative verb & complement. 6. Separation of transitive verb & object. 7. Separation of preposition & gerund. 8. Heedless misplacings.

1. Split infinitive. The heinousness of this offence is estimated in the article SPLIT INFINITIVE. Here the general result of that estimate is merely assumed, viz : (A) that *to love* is a definitely enough recognized verb-form to make the clinging

changes they have undergone, and endeavours to trace them back to their origin.' And so he went ahead and attempted to trace all grammatical, and other, features historically. It was a natural decision in the climate of opinion of the time.

And so for the next 75 years or so, until the 1960s, English grammar was presented historically or prescriptively, or in a somewhat uneasy mixture of both techniques. The voluminous works of Henry Sweet, Otto Jespersen, and others fall into this tradition. And it is these writers, directly or indirectly, who have influenced, and continue to influence, the writings and speech of most of the greatest writers and orators of the present century. Examples of their methods are given on pp. 100 and 102.

Since the 1939–45 war, first in linguistic journals, and then in books, several new approaches to English grammar have emerged, all broadly descriptive, anti-historical, and semi-scientific. Our language has been re-examined in isolation from its past and strictly without reference to the rules of Latin grammar, though not without some comparison with the grammatical practices of American Indians and some other non Indo-European languages. The primary question asked is 'How does it work?' rather than 'Is this or that construction correct?' Not surprisingly, in that these grammarians have brought into question a not wholly satisfactory tradition, they have had some successes. English grammar is indeed even more complicated in its present-day forms than Richard Morris, Henry Sweet, H. W. Fowler, and others seemed to admit.

The most comprehensive descriptive grammar published so far is that of Randolph Quirk and colleagues, entitled *A Grammar of Contemporary English* (1972). It pays little or no attention to the grammar of past centuries: 'our field is no less than the grammar of educated English current in the second half of the twentieth century in the world's major English-speaking communities' (p. v). Grammatical description is attempted by contrasting acceptable constructions with unacceptable ones, the second sort marked by an asterisk. Thus (p. 11):

> John hated the shed.
> John painted the shed.
> Fear replaced indecision.

All have the same tense (past) and the same structure (subject

(Tauchn.) I, 9, Mr. Hatchway *who had one of his legs shot away.* | 1849-50 Dickens, David Copperf. (Ch. D. ed. 1887) 189, *King Charles the First had his head cut off.*

1965—*Type* 'They banished him the realm' > (1a) 'The earl was banished the realm'; (2) 'He was banished the realm'

Instances of type (1) ('him was banished the realm') have not been met with. Type (1a) represents the transition form in which the opening noun does not formally show that it is the converted subject, (though occasionally the plural forms *are* and *were* do so). Cf. 'The earls *were* banished the realm.' In type (2) the subjects are *I, thou, he, she, we* or *they.*

(1a)   (1350-1400 Stanzaic Life of Christ (EETS) 1160, (the tree) that *was defendet hym to com till.*). | c1475 Gregory's Chron. 176, *iij sowdyers were banyschyde the towne of Caleys.* | 1548 John Bale, Kynge Johan 1121, *All Cantorbery monks are now the realme exyled.* | 1553 A. Robynson, tr. Utopia (EETS) 84, some peere of Englande, *that is bannysshed his country,* whiche must cleyme title to the crown of the realme. | 1565 T. Stapleton, A Fortresse of the Faith (Antwerp 1565) 127r., 6, *such as* for enormous crimes *were* excommunicated and *embarred the holy communion.* | 1567 T. Stapleton, A Counterblast (Louvain 1567) 345r., 345 v., *suche persone . . . were expelled the realme.* | 1571 Edm. Campion, Hist. England (ed. Vossen) 32, *Gathelus . . . was* uppon disfavor *exiled the country* with a number of his factions. | 1583, Philip Stubbes, The Anatomy of Abuses II, 42, *Adam* our first parent *was expulsed paradise* (OED). | c1586 Sidney, Arcadia (Sommer) I, 21b, By the King and Senat of Lacedæmon, *Demagorus was banished the countrie* (OED). | 1588 Shakesp., Titus I, i, 388, Let not *young Mutius,* then, that was thy joy, *Be barr'd his* entrance here. | 1593 Shakesp., 2 Hen. VI, III, i, 145, Foul subornation *is* predominant, And *equity exiled your highness' land.* | Ibid. III, ii, 244, Unless *false Suffolk* straight *be* done to death, Or *banished fair Englands territories.* | (1599 George Peele, The Love of King David (in Manly, Spec. II) III, ii, 28, *Faire Peace,* the goddess of our grace here, *Is fled the streete* of faire Ierusalem.) | 1601-1704 Hatton Corresp. (ed. M. Thompson) I, 129, *Harry Savile is banished* y⁰ *Court.* | 1602 N.D. (= Rob. Parsons), Warn-Word to Sir Fr. Hastings II, ii, people *being debarred the light* of reading the scriptures. | 1640 James Yorke, The Union of Honour 40, *King Edward the fourth . . . being expulsed the realme* by the powerfull Earle of Warwicke (OED). | 1648 D'Avenant, Love and Honour (Belles Lettres Ser.) IV, iv, 114, why should *ladies,* then, that imitate The upper beauty most to mortal view, *Be barr'd a numerous adresse?* | 1663 S. Butler, Hudibras III, 2, 1591, *These subtle animals . . . Are banish'd their well-order'd state.* | 1697 Congeve, Mourning Bride (Mermaid) III, i p. 448, If *piety be* thus *debarred access.* On high . . . , What is reward? | 1692 N. Luttrell, Brief Relation of State Affairs (1857) II, 369, Yesterday *Sir John Lowther was dismist the treasury.* | 1820 Southey, Life Wesley II, 493, *Whoever acted contrary . . . should be expelled the Society.* | 1898 Henry James, The Turn of the Screw (Dent) 18, *The child's dismissed his school.*

(2)   1384 Presentments of Juries (Surtees Misc.) 25, We wyll þat *scho be woydyd the town.* | c1440 Jacob's Well (EETS) 62, in þat wyse *þei ben . . . forbanysched þe kynges lond.* | c1470 Malory, Wks. (ed. Vinaver) 831, *I was* so vengeabely *deffended the courte* that I caste me never to com there more. | Ibid. 825, *I am banysshed the contrey of Inglonde.*

1557 Tottel's Miscell. (Arber) 6, I gape for *that I am debard.* | 1570-6 W. Lambarde, A Perambulation of Kent (1862) 179. *Godwine . . . and his sonnes were exiled the Realme* (OED). | 1579 Lyly, Euphues (Arber) 188, And surely if conscience be the cause *thou art banished ye court,* I accompt thee wise in being so precise that by the vsing of vertue, *thou maist be exiled the place of vice.* | 1583 Milbancke, Philotimus A a ij, I . . . commaunded *him to be voided his lodging* (OED). | c1593 Marlowe, Edw. the Second (Tauchn.) p. 116, *I'll* not *be barr'd the court* for Gaveston. | c1600 Shakesp., Sonnets XXVIII, 1, How can I then return in happy plight, *That am debarr'd the benefit of rest?* | 1608 J. King, Sermons 24, March 2, *He was exiled the world* (OED). | 1648 Hunting of Fox 11, Yet *were they . . . expell'd the University* (OED). | 1657 J. Smith, The Mystery of Rhetorique Unveiled 64, *they . . . were ejected the house of God* (OED). | 1666 John Bunyan, Grace Abounding (ed. Brown, Cambridge) 119, *You must be banished the realm.* | 1722 DeFoe, Moll Flanders (Abbey Classics) 39, *I* expected every day *to be dismissed the family* (J). | 1748 Smollett, Rod. Random (Tauchn.) II p. 5. *I . . . am debarred access* to my grandfather. | 1754 Richardson, Sir Charles Grandison (London) 24, 4, *he should be dismissed our service.* | 1759 David Hume, History of England I, 284, *he was debarr'd* all *intercourse.* | 1766 Goldsmith, Vicar XXVIII, *I was debarred the small comfort* of weeping by her. | 1778 Fanny Burney, Evelina (London 1904) 256, if their Lord had witnessed their impudence, *they* would have been instantly *dismissed his service.* | Ibid. 265, O that *they might ever be banished this peaceful dwelling!* | 1783 J. C. Smith, in: Medical Communications I, 146, *She . . . was dismissed the hospital,* perfectly cured (OED). | 1800 Coleridge, Death Wallenstein 3, 3, Could my will have determined it, *they had been* long ago *expell'd the empire.* | 1818 Jane Austen, Northanger Abbey (ed. Chapman) 116, Insup-

A page from F. Th. Visser, *An Historical Syntax of the English Language* (1973) plus verb plus object). They all permit the same syntactic operations, as in:

>The shed was painted by John.   (passive)
>Did John paint the shed?   (interrogative)
>It was John that painted the shed. (relative clause)

And so on. But 'invisible' constraints prevent some permutations:

>*Fear painted the shed.
>*Fear hated indecision.
>*John replaced indecision.

In other words the range of possible constructions is governed by meaning and not simply by the order of words.

All major sectors of English grammar, including syntax and accidence, are put through their paces in a systematic way, and the result is an indispensable book unlikely to be supplanted in the present century.

Of the various kinds of theoretical approaches to grammar the most influential is what has come to be called transformational/generative grammar. Its high priest is the American scholar Noam Chomsky (b. 1928), and its basic technique is also (but by no means only) contrastive.

One of its classical paradigms is formed by contrasting the statements

>John is easy to please.
>John is eager to please.

By transforming these superficially identical constructions into another mode their 'identity' disappears:

>It is easy to please John.
>*It is eager to please John.

In other words the adjectives *easy* and *eager* do not operate in the same way even though they may appear to at first sight.

In Chomsky's work,[25] and in that of his adherents, the contrastive method is ruthlessly exploited, and many new concepts have emerged. The words 'kernel', 'string', 'deep structure', 'surface structure', and many others have replaced much of the traditional terminology of English grammar. Historical grammarians have been driven on to the defensive. In many universities synchronic transformational/generative grammar rules the roost. It remains to be seen whether the complicated new rules can be transmitted to the educated general public who continue in their engagingly persistent way to resort to the old prescriptive manuals, and in particular to the battered old grammars which they used at the schools they attended.

7
Vocabulary

A word never—well, hardly ever—shakes off its etymology and its formation. In spite of all changes in and extensions of and addition to its meanings, and indeed pervading and governing these, there will persist the old idea.

J. L. Austin, 'A Plea for Excuses' in *Philosophical Papers* (1961), vi. 149

The Formation of Words

A 'chocolate' normally has a confectionery centre, a thin surrounding layer of chocolate, and often a decorative design or flavoured substance on top. It may be one of many separate chocolates in a box or bag or it may (if one regards it in this way) form part of a bar, capable of being broken up into segments. In other words a chocolate is often an aggregate of several ingredients, though it can be a single-ingredient object, without nuts, peppermint, or other flavouring or decorative additive.

In the same way, a 'word' can be a simple inherited sound-sequence assigned at some point in the past to denote an object or objects, and incapable of subdivision into any meaningful fractions. For example, the sequence /ʃɪp/, pronounced as in Modern English, had been assigned to the object 'vessel capable of moving on the sea' at some undiscoverable period before the earliest preserved records of the English language. The arbitrariness of the assignment of the sequence is partially but not radically affected by the circumstance that other ancient Germanic tribes used a very similar sequence of sounds to denote the same object: hence modern Dutch *schip*, German *Schiff*, and so on.

Once established, the sound-sequence /ʃɪp/ joined other sequences of sound—we might as well call them 'words'—all of which were notionally capable of expansion fore and aft, as it were, to modify the meaning of the basic word. One way of studying the

English language is to examine the procedures of expansion or modification of individual words.

Theoretically it is possible, no doubt, for any word to expand or contract until it reaches a point of unintelligibility (through sheer length) on the one hand, or until it lacks distinctiveness (by reduction to the point of near-extinction) on the other. For example, it is not usual for a simple element to expand much beyond the length of the word *indecipherability*, where the basic element *cipher* has been joined fore and aft by a number of affixes. And it is rare for a common word to become reduced to a point of near-extinction—as happened to the Old English word *ǣ* 'law'— and only then because it could be replaced by a word (*law*) that became familiar because of the historical circumstances that a Scandinavian ruler became the King of England. Similarly OE. *unnan* (which would have given modern **un*) was replaced in the fourteenth century by the French words *grant* and *allow*.

The rules governing word-formation vary from age to age, but some are very durable.[1] A noun like *ship* easily acquires postfixed elements, some of which do not occur in isolation (or, in linguistic terminology, are 'bound'), like *-ment* (*shipment*). Some require the application of another rule (in this case the addition of *p*) before being used, like *-er* (*shipper*). Other postfixed elements exist as separate words, like *man* (*shipman*), *shape* (*shipshape*), or *wreck* (*shipwreck*). It happens that the noun *ship* does not easily lend itself to the prefixing of 'bound' elements, but several other types of prefixed element have enabled it to form new words (*airship*, *warship*, etc.).[2]

Not all nouns can be 'used as' verbs but *ship* became a verb within the Anglo-Saxon period (*scipian*) and then became subject to new extensions, for example *shipping, shipped, trans-ship* (first recorded 1792), and *unship* (a. 1450; hence *unshipped, unshipping,* and similarly *unshiplike* (1842), *unshipment* (1846), and *unship-shape* (1883).

The formative elements that can be placed before and after the main parts of speech are numerous (scores, not hundreds). Some can appear before nouns, adjectives, adverbs, and verbs, for example *non-* (*non-observance, non-colonial, non-sexually,* and formerly *non-act*) and *un-* (*ungreediness, unable, unbearably, undo*). But there are constraints and complications of various kinds. For example, negativity can be expressed by any of several privative prefixes, *a-*, *im-/in-*, *non-*, and *un-*, but it does not follow that any adjective (for example) can be preceded by any of these at liberty (cf. *apolitical* (1952), †*impolitical* (1748–1843), *non-political, unpolitical*, and **alovely*, **inlovely, non-lovely, unlovely*). The constraints governing such matters are known intuitively by native speakers but foreigners find them difficult to learn.

Throughout history formative elements have displayed various degrees of permanence. In the Anglo-Saxon period the prefix *ge-* could be appended to hundreds of verbs and nouns with varying force. Before nouns it had associative significance, 'with' or 'together', for example *gebedda* 'one who shares a bed with another', *gescȳ* 'a pair of shoes'; or denoted the achievement of a result, for example *geweorc* 'something built, a fortification'. Before verbs it classically denoted the completion of an action, for example *ge-etan* 'to eat up' (cf. *etan* 'to eat'), *gewinnan* 'to win' (cf. *winnan* 'to fight, strive'). It was also more or less obligatory in the past participle of all strong verbs. It passed into obsolescence during the Anglo-Saxon period and survived into Middle English, usually in the reduced form *i-* or *y-*, only sporadically and in restricted areas. In other words it became archaic and then remained in the emerging standard language only as a useful literary device to suggest antiquity or distancing of one kind or another. Relics and fossilized forms containing the prefix survive to the present day, for example *alike* (OE. *gelīc*), *among* (OE. *gemong*), *enough* (OE. *genoh*), and *handiwork* (OE. *handgeweorc*), as well as the deeply archaic *yclept* 'called'. Earlier works of literature by Chaucer, Langland, Lydgate, and especially Spenser used the prefix very frequently in such words as *ybound, ybrought, yclad, ydight*, and *ywrought*. Such writers even prefixed *y-* to words of Greek, Latin, or French origin, as *ybaptised, ygranted, ymartyred*, and *yrobbed*. With no regard for function or etymology, the prefix was even used before present participles of French origin, like Sackville's *ycausing* and Milton's *star-ypointing*.

In the Middle English period just as quickly as the prefix *ge-* passed into general obsolescence the prefix *be-* advanced in a striking manner. The prefix was common enough in Anglo-Saxon, for example *beclyppan* to embrace, *befealdan* to fold round, *behātan* to promise, *beneoþan* beneath, but after the Conquest it was even added to loanwords from the Romance languages—for example the words *becalm* and *besiege*. Later again all kinds of problems arose by the bursting forth of words with initial *in-* or *en-*. Nearly every word of long standing in the language formed with *en-* appeared in the Tudor period written indifferently as *en-* or *in-*. Similarly with words originally formed with *in-*. For modern readers, old-spelling texts displaying pairs of words like *enable* and *inable*, *enaction* and *inaction*, are very confusing. The context normally makes the meaning obvious, though, once one makes allowance for the replaceability of the prefix.

It is not possible to assign causes to all these alternating silences, disappearances, and eruptions, any more than it is possible to say why rooks choose one tree rather than another. For deeply buried reasons they just 'happen' at certain periods and not at others.

In chapters 2, 3, and 4 some of the main types of word-formation at various periods have been described with examples. Prefixes and suffixes have slipped into and out of fashion. The suffix *-lock* (OE. *-lāc*), for example, survives only in *wedlock* (OE. *wedlāc*, pledge-giving, espousals, nuptials), but once was the second element of a number of other words, for example OE. *beadolāc*, *feohtlāc*, *heapolāc* (all meaning 'fighting, warfare'), and *rēaflāc* robbery. Had they survived they would have given us, for example, **fightlock*, and **reavelock*, on the face of it just as 'acceptable' words as *warfare* and *robbery*. The suffix *-ness* has had a continuous history in recorded English both in words expressing a state or condition (*brightness*, *goodness*, etc.) and in some words bearing a concrete sense like *fastness*, *wilderness*, and *witness*. In Middle English it vied with *-laik* (from Old Norse *leikr*): thus ME. *godnes/godlaik* goodness, *clænnes/clænlaik* cleanness. Curiously only one word, *forgiveness*, shows *-ness* in combination with a preceding verb.

Foreign words have been welcomed at all periods and sooner or later suffer the indignity of being absorbed into the syllabic and other patterns of the receiving language. For example, Old Norse *kalla* became Old English *ceallian* (that is, was placed in the class of Old English verbs that ended in *-ian*), and then had the same history as other Old English verbs ending in *-ian*. The Old French words *espine* (mod. *épine*) and *esperit* (mod. *esprit*), by a process known as aphesis, lost their initial *e-* and became *spine* and *spirit* respectively under the influence of native English words beginning with *sp-* (*span*, *spare*, *sparrow*, *spear*, etc.). Many loan-words reached their modern form by disentangling or dislodging themselves from earlier associations: for example, *window* is a Middle English rationalization of Old Norse *vindauga* (*vindr* wind + *augr* eye); and *penthouse* in an alteration of earlier *pentice* (ultimately descended from Latin *pendere* to hang, depend), a leaning or dependent structure, refashioned under the influence of the word *house*.

Many words in the language are broad imitations of sounds or are expressively symbolical, for example *bang, cuckoo, fie, huh, ping, rattle, swish, tut, twang, whoosh,* and *yuk*. These words, and some sound-combinations like *sl-* and *gr-*, are the only exceptions to the general rule that the connection between the sound of a word and what it denotes is arbitrary.[3]

It does not seem likely that the old processes of word-formation will cease for a long time to come. This is true not only of hallowed methods but also of those that are more fluid. Thus, childish and semi-literate words like *diddums* (= *did 'em*, did they (tease you, etc.)?, with addition of plural *s*), *din-din*(*s*) dinner, *howzat* (in Cricket), *jamas* (pyjamas), *yep* (yes), and *yum-yum* will doubtless come and go, as they always have, but the habit of making rough-hewn words like these will last. Other words lie about like plasticine for very long periods, able to be shaped and reshaped in spelling even though more or less stable in pronunciation, for example *curmudgeon,*[4] *didicoi* (gypsy),[5] *kerfuffle,*[6] and *smidgen* 'a small amount'.[7] In the future many more such words will drift out of a kind of primeval phonetic soup into the central body of the standard informal language.

Except in special circumstances—for purposes of linguistic analysis and the like—users of a language do not pause to consider why one formation exists and not another. But there are certain strongly held beliefs—one might call them myths—which lie near the surface of the day-to-day views of many speakers of the language. One of these is that shorter words are better than longer ones, *bet* (verb), say, rather than *wager* or *gamble*. Related to it is the belief that Saxon words are to be preferred to Latinate ones, for example *swear* rather than *blaspheme*. A third is that compound words formed from elements drawn from two different languages give the kind of pain to a fastidious person that would be felt if a thistle were placed in the hand of a blindfolded man, for example the Greek/Latin formation *television.*[8] In certain circumstances such myths seem to be unassailably true. Multiplication of syllables can induce pomposity; monolingual purity of origin seems at first sight an agreeable birthright; the yoking of beasts from unrelated species may not be ideal for the plough. It is only when one looks at such myths more closely that difficulties arise. Pretentiousness and officialdom are usually accompanied by an indefensible stretching out of syllables and an obscuration of meaning, leaving an impression that some of the poles and pillars of life have been removed. First, pretentiousness: 'She and Harvey hadn't finalized the parameters of their own interface, mainly because they still didn't agree on just how open an open marriage ought to be' (p. 41); 'None of his alternatives, in fact, seemed viable; none of them would survive a feasibility study' (p. 64). Such typical sentences from Cyra McFadden's remarkable satirical novel *The Serial* (1978), set in Marin County, California, neatly bring out the pretentiousness of people who had 'mutated over the years through Gurdjieff, Silva Mind Control, actualism, analytical tracking, parapsychology, Human Life Styling, postural integration . . .'.[9]

The jargon of officialdom is an easy target, more or less brought into focus and into disrepute by the late Sir Ernest Gowers in his *Plain Words*, but still lying ready to hand in the speech and writings of many politicians, civil servants, trade union leaders and representatives of management, and writers of manuals of instruction. The American word *gobbledygook*, first recorded in 1944, has proved to be a deadly arrow with which to reinforce the shafts of Gowers, and the 'gobbledygookers' are now very much on the defensive. There remains an uncrossable chasm between those who do not want to know what expressions like 'excessive basic rate adjustment' mean, and the inland revenue authorities who use such expressions as a necessary part of their rules. Others, trained in the interpretation of linguistic cruces in the *Odyssey* and *Beowulf*, find it difficult to detect clarity and certainty in instructions like the following (for the operation of a video cassette recorder): 'At PLAY or REC mode the STOP key must be actuated before pressing EJECT, F.FWD. or REW keys.' This elementary instruction is language at its most advanced to minds trained on the accentuation of the antepenult (*multiplicity*) and on Sievers-type C2 half-line metrical patterns (*þæt wæs gód cýning*).

The residue of unnecessary official jargon lying about will

continue to be pilloried by groups of people—notably contributors to features and letters columns of the more conservative newspapers and to journals like *The Underground Grammarian*[10] —who see English, or at any rate intelligibility, threatened by the impenetrable language of educated 'morons'.

The quest for Saxonisms is an unrealizable nationalistic dream. A Saxonism, as defined by Gowers in his edition of *Modern English Usage* (1965), is 'a name for the attempt to raise the proportion borne by the originally and etymologically English words in our speech to those that come from alien sources'. Such quests have had moderate success from time to time—*foreword* (first recorded 1842) has joined *preface* (first recorded in Chaucer, c.1386); W. J. Thoms introduced the term *folk-lore* in 1846 as a term meaning 'the traditional lore of the common people' rather than (say) **people lore*, and it has remained; and an uneven amount of currency has been given to native words (given first) in pairs like *betterment/improvement* and *forebear/ancestor*. On the other hand, the artificial 'native' coinages of William Barnes in the late nineteenth century—for example *faith-heat* (enthusiasm), *fore-ween* (anticipate), *sundersome* (divisible), and *word-strain* (accent)—have been eschewed for a century and are likely to remain so. Any good piece of modern English writing is likely to contain an even proportion of words of native and of foreign origin (those of foreign origin are italicized):

But in this dumb *colloquy* with the sand *dunes* he *maintained* that his *affection* for Ramsay had in no way *diminished*; but there like the body of a young man laid up in *peat* for a *century*, with the red *fresh* on his lips, was his friendship, in its *acuteness* and *reality* laid up across the *bay* among the sandhills.

(Virginia Woolf, *To the Lighthouse* (1927), Part I, Chapter 1)

It is obvious that the removal of words of alien (here Latinate) origin would destroy the fabric of the language. Nevertheless a vague desire for simplicity, however illusory, is widespread:

'I noticed once that you used the word "gubbins". Could we look it up?'
'I don't think it would be in any dictionary yet. I just happened to use it. It means, oh, say, nonsense, trivia, nothing to get het up about. I particularly like a word that has the sound of Anglo-Saxon in it. I don't go much for Latinate words, do you?'

'You sound as if you're offering me a piece of cake that you hate but that you don't want to throw out.'

'Latinate words are the ones that won't shut up, but I suppose they carry on to some purpose to someone.'[11]

Barbarisms—words formed in an unorthodox way—were anathema to the Greeks, though the inevitability of their existence was accepted. The creation of barbarisms—hybrids and other malformed words—in modern English must now be regarded as hardly more than a technical misdemeanour, however deplorable that may seem to some.

From the earliest period, English took on board Greek or Latin words and attached English prefixes and suffixes to them (*plainness*, *sympathizer*). Conversely prefixes and suffixes of Romance origin were added to native words *readable*, *disbelieve*). No one ever seems to have objected to such formations. In recent times hostility has been aimed at more obviously heterogeneous combinations of Latin/Greek/English elements, like *automation*, *breathalyser*, *coastal*, *helipad*, *impedance*, *speedometer*, *television*, and *triphibious*. Ingenious arguments are set down in Fowler/Gowers (1965) and 'well-formed' preferences are provided, for example **costal*, **impedience*, and **speed-meter*. But almost always such words are irreversibly established before objectors learn of their existence, and the objections are hardly more than academic exercises. Lexicographers, when setting them down in dictionaries, can hardly be expected to go beyond a formulaic 'irreg.', that is, 'irregularly formed from A and B'. In practice the life cycle of such objections is normally very short.

As in so many other areas of English, similar malpractices in past centuries have long since been forgotten and errant forms have attained respectability through use. The study of etymology accustoms one to intrusive *n*s (*celandine*, *messenger*, *nightingale*), homorganic or parasitic *t*s (*pageant*, *pheasant*, *tyrant*) and *d*s (*sound*), and initial letters like the *d* in *daffodil* (as against *asphodel*, ultimately the same word).[12] Etymological miscreants of many other kinds came into being in older times. The word *abominable* (L. *abōminābilis*) was frequently written as *abhominable* from the fourteenth to the seventeenth century, being regarded as from L. *ab* and *homin-*, *homō* man. *Brimstone* is 'properly' **brinstone*, displaying an ancient careless pronunciation made respectable by being called 'dissimilation'. *Gillyflower* is a sixteenth-century 'rationalization' of the earlier forms *gilofre, girofle* (from medL. *caryophyllum*), under the influence of the English word *flower*. False or unnecessary etymological adjustments were made in former times to the words *advance*—how natural French *avant, avancer* and Italian *avanti* seem by comparison!; *female* (properly *femel* or *femal*, cf. L. *fēmella*) under the influence of *male*; *debt* and *doubt*, the latinized spellings with *b* being reintroduced in medieval and Tudor times (cf. F. *dette, doute*); and hundreds of others.

The second *r* in *bridegroom* is redundant, the second element being a descendant of OE. *guma* man. *Icicle* (OE. *īs-gicel*), *lady* (OE. *hlāf-dige* kneader of bread), *nickname* (ME. *eke-name* additional name), and *stark naked* (ME. *start-naked* tail-naked), exhibit reductions and alterations of various kinds. Ancient hybrid formations include *beefeater, blackguard, heirloom, salt-cellar*, and *scapegoat* in which one element is English and the other French. *Architrave* and *ostrich* were derived by an ancient joining of Latin and Greek elements.

The English language absorbs, rejects, and adapts elements of vocabulary as it goes along. Its formative rules are no more than general guides, observed only when it is convenient to do so, and broken—because of the needs of euphony, analogy, or some other competing principle—at will. The passage of time conceals old wounds and past crudities. Nothing will or should prevent linguistic conservatives from objecting to changes and innovations as they occur. At any given time a fastidious speaker will necessarily make his own choice of vocabulary, avoiding some words and accepting others, as an aspect of good taste or of circumstance or context. In language, as in other aspects of life, good taste, however indefinable it may be, is a prize worth seeking.

Change of Meaning

Evelyn Waugh, in a letter written in May 1946, remarked 'I looked up *effete*. It means primarily "having given birth". The dictionary is an endless source of surprise and pleasure.'[13] He was right, of course, and his casual remark provides a convenient starting-point for an examination of some of the movements of meanings in words.

Latin *effētus* meant 'that has brought forth young' and, by a natural extension, 'worn out by bearing, exhausted'. This literal sense was adopted by some English writers in the seventeenth and eighteenth centuries—beasts of the field and the farmyard were spoken of as 'barren and effete'. Transferred and figurative uses are recorded from the same time. Evelyn (1664) wrote of the 'imprison'd and Effoete Air, within the Green-house' and Burke (1796) described France, 'the mother of monsters', as showing 'symptoms of being almost effete'. It is a short step from the effeteness of beasts, monsters, and domestic animals to the barrenness of the intellect or resolve of people, and the word has been applied in the sense 'that has exhausted its vigour and energy, incapable of efficient action' to governments, schools of painting, aristocrats, monastic systems, feckless individuals, and so on, ever since. Its nearest relative is, of course, *foetus*.

The history of the word *effete* shows that a Latin word and its range of senses can be brought into English and continue its life in its new surroundings. In the host language the danger is that it is confronted by and is threatened by other words of similar meaning. And it is also subject to other normal processes of survival—on which more in a moment.

A somewhat similar model is provided by the word *holocaust*. Brought into English in the thirteenth century in its original sense 'a whole burnt offering, a sacrifice wholly consumed by fire' (Greek ὁλόκαυστον, f. ὅλος whole + καυστός burnt) it gradually moved off in two directions—the sacrificial element became dominant and the idea of fire less so, or vice versa. Sacrifices of any kind—lives, fortunes, love, remarkably even of a college fellowship—were 'holocausts' from the fifteenth to the nineteenth century. On the other hand, in Milton's *Samson Agonistes* (1671), 'that self-begotten bird' the phoenix 'lay erewhile a Holocaust'; and later contexts show the word being used of any large consuming fire. The destruction of millions of Jews by the Nazis in the present century brought the word back into use, applied to a specific set of deadly events, no longer sacrificial but terrifyingly and wantonly punitive and destructive.

Its nearest relatives, *caustic*, *cauterize*, and *hypocaust* (heated place in a Roman villa) have links with the combustible sense of *holocaust* (Greek καυστός burnt is derived from καίειν to burn), but no trace of the meaning 'sacrifice' remains in them.

Stability of meaning is rare in any language. Unpredictable environmental factors of one kind or another disturb meanings, as well as spellings and other linguistic aspects. The Latin word *sīrus* (an adaptation of Greek σιρός a pit to keep corn in) is the antecedent of Spanish and French *silo* in the original classical sense. From Spanish the word entered English in the early nineteenth century as 'a pit or *underground* chamber used for the storage of grain, roots, etc.' (*OED*). But underground chambers and pits became unfashionable towards the end of the century, and a new 'above-ground' sense emerged, 'a pit, or an air- and water-tight chamber, in which green food is preserved for fodder by ensilage'. Grain silos are still normally (though not always) structures placed above the ground and they are usually cylindrical in shape. But there are silos and silos, and the most deadly of all, those containing guided missiles ready to fire, are once more set into the earth, with the ejection passage still cylindrical.

Environmental changes have transformed the shape of many familiar objects; for example the *beehive*, once conical in outline (hence beehive coke ovens of similar shape and the beehive tombs of Mycenaean times), is now rectangular. A *trolley* to begin with was a low-wheeled cart or small truck used in mines and at sawmills. Trolleys of various shapes and sizes are still commonplace at airports, in supermarkets, and elsewhere as convenient wheeled receptacles for luggage, food and other items of shopping, and so on. The word survives in another context—applied to the apparatus above an electric train or an electrically driven bus: for these the shape of the trolley varies considerably from a flexible iron network linking the vehicle to the source of power overhead to a wheel placed at the end of a pole above the vehicle.

The outline history of these five words alone—*effete, holocaust, silo, beehive*, and *trolley*—illustrates some of the powerful forces that have brought about semantic change in relatively modern times. When one turns to the language at large the mathematics of semantic change are daunting. The *OED* records nearly half a million words in alphabetical order, some as old as the language itself, some of moderate antiquity, and some that are relatively new. The words of the Anglo-Saxon language (except for words of which no record survives after the Conquest) are included, and all the ancient senses and their descendants are set down in ramified form. These old branches and ancient twigs ramified further in all the centuries that followed, and the new meanings are all assigned, for convenience of reference, to sections preceded by identificatory roman numerals, capital and small letters of the roman alphabet, arabic numerals, and so on. The result is an astonishingly rich network of chronologically and/or logically arranged senses. At any given time senses tend to merge or overlap, and the mathematical arrangement of the senses, and particularly of subordinate and specialized senses, needs to be treated with due caution. But the patterns of historical development of all words down to very recent times have been permanently established. They are of course modifiable and extendible as new information about them becomes available, but they are safe from the crude linguistic hypotheses and frettings of linguistic philosophers of earlier times and from the views of barrack-room lawyers of the present day.

It is unnecessary to set down here a catalogue of all the external events of the fifteen hundred years that English has existed as a distinguishable language—from the coming of Christianity and the decline and fall of paganism to the industrial revolution and its spectacular aftermath in the nineteenth and twentieth centuries. Suffice it to say that every major historical, political, and social event, every discovery and every new belief, since *c.*450 has brought change to the English language, and not least to the meanings of words.

It is best to assume at the outset that no single word in the language is a stable, unchanging, and immutable legacy from the past, however fixed, dependable, and definable it may seem at any given time. Ever-present elements of restlessness and instability— expansion of meaning, restriction, pejoration, amelioration, acceleration, retardation, association, differentiation, and so on— lie at the heart of linguistic instability. Words and meanings, like elements, have half-lives, however durable they may seem in their dictionary form. Paradoxically, in the chambers of the mind, we tend to cling to the words and meanings that we acquire when young like the treasures in the tombs of kings, tablets bearing sacred inscriptions.[14] But change comes to everything.

The least disturbance of meaning in the recorded history of the language can be observed in the primary terms of kinship, *father, mother, daughter, son, brother, sister,* and so on, and of colour, *green, yellow, blue, red,* etc.[15] They have not remained motionless in meaning and application—far from it—but relatively speaking there is a certainty about their relationship that is not affected by flood, fire, revolution, or other external circumstance. Individual numbers have also tended to remain systematically unchanged, 1 being recognizably and axiomatically separated from zero by the same interval as it is separated from 2, neither fractional nor plural, a half of 2, a quarter of 4, and so on.[16] Elsewhere flux and change are routine.

The meaning of 'meaning'—used as the title of a classic book (1923) by C. K. Ogden and I. A. Richards—cannot be reduced satisfactorily to a few simple propositions. It must needs suffice here to give examples of some of the types of change.[17]

The Anglo-Saxon verb *būgan* meant 'to bow, yield': it is in fact the antecedent of our verb *to bow*. In informal speech (it did not come into written form until *c.*1175) the corresponding adjective meaning 'tractable to, obliging, obedient' was **buhsom* / ˈbuksəm/. The sense 'obedient' was bequeathed to later generations, seemingly fixed and stable so long as it was applied only to living things. Its immobility ended when it was applied to inanimate things: 'obedient' easily developed into (*a*) 'yielding to pressure, unresisting', as in Milton's 'Wing silently the buxom air' (*PL* II. 842), and the two senses coexisted for a century or more. Two further branches of meaning emerged towards the end of the sixteenth century: (*b*) 'blithe, jolly, well-favoured' (applied to eyes, valour, speech, behaviour, etc.); (*c*) 'of good mien and of comfortable and comely appearance: applied especially to women'. Time moved on, the earlier senses withered and died, and only sense (*c*) survived. These changes can be represented diagrammatically as follows:

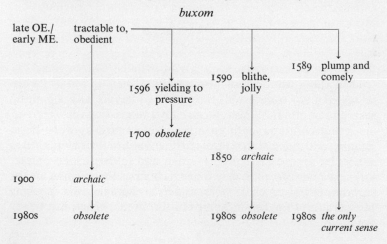

In another simple case, the word *hindrance* lost its primary sense 'injury, damage' ('That he should neuer . . . do any other beast anye harme or hynderance', Thomas More, 1529) by the early seventeenth century, but has survived in the weakened sense 'obstruction to progress' and in the corresponding concrete noun 'an impediment, obstacle'. Diagrammatically:

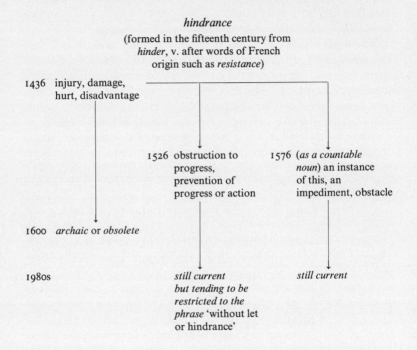

hindrance
(formed in the fifteenth century from
hinder, v. after words of French
origin such as *resistance*)

1436 injury, damage,
hurt, disadvantage

1526 obstruction to
progress,
prevention of
progress or action

1576 (*as a countable
noun*) an instance
of this, an
impediment, obstacle

1600   *archaic* or *obsolete*

1980s   *still current
but tending to be
restricted to the
phrase* 'without let
or hindrance'

still current

The Latin word *candidus* meant 'white, glistening' but it already possessed many transferred senses to do with innocence, stainlessness, purity, and frankness. Classically trained English writers in the seventeenth and eighteenth centuries carried over the basic meaning and many of the transferred senses into their works—it is impossible to read Clarendon, Dryden, and Johnson, for example, with true understanding unless one recognizes the range of meanings they bestowed on *candid*, *candidly*, *candidness*, and *candour*. The pattern of English meanings of the word *candour* can be set out like this:

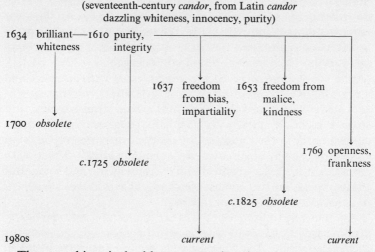

candour

(seventeenth-century *candor*, from Latin *candor*
dazzling whiteness, innocency, purity)

1634 brilliant——1610 purity,
      whiteness   integrity

1700 *obsolete*

                1637 freedom   1653 freedom from
                      from bias,   malice,
                      impartiality   kindness

      *c.*1725 *obsolete*

                                          1769 openness,
                                                frankness

                    *c.*1825 *obsolete*

1980s   *current*   *current*

These are historical tables representing the extant senses listed
in the *OED*.

Another way to observe the meaning of words is to examine the
areas in which near synonyms overlap. For example, the words
amusement and *entertainment* obviously have much in common.
In the *Concise Oxford Dictionary* (7th edn., 1982) the definitions
are as follows:

amusement: pleasant diversion; causing of laughter or smiles; pastime.

entertainment: In vbl senses (i.e. to amuse, occupy agreeably); hospitality;
                amusement (*much to my entertainment*); diversions or
                amusements for guests etc.; public performance or show.

Leaving aside discarded historical senses that are not recorded in
the *COD*, it might seem at first sight that there is little to choose
between the two words, despite the more elaborate presentation of
the entry for *entertainment*. And yet if one could imagine the
semantic space occupied by the two there is little doubt that the
'acreage' of the second word would be greater than that of the first.
Entertainment, to a greater or lesser degree, implies a ritualized
element of formal organization, for example a social gathering or
reception, or a public performance by an orchestra or the like, in
each case with the aim of diverting or amusing. Except in the
context of an amusement arcade (with one-armed bandits, Space

Invader machines, etc.) or an amusement park (in the United States, a commercially operated park with a roller-coaster, merry-go-rounds, etc.), *amusement* is a general unspecific concept requiring more involvement from the individual. In the language at large *entertainment* is much more commonly used than *amusement*. Thus in the computerized database called NEXIS (April 1983) there were 26,170 examples of *entertainment* and 5,222 examples of *amusement*. In this database *entertainment* is provided by a marine band, a musical group, street dancing, and so on. It is closely linked with 'hospitality'. On the other hand, the contexts held in the database for *amusement* place emphasis on enjoyment sought or discovered by the individual—'I read with amusement X's letter', 'with childlike amusement', and so on. But the two words are sometimes interchangeable as in the *amusement* or *entertainment business* or *industry*.

Another way to bring out the range of meanings of such nearly synonymous words is to place a set of contextual sentences for them side by side. Any such list (this group happens to be taken from *Webster's Third New International Dictionary*, 1961) clearly confirms that the semantic space occupied by the word *entertainment* is larger than that occupied by the word *amusement*:

It was amusement for him, not in deadly earnest.[18]

What are your favorite amusements?

His amusement knew no bounds.

He plays the piano for his own amusement.

He delighted in the entertainment of friends and relatives.

His serious entertainment of angelology . . . reveals the complications of a too strictly biblical theology.

She engaged a concert pianist for the entertainment of her guests.

This book is first-rate entertainment.

He provided entertainment for his guests, whimsical as well as culinary.

A serious novel as opposed to an entertainment.

The stream of life is the most permanently available of free entertainments.

> Last night another of these pleasant social entertainments was given at her home.
>
> Negro orchestras are in demand at white entertainments.

Another technique designed to draw attention to the meanings of words by contrastive methods was demonstrated by the American scholars J. J. Katz and J. A. Fodor.[19] In their treatment of the word *bachelor* they observed that the main strands of meaning[20] can usefully be contrasted in something like the following way:

1. young knight: human, male, adult, trained in war.
2. university graduate: human, until modern times exclusively male, adult, scholarly.
3. unmarried man: human, male, adult, unlimited range of personal qualities.
4. young male seal: non-human, male, not adult, may be legally killed for its fur.
5. a size of roofing slate: a thing, i.e. asexual, one of a series according to size (long wivets, long bachelors, short bachelors . . . long days, short days, etc.).[21]

The contrastive method was intended to make it possible for like items eventually to be gathered together, that is, all words denoting a human being, exclusive maleness, person trained for war, person trained in scholarship, in other words a conceptual dictionary. But such a dictionary, except for relatively simple examples like *Roget's Thesaurus*, remains something of an alchemical dream.

I referred above to various abstract concepts which bring about unpreventable linguistic change. It is beyond the scope of this book to illustrate all of them. All I can do here is to give brief indications of the way in which words move about between conceptual flagpoles, programmed, as it were, by their nature to follow a predestined course until they are disturbed by their circumstances or by some external events.

Certain adjectives acquire clear acceptability in one set of contexts (or collocations) and diminishing acceptability in others. It has been pointed out,[22] for example, that the adjectives *pretty* and *handsome* share common ground in the meaning 'good-looking', and that their distribution is largely, though not exclusively, governed by the words they qualify. Thus:[23]

pretty {
bargain
boy
face
features
laughter
penny
state of affairs
sum
woman
words
}

handsome {
contribution
house
inheritance
man
newt
proportions
quality
resolution
saddle
woman
}

The means by which this distribution came about reflect the history of the words concerned. Constraints and permissions of various kinds—why one really cannot say 'what a handsome state of affairs', for example—lie beyond the governance or control of the individual. We can go no further in the matter than Wittgenstein did: 'A meaning of a word is a kind of employment of it. For it is what we learn when the word is incorporated into our language.'[24]

Some classes of words are governed by the social circumstances in which they are used. Many of them may have started out free of childish, hurtful, fanciful, restrictive, or other impediments, but are drawn by this or that force towards their present status. The standard translation of the Latin word *equus* is 'horse'. *Horse* was already (in the form *hors*) the normal word for this 'solid-hoofed herbivorous quadruped' in Anglo-Saxon. The concept 'horse', however, even in its male adult form, can be indicated by a range of synonyms of widely different form, both now and in the past. In the fourteenth-century poem *Sir Gawain and the Green Knight*, for example, the requirements of the alliterative metre led to the use of numerous poetical synonyms, some more martial and less neutral than others, for example *blonk, caple, corsour, fole, horse, mounture*, and *stede*. With the demise of warfare on horseback, the invention of the internal combustion engine, and the introduction of the combine harvester on farms the traditional roles of the horse have been largely reduced to the competitive (racing, hunting, show-jumping) and to the control of crowds (police horses). Even so the words *gee-gee* (childish), *mount* (racing), *nag* (slang), and *steed* (poetical) give some indication of the complex relationship between a word and the object it denotes, not to mention the somewhat more specialized words *cart-horse, draught-horse, dray-horse, pack-horse*, and *racehorse*, names for male/female, old/young horses, and so on.

Amelioration of meaning spread over a period can be illustrated by such words as *boy* (fettered person → male servant → male child), *caitiff* (prisoner → poor wretch → base fellow, villain), and *meticulous* (over-scrupulous → very careful, accurate). The opposite process of pejoration is shown by the history of *knave* (male child → male servant → rascal). In several words a specific sexual sense has placed earlier general senses at risk, for example *ejaculation, erection*, and *intercourse*. The word *gay* in the sense 'homosexual', to the fury of many people, is tending to drive out the traditional senses 'light-hearted, carefree' at the present time. Such changes are always uncomfortable when they seem to threaten the props of society, but no amount of praying, begging, or of formal legislation will stop them happening.

The completion of the *OED* put an end—or largely put an end—to idle speculation about semantic change. But the boundaries of semantics are broader than those of traditional philology. New methods of analysis, new dichotomies, new functionalisms and relativisms, are now all the rage. Generative semantics, semiotics, deontic modality, illocution, and other conceptual approaches require more complex Venn diagrams, truth-tables, and phrase-markings than can be provided in a small book like this. But they are seeking general truths, not semantic patterns and developments for the English language alone. It remains to be seen how fruitful they will be and how communicable to anyone except philosophers of language themselves.[25]

Dialect

The carved stones, slabs, and wheel crosses in churchyards in Cornwall are permanent reminders of older generations. Unfortunately the speech patterns of Sennen, Mevagissey, and Tintagel have no such memorial stones or crosses. So it is with East Anglia—Burgh Castle and Framlingham Castle, impressive squat layers of flint and stone, look out over well-mapped marshes and farmland, but East Anglia lacks a continuous record of its linguistic history from pre-Conquest times. Dialects are relics of forgotten and mostly unrecoverable patterns of speech but retain within them the ingredients needed for perpetual renewal and modification.

Within the British Isles, now as in the past, the English language exists and persists in an uncountable number of forms. Only one form—that taught to foreigners—is 'standard'. This broadly rationalized prestigious form of English is a lineal descendant of a dialect that began to acquire its potency in the fourteenth and fifteenth centuries. Its importance and its individuality went hand in hand with the fortunes of London and of people who moved into the London area for commercial, political, or other reasons. Historically it contains some elements from the south-east, especially Kent, and some from the east Midlands as far north as the city of Lincoln. But for the most part its constituent elements are those that came to be accepted as the 'best' form of speech among educated speakers in London itself.

Standard English is the variety considered most suitable for use on the spoken channels of our broadcasting systems emanating from London. For the most part it is the variety towards which the speech of university teachers and schoolteachers south of the Midlands tends to become accommodated. It has a grammar that can be set down in reasonably undisputed form in textbooks, a nearly immobile set of phonemes (or speech-sounds)—except in so far as these are exaggerated for special purposes (Sloane Rangerness, archness, snobbery, preciosity, and so forth)—and a vocabulary which, subject to the usual limits of education and intelligence, is 'understood' throughout the country. It has no features that are restricted to any small parcel of land or to a particular city, village, or hamlet: the *chines* (small ravines) of Bournemouth, for example, are not part of the central core of Received Standard. It is seen as unequivocally 'English' by people in Beijing, Kaliningrad, and Tokyo, who learn it as they might learn the lines of a gigantic play. It is a form of English in which ears are *ears* (not *lugs*), in which the range of prepositions does not include *outwith*, and in which a church is called a *church* (not a *kirk*). It shows little interest in multiple terminology for left-handedness, freckles, or the last of a litter of pigs. It is the form spoken by the monarch on public occasions and by public orators at southern universities.

It is not shackled to rural particularities, and is little influenced by the languages of the Celtic speakers whose ancestors moved to the British Isles long before any Saxons or Vikings appeared. In practice Standard English can be learnt very quickly by regional speakers if the right motivation exists. By contrast it is more difficult to abandon Received Standard and comfortably pass as a native in any provincial region.

Rural and regional particularities are not easily scooped up and deposited in dictionaries and grammars even with the aid of modern technology. What has emerged as the stock-in-trade of modern scholarly investigators of English dialects are shaded and dotted maps showing where one linguistic feature ends and a competing one begins, or to what extent two or more competing features overlap. The crisscrossings are as complicated as the scent trails of foxes and badgers and less discoverable. The words and meanings of many dialects are recorded in the greatest dialect dictionary of all time, Joseph Wright's *English Dialect Dictionary* (1896-1905). More recently the several volumes of a *Survey of English Dialects* (1962-8), edited by Harold Orton and others, have been published. A large number of glossaries have also appeared dealing with the vocabulary of particular counties. There is a *Linguistic Atlas of England* (1978) edited by Harold Orton, Stewart Sanderson, and John Widdowson, and there are tapes and cassettes of local varieties of speech.

Ordinary people—people not trained in the professional study of the language—have no difficulty in recognizing regional varieties of English. A. H. Halsey, an Oxford sociologist, revisited his birthplace, Kentish Town, and reported:

I turned into a workmen's café on Camden High Street and sat over thick, stale tea of the traditional brew, to eavesdrop on the conversation of those displaced from the domesticities. They were all male, including the Polish cockney proprietor. Two retired long-distance lorry drivers carried on a desultory argument in guttural Glaswegian dialect, about the best route to Guildford. An old tramp sat in the corner, muttering obscenities to himself in West-country tones which rose and fell like the tide on some dimly remembered Devon coast. Two younger men were local cockneys, exchanging rapid diphthongs and lazy consonants.—That is the familiar fast and lively talk which was my own mother tongue.[26]

Virginia Woolf read the works of George Borrow (1803-81) and in a letter of 1936 to her friend Ethel Smyth remarked, 'But Lord, how I wish I could write that particular racy English eccentric East Anglian nonconformist style.'[27] One of the greatest writers and speakers of standard English in the present century, Virginia Woolf, looks half with envy and yet with not quite unwrapped pleasure at the written work of a man from another region who would not quite have fitted into her circle.

These are generalizations. A West Country doctor recently drew my attention to what ordinary people regard as typical dialect words. Would I 'tell him something about' some words used by his mother who was also of West Country origin? They were *cleachy*, used of soup when it is no longer warm ('Drink your soup before it becomes cleachy'); *shrammed*, very cold ('Let me get near the fire, I'm shrammed'); *smeach*, smoke-laden air ('What a smeach. Open the door.'); and *scrage*, a slight contusion of the skin ('I've got a scrage on my ankle'). These are archetypal dialect words, richly associative, tinged with antiquity, seemingly wrapped like small gifts in the folds and orchards of the West Country. But like everything linguistic they are exceedingly difficult to pin down. Women from the West Country and mothers of doctors are not members of a stationary clan locking words away in their locality and saying that no one else may use them. *Shram*, for example, is a widely used dialectal word meaning 'to benumb or paralyse with cold'. By its nature it is chiefly used in the passive (*to be shrammed*). It turns up in Thomas Hardy's Wessex poems ('half shrammed to death'), and variants like *scrammed*, *shrimmed*, and *shrimped* are recorded in the classic collections of regional English of the last three hundred years or so. It cannot be doubted that they all answer ultimately to an Anglo-Saxon verb of the type *scrimman* (recorded once), with an alternating stem-vowel -*i*- or -*a*- in the past tense as, over the centuries, it hovered between being a strong and a weak verb. But the word in its variant forms lay about in the casual speech of countryfolk for centuries before Francis Grose first recorded it in his *Provincial Glossary* in 1787. During this time the meaning veered between 'chilled, numbed' on the one hand and 'shrivelled, withered, shrunk' (originally or contextually from cold) on the other.

The other words listed by the doctor are equally elusive and just as evocative. All that one can do is pursue them in the *English Dialect Dictionary* and the *OED* itself. Nothing short of a national poll could establish their geographical distribution with any certainty.

The impossibility of setting precise boundaries to regional words comes about partly because of the reluctance of writers and scholars until very recent times to set down precise details of non-standard words.[28] Sir James Murray and his colleagues realized that the recording of dialectal vocabulary must be kept within limits if they were ever to complete their work, and this tradition has been continued in the *Supplement to the OED*. For example, in Volume 3 (*O–Scz*) of the *Supplement* there are only about 30 words that are stated to be more or less restricted to dialectal use:

outen *prep.*, overner, overun, pearten *v.*, pedgill *v.*, piggle *n.* and *v.*, pilkin, pillaloo, pit-yacker, poddle *v.*, polis, puckle, pulamiting, punkie, pussivanting, raft *v.*[3], ran-tan *v.*, ranterpike, ranty, ratch *v.*, rit, rodham, score, Scouse, scow *v.*[3], screef *n.* and *v.*, screel *n.* and *v.*, scroddy, scrooch *v.*, and scrunty.

When one considers that there are some 18,750 'Main Words' in this volume divided into some 28,000 senses, the proportions become dramatically clear. When one examines the credentials of the thirty words the reasons for inclusion seem to be:

(*a*) They are used by well-known writers: R. D. Blackmore (*poddle* v.), Charlotte Brontë (*scrunty*), Thomas Hardy (*raft* v.[3]), D. H. Lawrence (*pedgill* v., *piggle* v., *pulamiting*, *ranty*, *scroddy*), George Meredith (*pilkin*), A. Quiller-Couch (*pillaloo*, *pussivanting*).

(*b*) They are used in countries abroad as well as in a UK region (*outen* prep., *pearten* v., *screel* n. and v.: Scotland, Northern Ireland, and Barbados; *scrooch* v.: slightly non-standard in many English-speaking countries).

(*c*) They are 'discovered' by tourists (*overner*, *overun*), sociologists (*pit-yacker*, a Geordie word for a coal-miner), folklorists (*punkie*, a lantern in a hollowed-out vegetable; *ran-tan* v., to make an unruly noise at the house of a man known to have beaten his wife; *scow* v.[3], to loiter, idle), naval historians (*ranterpike*, a schooner or brigantine on the River Clyde), columnists in national newspapers (*ratch* v., to forage for food, etc.; *rit* n.[3], the smallest pig in a litter).

(*d*) They become technical terms in geography textbooks (*rodham*, a raised bank in the Fen district of East Anglia; *score*, in East Anglia, a narrow steep path leading to the sea; *screef*, a layer of vegetation; (as verb) to clear surface vegetation from the ground).

Of all these words only *Scouse* and perhaps *polis* (representing a Scottish and Irish pronunciation of *police*) have moved into the general language as nationally recognized words. The remainder lie imprisoned within restricted areas.

In practice the recording of regional language has been restricted by various factors. For example, the Survey of English Dialects undertaken by Eugen Dieth and Harold Orton in 1946, like other surveys undertaken in Europe, was based on a questionnaire designed to elicit clear answers from elderly people living in rural communities. The questions were so designed that the informants were normally unaware of the actual point brought out by their answers. Farmers who answered 'spade' when asked 'what do you dig the ground with?' were not to know that the point at issue was the *pronunciation* of 'spade', not the choice of word (e.g. *spade/shovel/spit*). Much was overlooked. For example, it would have been useful to elicit local terms for the sparrow, the cuckoo, the butterfly, the centipede, the clothes-horse, dumplings, a dunghill, and many other animals, insects, and objects.[29]

More recent work on regional English has tended to turn away from the fading or faded language of rural areas and some progress has been made in the recording of the regional speech of socio-economic groups in places like Gateshead (Durham), Bethnal Green (London), and Norwich.[30] What we lack, however, is a ruthlessly systematic linguistic equivalent of Pevsner's books on the buildings of England. William Labov's *The Social Stratification of English in New York City* (1966) blazed the trail, but no equivalent scholar of stature has emerged yet in England. We still know far more about the distribution of *byre/shippon/mistall/cow-stable/cow-house/cow-shed/neat-house/beast-house* for 'cow-shed' (see p. 129) than we do about urban synonyms for pedestrian crossings, lollipop men, machines used to wash cars, forecourts of petrol stations, bollards, sleeping policemen, pay-out desks, supermarket trolleys, traffic wardens, telephone booths, and hundreds of other items found in every city in the United Kingdom.

The nature of class-structured dialects is also a matter of perpetual discussion and disagreement, from the middle- and upper-class diversions of U and non-U to the politically divisive vocabulary of various social groups. For example, most professional linguistic scholars regard it as axiomatic that all varieties

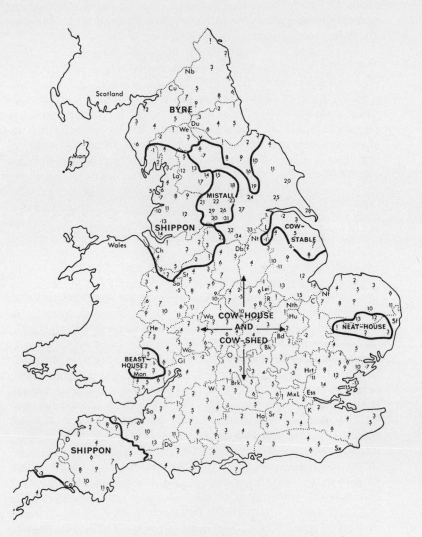

Words for the cow-house. From M. F. Wakelin, *English Dialects:
An Introduction* (1972)

of English have a sufficiently rich vocabulary for the expression of all the distinctions that are important in the society using it. By contrast, Professor John Vincent, a historian, regards such a view as

a nasty little orthodoxy among the educational and linguistic establishment. However badly you need standard English, you will have the merits of non-standard English waved at you. The more disadvantaged you are, the more extravagantly your disadvantages will be lauded as 'entirely adequate for the needs of their speakers', to cite the author [Professor John Lyons] of *Sociolinguistics*. It may sound like a radical cry to support pidgin, patois, or dialect, but translated into social terms, it looks more like a ploy to keep Them (whoever Them may be) out of the middle-class suburbs.[31]

Resolution of such opposite views is not possible. Nevertheless the future of dialect studies and the study of class-marked distinctions are likely to be of considerable interest to everyone.

Slang

Like everything else linguistic, slang[32] can be approached from different angles. Seen as a sizeable distinguishable element in written English it can be plainly identified from the sixteenth century onward. Prior to that it lay about in unrecorded private speech. The first formal recording of slang in dictionary form came in B.E.'s *Dictionary of the Canting Crew* in 1699. As a phenomenon of modern times it can be pursued to many public and private lairs. It is stretched on class-structured racks. It crosses generation gaps but is sometimes mainly restricted for a period to a particular generation. It is not forbidden in any social class in the spoken language but is more prevalent in some classes than in others. It forms an engaging proportion of the total informal realm of the English language. It is often geographically restricted, or more or less confined to the members of a set or group. It is seen at its raciest and most furtive in the language of illicit pleasures or of crime. Its ingredients are often transferred from the sack in which it arrived to other containers and from there into the normal unconstrained neutral store of words making up the English language. It can also be kept in its slang sacking for decades or even for longer periods, seemingly rejected for formal public use. The

Slum (slvm), *sb.*[1] [Of cant origin, and in all senses except 2–4 only in canting use.]

I. †1. A room. *Obs.*

1812 J. H. VAUX *Flash Dict., Slum,* a room. **1823** BEE *Dict. Turf* s.v., Thus we may have 'the little slum',..'the back slum', and a slum in front. **1824** *Hist. Gaming* 28 Regaling..in the back parlour (*vulgo* slum) of an extremely low-bred Irish widow.

2. A street, alley, court, etc., situated in a crowded district of a town or city and inhabited by people of a low class or by the very poor; a number of these streets or courts forming a thickly populated neighbourhood or district where the houses and the conditions of life are of a squalid and wretched character. Chiefly *pl.,* and freq. in the phrase *back slum(s).*

(*a*) **1825** WESTMACOTT *Eng. Spy* II. 32 The back slums lying in the rear of Broad St. **1851** DICKENS *Lett.* (1880) I. 251 When the back slums are going to be invaded. **1871** L. STEPHEN *Playgr. Eur.* (1894) ix. 203 The unspeakable ugliness of a back slum in London. **1880** R. S. WATSON *Visit Wazan* iv. 72 The back slums are not more inviting than those of many European towns.

(*b*) **1845** *Athenæum* 18 Jan. 75 In the thick of the once renowned 'slums' of St. Giles's. **1860** *All Year Round* No. 74. 570 An obscure cabaret—say pothouse—lying in a slum. **1889** JEROME *Idle Thoughts* 117 A little mite sitting on a doorstep in a Soho slum. **1894** SALA *London up to Date* vi. 79 Large tracts of indescribably dirty, profligate, and felonious slums.

fig. **1870** LOWELL *Among my Bks.* Ser. I. (1873) 84 The slums and stews of the debauched brain.

b. *Theatr.* (See quot.)

1886 *Stage Gossip* 69 Such lowly edifices of the drama as wooden buildings of humble erection and booths are frequently designated 'slums'.

3. Representation of slum life or conditions.

1885 *Pall Mall G.* 7 Apr. 10/1, I should like to know who would stand five acts of 'slum'.

4. *attrib.* and *Comb.,* as *slum-burrow, -literature, -people,* etc. ; **slumland,** the slums; **slum-sister,** a woman devoted to charitable and educative work in the slums.

Many combs. of these types occur in recent newspaper usage.

1863 B. JERROLD *Signals of Distress* 7 It is a genuine bit of slum-literature. **1878** GORDON *Jrnl.* in Hill *G. in C. Africa* (1881) 326 These slum people liked their visitor. **1887** *Contemp. Rev.* Dec. 772 That class rarely stray..from their slum-burrows and dens. **1890** *Guardian* 31 Dec. 2096/1 This 'slum-sister' gathers children for instruction on Sunday afternoons. **1893** *Graphic* 25 Mar. 298/3 The appearance of respectability..deprives him of the glamour of slumland.

II. †5. Nonsensical talk or writing; gammon, blarney. Also, gipsy jargon or cant. *Obs.*

1820 in *Grose's Dict. Vulgar T.* (1823) s.v., And thus, without more slum, began..To settle..The rigs of this here tip-top nation. **1822** J. WILSON *Noctes Ambros.* iv, He may have written some pretty things, but he is taken now to slum, scissorsing, namby pamby, and is quite spoiled. **1823** BEE *Dict. Turf* s.v., The gipsey language, or cant, is slum. *Ibid.,* Loose, ridiculous talk, is 'all slum'. 'None of your slum,' is said by a girl to a blarneying chap.

b. *Up to slum,* knowing, wideawake; not to be 'taken in' or 'done'.

1857-9 in *Slang Dict.*

c. 'An insinuation, a discreditable inuendo.'

1865 *Slang Dict.* 236.

6. A begging-letter.

1851 MAYHEW *Lond. Lab.* I. 224 A slum's a paper fake.

The origin and development of the word *slum* is shown by the *OED* entry (1912) for the word rate of loss is considerably higher than it is for any other segment of the language.

> 'What about that polony he was with?'
> 'She doesn't matter, she's just a buer.'

Language like this is lying around like gravel in modern fiction. It happens to be an extract from Graham Greene's *Brighton Rock*, published in 1938, but the strange words *polony* and *buer*, and words from any of the other areas of slang, are likely to turn up in great profusion in the dialogue of hundreds of modern fictional characters. The authors, in this case Graham Greene, may or may not be able to say how they first came across such words. Both words (as so often in the language of slang) are of obscure origin. 'Polony' has nothing to do with Poland or with Bologna or with sausages. It is just a derogatory word for a young woman. Its spelling is not fixed and no one has found it used in print before 1934. For Greene it must have come from his drawer or notebook marked 'Recent Slang' or from some casual source. *Buer* is also found in a variety of spellings. It has been found in print in its various disguises from 1807 onwards used to mean 'a woman, especially one of a loose character'. In other words it is one of an extremely large class of slang expressions. It is recorded chiefly in regional works written in northern counties of England and in the language of tramps.

The crudities of the slang of *Brighton Rock* have acquired a special kind of innocence as the book has now gently receded into the past. Anyone shocked by its relative explicitness would need to acquire new protective coverings of the mind for much of the fiction of the 1980s. In William Boyd's *On the Yankee Station* (1981), Lieutenant Larry Pfitz, an American pilot on the USS *Chester B. Halsey*, takes a scunner to a member of his ground crew. After landing bumpily on the deck of the aircraft-carrier he grabs Arthur Lydecker by the arm:

Fuckin' bumpy landing again, you fuckin' shithead creep. How many times I told you to get those tyre pressures reduced? You're on a fuckin' charge.

The venom is unmistakably expressed in the all-too-familiar language of abuse.

Russ, a cockney layabout in Martin Amis's *Other People* (1981), believes himself to be sexually irresistible to women:

Is the feeling of self-loaving I can't bear. Inna mornins. *Used* again. I'm just a bloody pushover, I am. I'm just bloody anybody's—providing they're film stars, I'm a cinch.

The novelists are not exaggerating or showing off. With more or less exact phonetic accuracy, they are simply lifting the lid of the dustbin of slang.

There are innumerable such bins of slang, not all of them unattractive, but most of them quite specialized. The armed services, gambling casinos, racecourses, opium dens, brothels, and so on abound in slang. The slang of many public schools in England is, or was,[33] highly ritualized. For example, in *Words on the Air* (1982), John Sparrow reminded us that the prefects at his school, which happened to be Winchester in the 1920s, could inflict punishments on the younger boys.

The instrument employed was regularly a cane; in my old school it was an ash-plant, called a ground-ash.

Similarly Stalky, Beetle, and M'Turk in Kipling's *Stalky & Co.* were all very familiar with this particular instrument of educational torture:

Prefects' meetin'! Prefects' meetin'! hissed the tables, and they imitated barbarically the actions and effects of the ground-ash.

Outside Winchester and the school in *Stalky & Co.* I have found the *ash-plant* in only one other school, Rugby, and the word seems to have been abandoned there long before *Tom Brown's School Days* (1857). Elsewhere, at Eton, Harrow, Repton, Oundle, and so on, the cane doubtless rose and fell until quite recent times, but it was not called a ground-ash or an ash-plant and the infliction itself was not called 'ash-planting'.

The penalties, rewards, homework, writing utensils, cribs, monitors, prefects, members of staff, lavatories, meals, gymnasiums, playing fields, drill, and so on, of school life are covered by a wide range of informal expressions in every school in the land. No one has recently collected this rich vein of language. Even the perimeters lie unmarked.

Carl Sandburg once said that 'slang is language which takes off its coat, spits on its hands—and goes back to work'. To the Victorian lexicographers Albert Barrère and Charles G. Leland, it was 'simply a collective name for vulgar expressions, the most refined individual being the one who uses it least'. Fastidious writers like Virginia Woolf disliked it, as when she criticized the work of a contemporary called Stephen MacKenna: 'I did read MacKenna, and wondered what sort of man he was. I think a very queer mix: I liked him, but then his slang worried me—but I liked his life.'[34] I have already called it 'dustbin language'. All such definitions are inadequate. Slang can be ephemeral but it can also be durable. The word *slum* (see p. 131), before 1820 or so restricted to the canting language of rogues and thieves, is now the normal term for an overcrowded and squalid section of a city. *Quid*, first recorded in 1688, is still a slang word for a pound sterling. Slang can and does occur at all levels of society and not only among disreputable or disapproved-of groups. It can be intensely personal and explicitly clinical. It can be unacceptably offensive and hurtful. But it can also have the comforting formality of a flower in a buttonhole (*everything tickety-boo?*), or of any other sign or symbol of pleasure or respect.

Old slang—that recorded in old dictionaries—has acquired respectability because of the passage of time. For B.E. Gent. in 1699, slang meant the 'terms ancient and modern of the canting crew', in other words the language of gypsies, beggars, thieves, and cheats. He believed that his dictionary of slang would be 'useful for all sorts of People, (especially Foreigners) to secure their money and preserve their Lives; besides very Diverting and Entertaining'. The 'Tag-Rag and Long-Tail' language of the Canting Crew is exemplified by such definitions as:

Abram-cove, a Naked or poor Man, also a lusty strong rogue.
Academy, a Bawdy-house, also an University, or School to learn Gentleman-like Exercises.
Curtals, the Eleventh Rank of the Canting Crew.
Nick-ninny, an empty Fellow, a meer Cod's Head.

These are typical entries. One feels as if one is watching a romantic and distant operatic world, inhabited not quite by an underclass, but rather by blunt and brutish not-quite-human people called 'Nigmenogs' and 'Rantipoles', born only to thieve and beg, and to provide others (especially foreigners!) with visible evidence of deviation from normal behaviour.

In the eighteenth century the operatic element receded and the words advanced towards a kind of recognizable explicitness.

Captain Francis Grose widened the frame of slang in his *Dictionary of the Vulgar Tongue* (1785). He lists *idea pot* in the sense 'the head' and *inexpressibles* meaning 'breeches'. *Obstropulous*, a vulgar misrendering of 'obstreperous', makes its appearance along with numerous Malapropisms:

I was going my rounds, and found this here gemmen very obstropulous, whereof I comprehended him as an auspicious parson.

Testicles turn up as *twiddle-diddles* and a woman's genital area as her *tuzzy-muzzy*. Synonyms for knaves, whores, hoydens, pickpockets, beggars, and other miscreants stand alongside names for chamberpots, pawnbrokers' shops, and privy parts. *Peeping Tom*, 'a nickname for a curious prying fellow', makes its first appearance in the language.

The collecting of slang became a major linguistic industry in the nineteenth century. Hotten, Baumann, Farmer and Henley, Ware and others built ever larger and more intricate sandcastles of slang by enlarging those they found on the beach already or by focusing on the slang of particular groups.

The 1914-18 war probably caused more slang to come into being than at any other time in the history of English. As the regiments, squadrons, and battalions came together from all over the English-speaking world, they brought their informal language with them. The effect was explosively generative. Many people collected it, but the greatest collector of all turned out to be Eric Partridge, and the *annus mirabilis* of slang proved to be 1937, the year of publication of the first edition of his *Dictionary of Slang and Unconventional English*. Many revisions followed and when he died in 1979 Partridge had assembled an unparalleled record of English-language slang. Services' slang is abundantly preserved in this dictionary, but he added to the ancient piles of dustbin words, surfing slang, jazz terms, mock auction slang, nicknames of Association Football teams, rhyming slang (*Adam and Eve* for 'believe'), back-slang (*yob* 'lout, hooligan' from 'boy') the language of beatniks, drug addicts, mods and rockers, and all the rest. Since his death new slang continues to emerge in every English-speaking area, and to move from one area to another. For example, Citizens' Band slang is now in the course of being 'absorbed' in the United Kingdom from North America, a process which will doubtless leave casualties and altered meanings strewn in its path. This new strand of slang can be exemplified by the story of the American clergyman, a CB operator himself, who went by the 'handle' of 'Marryin' Sam':

The bride was 'Little Lulu' and the groom was 'Stanley Steamer'. They didn't say 'I do'; they said '10-4'. And the clergyman didn't pronounce them man and wife; he said 'Put the hammer down'.

The disguising of language by the informalities of slang is doubtless as old as the Anglo-Saxons. One of the shaping forces of English is the conservativeness of its users and much of the history of the ordinary language—just as with the word *slum*—lies regrettably lost in unrecorded reticences of the period before modern recorders of the language emerged. Slang is a valuable source of enrichment of the language. Incredibly, many people today still express surprise when such words make their way into dictionaries, however clearly they are labelled, as if a well-kept garden were being invaded by weeds.

8

Pronunciation and Spelling

> The pronunciation is the actual living form or forms of a
> word, that is, *the word itself*, of which the current spelling
> is only a symbolization.
>
> Introduction to the *OED*

It is not really understood how the spoken language operates—
whether as the output of a servo-mechanism—that is, a complex
system with feedback loops monitoring itself and modifying itself
as it goes along—or by something else equally complex. To most
speakers it simply doesn't matter how it operates so long as it does.
One can but marvel that millions of people can communicate daily
by speech and manage their linguistic relationships with no more
than relatively unimportant misunderstandings.[1]

It is all the more mysterious how it comes about that if one moves
just a few miles away from one's own habitat a different set of linguistic sounds is encountered—still those of recognizably the same
language but subtly and charmingly different—and that one does
not even need to move outside one's immediate area to encounter
other observably different sets of sounds representing social or
educational rather than geographical distancings from oneself.

These general considerations are true of all languages which in
historical time have remained geographically static. Variation is
governed by the social arrangements within a group or clan, or by
a geographical boundary like a river or a line of mountains. And
within the borders and limits of a given set of variants of one
language it is quite normal to find other people using totally
unintelligible sets of sounds (foreign languages like Welsh) or half-
way houses (one's own language spoken by foreigners).

Over the centuries the movement of clans and tribes of people
has produced the kind of crop that would emerge if a blind god
had sprinkled seeds at random on a field—a vast array of diverse
patterns, usually not even interlocking or decussated, but crossed
and intersected by every kind of structured diversity.

Of all the main languages of the world none is more widely disseminated and more subtly sliced and severed than English, and all within the space of only 1,500 years. From the diversity of the earliest records of the Anglo-Saxons it can be assumed that they were already divided into a multitude of linguistic subgroups using different modes of pronunciation, grammar, and usage, even though they remained (as far as we can tell) mutually intelligible.

I regard it as axiomatic that the traditional classification of Anglo-Saxon dialects into four major groups—Northumbrian, Mercian, West Saxon, and Kentish—is an over-simplification. If more information about them had survived, the parental groupings of the numerous varieties of English now spoken in Britain would have been more than quadrilaterally complex. Even now, if all recorded forms of every surviving text were fed into a computer databank in an unregularized form, and without prior assumptions, new distributional maps would emerge, and the overlaid rules of the main types of *Schriftsprache* could perhaps be stripped away to take us nearer to the tribal variations of speech extant at the time of Offa, Alfred, and Ælfric. Regional variation of speech at the time of the first discernibly professional analyses of dialects—in practice not before the seventeenth century— points firmly in the direction of great complexity. It seems most unlikely that this complexity developed from a simple base of four 'blocks' of Anglo-Saxon speech.

Be that as it may, we must work with the evidence we have. The establishment of the mode of pronunciation of the earliest form of English is traditionally and necessarily based on an assumption of close equivalence between sound and symbol. Phonologists assume near-coincidence between spellings and sounds in the earliest records of our language: that OE. *hūs* 'house' is /huːs/; OE. *hlūd* 'loud' is /hluːd/, with initial *h* fully pronounced and with a long *ū*; *hring* 'ring' is /hrɪŋ/, also with *h* fully pronounced but with ŋ not ŋg; and that OE. *wlanc* is /wlank/, with the approximant *w* fully pronounced before the following *l*. In my view it is likely that some Anglo-Saxon tribes, or groups of people within tribes, had already adopted the later ways of pronouncing such words.

Traditional phonology is based on the assumption that three major phonetic changes at a later period brought radical changes to the classes of words into which these four words fall—that

/huːs/ became /haʊs/ as part of the Great Vowel Shift; that *h* followed by the liquid consonants *l* and *r* was lost at the beginning of the Middle English period; and that words beginning with *wl* (an approximant followed by the liquid consonant *l*) disappeared in the course of the Middle English period. We should, however, allow for the possibility that dissident pronunciations existed among minority groups within the Anglo-Saxon period, and that the historical process was one in which these 'subversive' forms gradually replaced the ones maintained by the conservative scribes in their written texts and by linguistic conservatives in their speech.

Modern parallels are provided by the substitution of /ɒ/ for /ɔː/ in words like *cloth*, *cross*, and *lost*, and *off* in the twentieth century except in the speech of those answering to what might be called the Nancy Mitford tradition; and the emergence of the aspirateless /w/ in words like *whale*, *when*, *whether*, instead of /hw/. In both cases it is not a 'law' of phonetics or of physics that has brought about the change but the reduction of two socially competing forms to one. This 'Mitford factor' is of profound importance in the interpretation of phonetic data. It may be expressed in the following terms. At any given period linguistic conservatives regard selected parts of the pronunciation system (as well as other parts of the apparatus of speech) as necessary ingredients of social superiority or acceptability. The maintenance of social values in part depends (they believe) on the preservation of such elements of speech and the rejection of rivals. Other social groups, not out of perversity but because of a different line of inheritance, display different, and therefore potentially threatening, modes of speech. In the slow turning of the centuries the rivalry of such competing systems produces an alternation of socially triumphant variants. In the period since 1800 most of the observable changes to RP have been brought about by the Mitford factor—in other words by sociological change and not by phonetic change. Some have already been listed in chapter 4 (pp. 38–42). Others include the substitution of /eɪ/ for /iː/ in words like *deity*, *homogeneity*, and *spontaneity*; and the replacement of a soft *g* in *gynaecology* by a 'hard' one (until *c.*1900 initial soft *g* only; till about 1930 optionally hard or soft *g*; from *c.*1930 hard *g* only). In the present century the stress-patterning of many words has wavered between one syllable and another (examples on p. 42). Conflicting analogical patterns have disturbed the pronunciation of a great many other words:

	Traditional	Now dominant or increasingly common in RP
centenary	/iː/	/ɛn/
centrifugal	stress on 2nd syllable	secondary stress on 1st syllable, main stress on 3rd syllable
dissect	1st syllable /dɪs-/	1st syllable /daɪ-/
harass	stress on 1st syllable	stress on 2nd syllable
pariah	/ˈpær-/, stress on 1st syllable	pronounced like *Isaiah*
pomegranate	three syllables, /ˈpɒmgræn-/	four syllables, medial *e* pronounced[2]

People using the traditional pronunciations listed above still abound. They feel in varying degrees threatened by, hostile to, or just somewhat annoyed by the newly emerging forms. The Anglo-Saxon monks and scholars of Winchester and Wimborne must have felt the same as they heard townsfolk using untraditional pronunciations.

The study of pronunciation

In one of the greatest scholarly linguistic monographs of the present century, *English Pronunciation 1500–1700* (1957), E. J. Dobson set down in abundant detail the way in which we can ascertain with reasonable certainty how Standard English was pronounced during those two centuries. The evidence is drawn from the work of contemporary orthoepists (scholars concerned with the nature of correct speech), from rhymes in metrical verse, and from many other sources. After 1700 the mood remained rigidly prescriptive. The subtitle of John Walker's *Critical Pronouncing Dictionary and Expositor of the English Language* (1791) pointed the way:

In which not only the meaning of every word is clearly explained, and the sound of every syllable distinctly shown, but where words are subject to different pronunciations, the reasons for each are at large displayed; but the preferable pronunciation is pointed out. To which are prefixed, principles of English pronunciation . . . Likewise rules to be observed by the natives of Scotland, Ireland, and London *for avoiding their respective peculiarities* [my italics].

Walker concluded that the pronunciation of London 'is undoubtedly the best': 'that is, not only the best by courtesy, and because it happens to be the pronunciation of the capital, but best by a better title, that of being more generally received'.

In the *OED*, Sir James Murray adopted as his standard the late-Victorian speech of educated Londoners. His phonetic system was greatly influenced by the views of A. Melville Bell, whose system of Visible Speech, introduced in the 1860s, was based on a set of forty-three special phonetic symbols indicating the position of the lips and tongue in making sounds. More or less at the same time Murray's friend Alexander J. Ellis had decided that 'no accented letters, few turned, and still fewer mutilated letters should be employed'. Ellis therefore invented a new system of symbols called Palaeotype, and for the representation of regional English speech an even more complicated system called Glossotype.

Fortunately by 1882, when he sent the first section of the *OED* to press, Murray had settled for a more comprehensible system, which is still reasonably transparent to people not trained in phonetics. The *OED* system and various methods of indicating pronunciation by respelling (first introduced in the Oxford family of dictionaries by H. W. and F. G. Fowler in the *Concise Oxford Dictionary*, 1911) remained dominant in Oxford and in many other lexicographical centres until fairly recently. But these systems have come to be widely discarded in favour of the International Phonetic Alphabet (or IPA), a system that was first introduced in 1888 and is now internationally recognized and flexible enough to be usable for all languages, not just for English.

The first half of the twentieth century was dominated by the work of Daniel Jones at University College London. In 1909 he set down all that he considered one needed to know about English speech-sounds in *The Pronunciation of English: Phonetics and Phonetic Transcriptions*. In sixty-nine pages, with the utmost clarity, he described the careful conversational style, or StP (standard pronunciation) as he called it, with which he was concerned. The organs of speech were described and illustrated. English consonants were carefully classified according to the part of the speech tract involved (often with the tongue) in articulating them, and according to the manner in which they are articulated—

plosive, nasal, lateral, rolled, fricative, and so on. The vowels were then characterized in terms of the position of the tongue, lips, and larynx. This brief set of models, tables, and diagrams was then exploited with admirable clarity in a section called 'English Speech Sounds in Detail'. In 1917 Jones's *English Pronouncing Dictionary* was published, a 419-page alphabetical list of words and names accompanied by phonetic transcriptions. Both were books that the general public, or the university student, could turn to with the certainty that one could find an uncomplicated answer to what one was looking for.

Until the 1960s, great emphasis was placed on the historical development of the pronunciation of the language. The articulatory facts of life were subsumed within an intricate system by which, it was explained, some selected sounds turned into some other sounds under the influence of an adjacent sound (*i*-mutation, etc.), or because of vowel-harmony (*ablaut*), or for some other reason (assimilation, fronting, etc.). One formed the impression that sound changes occurred at some specified periods but not at others because of certain phonetic conjunctions that happened to exist at the time. Scholars came to believe in a general theory of drift or seepage. It seemed clear that whole communities changed elements of their speech, sometimes quite dramatically, because of the existence of adjacent palatal consonants, yods, or back vowels, or because of some other anticipatory or retroactive circumstance.

In the last few years I have discussed the nature of RP with many people, some of them phonetically trained, more of them not. What has emerged is a reiteration of three main views:

No one was aware of a phonological change that had happened in his or her speech in his or her lifetime, that is of an ungovernable and irreversible change in a particular vowel, diphthong, or consonant to one that was demonstrably new.

Everyone believed that new borrowed or imitated modes of pronunciation, shiftings of stress, and so on, were coming into existence all the time, whether from America, from popular songs, from broadcasters, or from some other source, and that others were being abandoned (the Mitford factor, see above). These new pronunciations had been resisted with various degrees of determination by my informants. But all realized that, in most cases, it was only a matter of time before they became dominant.

Almost everyone over the age of thirty spoke of the 'unintelligibility' and 'inarticulacy' of younger people, although it was admitted that this alleged unintelligibility seemed to set up no discernible communication barriers among even the more uneducated young people themselves. Expressed another way, new patterns of speech are coming into being, shaped by young mouths, and at present unanalysed and probably unanalysable because of the informal circumstances in which most speech occurs.

In other words the plotting of language change in the twentieth century seemed to be much less of a developmental process than a swopping one, the changing of one basket of sound for another. Paradoxically and unaccountably, future fashionable RP strands of linguistically acceptable speech are probably lying about in the informal speech of younger people—unstudied, unpinpointed, and unrevealed because they are not yet 'standard'.

The most recent professional study of English pronunciation— a wide-ranging synopsis of spoken English in all English-speaking regions by J. C. Wells called *Accents of English* (1982)—gives as the main causes of linguistic change all the old traditional ones, the 'principle of least effort', 'persistent infantilism', 'splits', and 'mergers', and so on. One cannot prove that he is wrong. But it seems much more likely to me that change comes about because of the adoption by RP speakers of already existing alternative features from other varieties of English. Putting this another way, the causes of apparent sound change in RP lie deeply embedded in the births, deaths, and marriages columns, and in the spaces in newspapers devoted to social elevation and to the declaration of wills. The *nouveaux riches* tend also to be the '*nouveaux parleurs*', and they bring some of their language habits with them to their new way of life. The video cassette industry, microtechnology, and every other walk of life in which young people predominate, supermarkets, oil-rigs, peace movements, discothèques, skiing, windsurfing, and so on, are the areas in which new modes of speech are now being formed, and these new patterns will not become dominant for another half-century or so.

Phonemes, allophones, and the concept of phonological 'space'

Easily the most important modern theoretical developments concerning speech are those to do with the nature of the 'space'[3] surrounding identifiable separate sounds. English speakers perceive the *l* in *lip* to be the 'same' sound as the *l*s in *lap* and *willow*, though they are not. The acoustic 'space' within which the phoneme *l* moves is generous. Its nearest rival is the space occupied by the phoneme *r* in *rip*, *rap*, and *burrow*. Any speaker of Japanese will confirm that the phonemic space of RP *l* overlaps with that of RP *r* to the point that Japanese speakers have the greatest difficulty in separating the two sounds ('seeing is bereaving'). Similar considerations apply to every distinguishable 'separate' sound in the language. Each phoneme (or separate sound) is acceptable, intelligible, and unambiguous, provided that it does not stray too far into the 'space' occupied by its most closely related neighbour. The slightly different initial sounds in *cool*, *cup*, and *keep* are called allophones of the phoneme /k/. They are sufficiently like one another to be treated as 'the same'. Similarly with the vowels in RP *pick*, *pip*, and *pit*.[4] Any standard book on the subject, for example, A. C. Gimson's *An Introduction to the Pronunciation of English* (3rd edn., 1980), deals with such matters at length.

The relationship of spelling and pronunciation

It is a commonplace that English spelling is quite seriously unrelated to pronunciation. The reasons are well known to linguistic scholars, but hardly at all to laymen. In general terms, written English has remained relatively static since the invention of printing towards the end of the fifteenth century, but spoken English, in its received form, has changed repeatedly since then. Loanwords have also been adopted from languages which have different spelling systems. As a result the phoneme /f/, for example, can be represented by a number of different spellings, for example *f* (*firm*), *gh* (*rough*, *draught*), *ff* (*offer*, *gruff*), and *ph* (*philosophy*). The phoneme /kw/, once written as either *cw-* (OE. *cwēn* queen) or *qu-* (*quick* from OE. *cwic*) can now be spelt only as *qu-*. But *qu-* is sometimes pronounced /k/ (*quay*). The letter *h* can be silent (*honour*) or fully pronounced (*hand*). The sequence *-ough* can be pronounced /ʌf/ (*tough*), /aʊ/ (*slough*), /əʊ/ (*dough*), or /ə/ (*borough*). The phoneme /s/ can appear written as *c* (*cinder*), *s* (*send*), *sc* (*scent*), or *ss* (*assist*); conversely the letter *s* can be pronounced as /s/ (*seven*) or /z/ (*is*). Occasionally it is silent (*aisle*, *demesne*, *island*). The digraph *ch* represents a single phoneme, but it can be /tʃ/ (*chain*), /ʃ/ (*charade*), or /x/ (*loch*). The trigraph *sch* is pronounced differently (in British English) in *eschew*, *schedule*, *schism*, and *school*.

All such variations can be accounted for historically. If one examines older works in their original spellings the variations are very numerous. By the same token if one were to attempt to impose a universally acceptable spelling system in all English-speaking areas now, local phonetic differences would lead to wide variations: for example, all words with medial *-t-* would need to be respelt with *-d-* in the United States and parts of Canada (**medaphysical*, *split the *adom*), and many areas would need a symbol /æ/ in words like *dance* to distinguish it from RP /ɑː/. Variation in the pronunciation of diphthongs and triphthongs would produce a nightmarish array of distinctive symbols. The amount of *t*-ness at the end of the word *chants* (as against *chance*) would require a different variety of *t* from that in *chant* or *chat*. In the face of a line of spellings like *choler, debt, doubt, receipt, salmon, sceptre*, and *victuals*, all containing unpronounced elements, one is tempted to admire Middle English scribes who wrote these words as *colere, dette, doute, receite, samon, ceptre*, and *vitailes*.[5] Equally 'strange' —and all with spellings that disguise their original Middle English forms—are *absolve, admonish, captive, corpse, describe, elephant, falcon, language, picture*, and *throne* (ME. *assoil, amonest, caitif, cors, descryve, olifaunt, faucon, langage, peynture*, and *trone*).[6] But anyone who has examined Middle English knows that all texts from that period are likely to contain multiple spellings for the same word, and that a dictionary of Middle English contains almost as many cross-references as lemmas. Lexicographers of dead languages sometimes speak of 'the agonizing problem of lemmatization', that is under which spelling, for example, to place the more than fifty variants of the Latin word *episcopus* 'bishop' that are found in Middle Dutch. The problem has eased in modern English. There are still problems, but they seem to have been reduced to a more or less irreducible minimum.

The English spelling-system is best left alone, except in minor particulars.[7] Attempts to simplify or respell the language are likely to be unavailing for a long time to come.

It is of interest to speculate about the amount of dislocation to the spelling system that would occur if English dictionaries were either proscribed or (as when Malory or Sir Philip Sidney were writing) did not exist. In other words, how much the regular writing down and printing of the language would be put at risk if educated speakers of the language had only unglossed books as guides to the spelling system and nothing to settle disputed spellings.

The props and stays of the written language are dictionaries like the *Concise Oxford Dictionary*. In them, for nearly all words in the language, only one spelling is recorded: for example, no variants are listed in the series *crackling, cracknel, cracksman, -cracy, cradle, cradling, craft, craftsman, crafty, crag, crake, cram, crambo, crammer,* and *cramp* on p. 221 of the current (seventh) edition of *COD*. An almost unqualified belief in a one-to-one relationship between most words in the language and the way they are spelt has been maintained since at least 1755 when Dr Johnson's dictionary was published. Before 1700 fixedness of spelling was not insisted on with anything like the same rigidity.

This seemingly rigid system of spelling in modern dictionaries is put at risk by two main factors. First, people temporarily without access to a dictionary, for example when writing family letters (when spelling does not 'matter' as much as it might in other circumstances) or when writing an examination script with an invigilator present, set down many approximate spellings: for example, *appartment* (for *apartment*), *concensus* (for *consensus*), *crucifiction* (for *crucifixion*), *ecstacy* (for *ecstasy*), *gutteral* (for *guttural*), *idiosyncracy* (for *idiosyncrasy*), *millenium* (for *millennium*), *miniscule* (for *minuscule*), and *supercede* (for *supersede*). In other words some spellings are less well maintained in the mind than others; many need to be signposted. I have seen all the above spellings, and many more such, in the examination scripts and also in the essays and letters of Oxford undergraduates, not to go further afield. One wonders how often descriptivists withhold the correcting pen when such spellings occur in work submitted to them for publication or adjudication. How carefully should lexicographers set them down in their dictionaries? And should they mark them as 'erroneous' or merely as 'variants'? Such problems remain unsolved.

The one-to-one correspondence of word and spelling is also put at risk by the existence of acceptable and in no way to be questioned variants—words for which one publishing house will opt for one form and another house for a second. *The Oxford Dictionary for Writers and Editors* (1981) lists many such variants and needs nearly 450 pages to set them down. This unstable optional area of written English can be illustrated by a few examples:

absinth, the plant; *absinthe*, the liqueur
antenatal (one word)
ante-post, of racing bets (hyphen)
baptize, not *-ise*
Czar etc., use *Ts-*
Djakarta, Indonesia, use *Jak-*
equinoctial, not *-xial*
feoff, use *fief*

When one recollects that some 25,000 words and names are listed in this book alone the area of fluidity or instability—the area where printers need to make a deliberate choice—is plainly not inconsiderable. The waves are beating against the rocky promontory of fixed spelling all the time and it is extraordinary that printed work emerges for the most part in a fairly uniform manner.

It might be of interest to end this chapter with a list of some of the factors since the Conquest that have guided our rebellious written language towards its present relatively stable form.

Norman scribes. They helped to establish *ch*, *sh*, *th*, and *wh* from an array of earlier variants; also to regularize *cw-* and *qu-* as *qu-*.

Caxton and other printers. They trained compositors to reduce the number of variant spellings except as line-fillers (the addition of a final *-e* was a useful device to eke out a line, while seemingly not affecting the aesthetic appearance of a word in their eyes).

Robert Cawdrey and later lexicographers. The convenience for lexicographers of a strict alphabetical ordering, not just of the initial letter but of the following letters as well, is self-evident.

Noah Webster. The establishment of several categories of distinctive American spellings (*catalog, color, esthetic, program*, etc.).

Word Processors. The capacity to restrict the range of preferred spellings to those allowed by the dictionary drawn on as the computerized base.

All such factors have placed new constraints on a system that is by nature flamboyantly inconsistent and, in many respects, ungovernable. There are plenty of signs that, as a society, we are moving back into a period that more closely resembles the time before printers arrived and before cursive writing became compulsory, in other words to a period when the maintenance of written standards depends on a diminishing number of experts or shamans. The normalization of written English, maintained for the last century or so at great cost and with mixed results, might once more be put to the test while computer operators, the new rune-masters, govern its complex rules.

9

The Syntactical Arrangement of Words

> It was an effort to think I might have had a good brush
> with you and did not. No grammar in that sentence. No
> cohesion in my mind.
>
> Virginia Woolf to Ethel Smyth, 4 September 1936,
> in *Letters* VI (1980), p. 70.

'The grammatical arrangement of words in speech or writing to show their connection and relation; a set of rules governing this relationship; an analysis of such rules.' This slightly adapted definition of *syntax* (from Greek *syn* 'together' and *taxis* 'an arranging') in the current (seventh) edition of the *Concise Oxford Dictionary* will serve as an introduction to a notoriously difficult subject. Educated speakers of English can string together sentences in both spoken and written form without having an explicit book of rules at hand. By contrast numerical problems of comparable complication cannot be solved without the aid of a pocket calculator, log tables, or some much more complicated devices. Somehow categories of words—nouns, verbs, pronouns, etc.— become established as distinguishable entities in our minds at an early age, and also the means of cementing them together in an acceptable orderly sequence. We also learn that some of them have a fixed and unchanging form (*but*, *with*, *sheep*) but that the vast majority are malleable, however slightly, by inflexional additions or other modifications (*hat/hats*, *bird/bird's/birds'*, *goose/geese*) and must be altered in such ways to meet the needs of a given context.

This chapter will be concerned with the morphological elements and grammatical rules within which speakers and writers feel that they can proceed without error or ambiguity. I shall also attempt to show how the 'rules' and 'feelings' change over the centuries, with legacies of varying degrees of acceptability for very long periods.

When I was at school I was taught that a sentence (which itself needed no explanation) consisted of a subject and a predicate. The subject was obvious (*The cow*) and the predicate was the rest (*jumped over the moon*). More advanced grammar had to do with the way in which subordinate clauses were attached to main clauses, and what they were called—noun clauses, adverbial clauses, and so on. I was also taught that there were certain hazards to avoid—split infinitives, confusion of *may* and *might*, prepositions at the end of sentences, and so on—and marks were awarded in the matriculation (roughly O-level) examinations to those who could spot such errors in sentences specially constructed for the purpose. From time to time, my teachers would murmur, 'just as in Latin' (no one ever said 'just as in Greek' as no one knew any Greek at my school). English appeared to be a language with minimum inflexions but with inflexions nevertheless—closer, that is, to Latin and its European descendants than to certain nameless languages (doubtless they meant Chinese among others) which appeared to fit words together without a connecting array of inflexions. When a sentence did not seem to be a complete sentence, something called 'ellipsis' was brought in to account for the missing element.

This comfortable, and sometimes irritatingly imprecise, method of analysis has a long history and has been beneficial to millions of English students throughout the world over many generations. It has by no means died out.

It is well illustrated, I discovered much later, in C. T. Onions's *An Advanced English Syntax* (1904 and later slightly corrected editions). Five types of predicate were identified and presented in the following manner:

First

Subject	Predicate	
Day	dawns	predicate contains a verb
My hour	is come	

Second

Croesus	was rich *or* a king	predicate contains a verb and
Many	lay dead	a noun or adjective

Third

Cats	catch mice	predicate contains a verb and
Many hands	make light work	an object

Fourth

Subject	Predicate	
We	taught the dog tricks	predicate contains a verb and
I	ask you this question	two objects

Fifth

Nothing	makes a Stoic angry	predicate contains a verb, an
People	called Duns Scotus the	object, and an adjective or noun
	Subtle Doctor	

The whole point of analysis was to apportion the right label to the constituent parts of simple sentences like 'I stood on the bridge at midnight', or of complex sentences like

I had a strong hope, which never left me, that I should one day recover my liberty; and, as to the ignominy of being carried about for a monster, I considered myself to be a perfect stranger in the country, and that such a misfortune should never be charged upon me as a reproach if ever I should return to England; since the King of England himself, in my condition, must have undergone the same distress. (Jonathan Swift)

Dr Onions analysed this passage on pp. 26–7 of his book (6th edn., 1932).

Other grammatical notions came into it, of course. 'A wild beast fed him' is an active expression. 'He was fed by a wild beast' is its passive equivalent. Many verbs govern an infinitive preceded by *to* (I *expect* to arrive tomorrow); others proceed without *to* (I *can* drive a car, I *may* come tomorrow). Some, like *dare* and *need*, hover between the two uses (He *dare* not speak/Does he *dare* to say so? He *need* not know/The clothes *need* to be dried).

A range of sentences forming statements, commands, questions, and exclamations cause us to draw on a more sophisticated battery of orderings and arrangements. It is a long way from the simplicity of 'I am happy' (a statement) to 'May I never see his face again!' (a wish in the form of a request); from 'Are you ready?' (a simple question) to 'What mean these torn and faded garments?' (a more complex question); and from 'Alas! Alack!' (an exclamation) to 'Oh, what a fall was there, my countrymen!' (a more complex exclamation).

Temporal clauses (*When it is fine*, I go for a walk), local clauses (The house stood *where three roads met*), causal clauses (*Since you insist on it*, I will consider the matter), concessive clauses (*Although you are rich*, you are not happy), absolute clauses (*The signal being given*, we set off), relative clauses (This is the house *that Jack built*), and many other types of clause seemed to account for the sentences that appeared in the books we read and the sentences we used in the English we spoke. In broad terms they still do.

Case-endings in English, set against the traditional array of those in Latin and Greek (nominative, accusative, genitive, dative, ablative, and instrumental) are extremely simple. Only two can be clearly distinguished—the possessive (*man's, men's, ladies'*) and an unchanged form in all other cases (He met the *man*; he went up to the *man*; etc.). Old English had four case-forms (nominative, accusative, genitive, and dative), and occasional examples of a fifth, the instrumental. Most of these cases had distinctive endings in the various classes of nouns. It is obvious that the system in present-day English is radically different, and that the notion of case (i.e. a form or modification of a declinable word) is now of very little significance. The survival of the objective case in English pronouns (*me, him, her, us, them, whom*), however, causes many difficulties, as in the notorious type **between you and I* (correctly *me*).

In such traditional grammar the notion of possessiveness (that is, the genitive case in Old English, Latin, etc.) is conveyed by an apostrophe or by *of*. The apostrophe is used in various types of construction:

The doctor's house	(simple attributive)
This house is the doctor's	(predicative)
My father's brother's daughter	(double possessive)
The Emperor of Germany's mother	(group genitive)

Of is used where fully inflected languages would use a partitive genitive (This is an old book *of my mother's*; *of all men* the most accomplished), an objective genitive (love *of God*; their fear *of the enemy* was great (that is, they feared the enemy greatly)), a genitive of description (a man *of great honesty*), and an appositive genitive (the continent *of Africa*). The apostrophe and *of* are sometimes interchangeable (e.g. the sun's rays *or* the rays of the sun).[1]

Traditional grammar places great stress on prepositions and the positioning of them in a sentence; on tenses of verbs and tense-equivalents, including the complications of the continuous tenses (he *is writing* the book all over again; we shall *be going* home tomorrow); the subjunctive mood; the infinitive (including the split infinitive, *to continually refer*); impersonal verbs (verbs with a vague subject 'it', *it is raining, it is time to go home*); anomalous verbs like *shall/will, should/would, can/could, may/might, dare, need, must*, and so on; and many other matters.

Traditional grammar was largely unchallenged before the 1960s. It was nurtured and supported by generations of teachers at schools and universities. And it neatly dovetailed in with the nomenclature used for the teaching of ancient languages like Greek, Hebrew, and Latin, and of modern European languages. A brief account of the setting down of traditional grammar from the early seventeenth century onward is given in chapter 6.

Revolutionary new methods of parsing, most of them synchronic (or descriptive), that is without any reference to older forms of English, have swept into prominence in the last twenty years or so. The messianic figure was Noam Chomsky and the starting-point his book *Syntactic Structures* (1959). He sought a simple linguistic theory which would 'generate all the sequences of morphemes (or words) that constitute grammatical English sentences' (p. 18). For him a 'constituent analysis' of the sentence *The man hit the ball* would require (and I quote from Chomsky):

1. (i) $Sentence \rightarrow NP + VP^2$
    (ii) $NP \rightarrow T + N^3$
    (iii) $VP \rightarrow Verb + NP$
    (iv) $T \rightarrow the$
    (v) $N \rightarrow man, ball$, etc.
    (vi) $Verb \rightarrow hit, took$, etc.

In each case $\rightarrow$ represents the word 'rewrite', and each statement in (i) to (vi) is an instruction of the type 'rewrite X as Y'. The following series (2) shows what happens to the sentence *The man hit the ball* if it is rewritten in terms of the 'grammar' (1) given above:

2. *Sentence*

$NP + VP$	(i)
$T + N + VP$	(ii)
$T + N + Verb + NP$	(iii)
$the + N + Verb + NP$	(iv)
$the + man + Verb + NP$	(v)
$the + man + hit + NP$	(vi)
$the + man + hit + T + N$	(ii)
$the + man + hit + the + N$	(iv)
$the + man + hit + the + ball$	(v)

This *derivation*, as Chomsky called it, can be represented in a diagram:

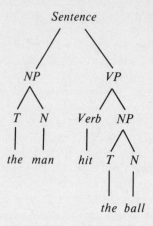

From such elementary rules and diagrams has emerged a school of grammar that has shaken the foundations of traditional grammar. In its developed form it has been taken up by scholars of foreign languages. It has also been applied as a technique to older forms of English, and older forms of other languages. Transformation is one of its techniques: the apparent grammatical identity of the sentences

> She made him a good husband
> She made him a good wife
> She made him a good dinner

is removed when algebraic symbols are assigned to their parts and tree-diagrams of the type shown above are provided for each of them. Its weakness is that it depends on intuition about grammatical acceptability. But a more fundamental weakness lies in its failure to produce a grammar of English that can be consulted and cherished as an aid to the disentangling and ascertainment of the language that lies about us. Despotic professors of linguistics vying with one another about the nature of grammatical embeddedness and 'disambiguating' sentences by contrastive methods have failed to notice that they have taken the subject beyond the reach of intelligent laymen.

The parts and parcels of speech can be understood, rather grimly and with pedantic pleasure, from Onions, Fowler, and the great historical grammarians like Poutsma and Visser. The syntactical arrangements of English can be made to stand out very clearly, but only like dead flowers in a dry landscape, by nonsense sentences of a type invented by Chomsky ('Colourless green ideas sleep furiously'). The differences between acceptable constructions like 'Have you a book on modern music?' and unacceptable ones like 'Read you a book on modern music?' need no Chomskyan signposts for a native speaker, and have very little to do with statistical probability but a lot to do with common sense. Anyone knows that *have*, as an anomalous verb, is likely to behave differently from *read*.

Much ground has been lost and many fine minds blunted on the complications of transformational generative grammar. But traditional approaches to grammar have been successfully developed in a synchronic (or descriptive) form, that is with historical elements stripped away, and yet not partial or negative or idiosyncratic, by Randolph Quirk and colleagues in *A Grammar of Contemporary English* (1972).

Subject and predicate come sailing back into view. SVO (= subject/verb/object) and SOV (= subject/object/verb) stand as lighthouses to those adrift in the stormy sea of grammar. The acceptability of *some* adverbs in *some* contexts is brought out:

John searched the room
{
carefully
slowly
noisily
sternly
without delay
}

but not when the verb is stative:

The girl is now a student . . .
She saw this . . .
John knew the answer . . .
{
*carefully
*slowly
*noisily
*sternly
*without delay
}

(p. 41)

The tree-diagrams present a pleasant and intelligible face, for example (p. 65):

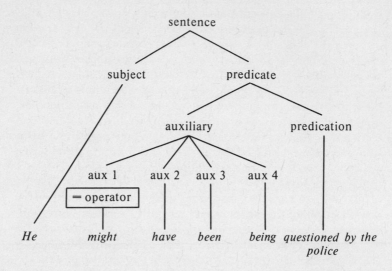

In every section of this invaluable work new light is thrown on ancient problems—phrasal verbs (*bring up, put off*), phrasal-prepositional verbs (*catch up on, come up with*), constraints of various kinds (for example, verbs which have no passive, *he lacks confidence* but not **confidence is lacked by him*), intensifiers, duratives, sentence adverbs, and so on. One disadvantage from the point of view of the literate widely-read person who is concerned about constructions in (say) the works of Virginia Woolf or Evelyn Waugh is that there are no literary examples at all in this clinical and compendious work. The examples are like lifeless membranes in a laboratory, lacking even the flexibility and unpredictability of living speech. Moreover, people suffering from the 'split infinitive' syndrome, those concerned with the dramatic problems of taste, choice, and acceptability described by H. W. Fowler—battered ornaments, pairs and snares, sturdy indefensibles, and all the rest (to use his terminology)—are given little or no help. Such problems, it would appear, do not exist. The choice lies between the older grammars which cite evidence from Swift, Tennyson, and Conrad as if they were contemporaries writing in the same medium, and the quasi-scientific grammars of Randolph Quirk and his colleagues and adherents who seldom get beyond the factuality of utterances like 'Their safe arrival in Cairo' and 'Lobster Newburg is difficult to prepare'.

Syntactic Change

In this book I have been much concerned with showing that linguistic rules and attitudes change as the centuries pass. It is self-evident that the same principle applies to syntax. In Old English, an inflected language, customary but not obligatory rules affected the normal subject-verb-object rule: *sēo cwēn beswāc þone cyning* 'the queen betrayed the king' could be changed to *þone cyning beswāc sēo cwēn* without change of meaning. The endings un-mistakably revealed the subject and object. In post-Conquest English the ordering of words can and normally does reverse the meaning. In Old English two negatives strengthen the negativity of a sentence (*næs mē næfre gewunelic* 'it was never customary for me'). In post-Renaissance English one negative normally cancels the negativity of a second one. In Old English the title of a monarch or other person of rank normally followed the name (*Ælfred cyning*), whereas of course the order is now reversed (*Queen Elizabeth*). Old English had no distinctive future tense: the present tense was used to express future time: *gā gē on mīnne wīngeard, and ic selle ēow þæt riht biþ* 'go into my vineyard, and I will give you what is right'. The future tense came into being as the verbs *sculan* and *willan* lost their ancient power as finite verbs and turned into future auxiliaries. Old English had a present participial form but it ended in *-ende* or (in some regions) *-inde* or *-ande*. The *-ing* form emerged after the Conquest from an array of disintegrating and jostling forms, with the process still not fully understood by scholars. Visser in the Second Half of Volume III of his *Historical Syntax of the English Language* (1973) devotes nearly 200 pages to the development of 'the second verb as a form in *-ing*', as in 'I've so much enjoyed talking to you', 'Have you tried shopping in the Berwick Market?', 'He wouldn't have risked killing me', 'What are you getting at?', 'You are being silly', and so on. His examples are drawn from medieval chronicles and poems and stretch out in great historical swathes down to the works of Aldous Huxley and Kingsley Amis. No construction is everlastingly stable, no cherished rule remains unbroken. At any given time it is safe to assume that permissible patterns of syntax are ascertainable if one has the means of identifying and classifying them. Go back a century or so and the rules are radically different even if on the surface they appear to be the same. Go back two centuries and more and one must call for help from scholars with a particular knowledge of the rules and constraints of the time. It is risky without such help to read the works of any writer whose writings were published more than two centuries ago. And it is unhelpful when scholars yoke constructions together without regard to chronology, geography, type of writing, and social class. We still lack an authoritative grammar based on spoken *and* written British English of the period since 1945, let alone one that looks further afield. Also lacking is a systematic synchronic treatment of the syntax of (for example) Chaucer, Shakespeare, and Milton. It seems wrong that so much scholarly endeavour is devoted to the algebra and tree-diagrams of impenetrably complex modern syntactic problems when the language of some of our greatest writers remains inadequately analysed.

10

Dispersed Forms of English

This is my ocean, but it is speaking
Another language, since its accent changes around
Different islands.
Derek Walcott in *New Yorker*, 14 Mar. 1983, p. 48

Fifteen hundred years ago Germanic-speaking tribes in north-western Europe intensified their raids and journeys of exploration 'abroad'. Their systems of speech went with them and the local parcels of speech emerged in due course in new localities in broadly differentiated forms. Great language blocs became established, each at a later stage unintelligible to the others, and these became known eventually as English, German, Dutch, Swedish, and so on. What started out in some Germanic tribes as **brauðam* /ˈbrɑuðəm/ ended up in English as *bread*, in German as *Brot*, in Dutch as *brood*, in Swedish and Danish as *bröd*, and so on, all superficially similar but in practice as different as finches, sparrows, and robins. Their syntactic patterns and their systems of accidence, with no restraining authority from any central source of power, formed new shapes and admitted new licences. The social and political worlds of the speakers of Friesianized, Scandinavianized, and Briticized 'Common Germanic'—not to speak of those who moved further afield like the Icelanders and the Goths who drifted to the Crimea—became themselves complex entities subject to further subdivision and to local differentiation. In other words Germanic turned out to be a fissiparous language.

In the seventeenth and eighteenth centuries, English-speaking groups of people went abroad in ships to navigate waters already known or partially known to them and to start a new process of colonization. Most of the territories to which they moved already had aboriginal inhabitants, less advanced in material ways than themselves. It was necessary to drive them back, or to assimilate them, or to arrive at some kind of compromise, politically, socially, and linguistically. These processes took their course. It was not foreseen that this was the beginning of a new process of severance.

The geographical dispersal of the speakers of a language, after a lapse of time, inevitably leads to the separation of local speech patterns from those of the mother country. The most powerful model of all is the dispersal of speakers of popular forms of Latin in various parts of western Europe and the emergence in the early Middle Ages of languages now known as French, Italian, Spanish, Portuguese, and of subdivisions (like Catalan) within these languages, none easily comprehensible to the others.

The political results of the dispersal of English speakers abroad are well known. So too are the linguistic results although these are not so easily measured or classified. There are no constitutional processes leading to declarations of linguistic independence as there are in politics. No flags are run up as signs or symbols of linguistic sovereignty. There are no governor-generals of language, and no linguistic Boston Tea Parties. Languages break free without ceremony, almost unnoticed by the speakers themselves except in unimportant and unsystematic ways. It took many decades for settlers (apart from a few individuals) to notice that the English they were using in their new surroundings was gradually drifting away from the home variety. A stage followed in which linguistic conservatives clung to an idealized form of the language brought from the mother country, and suffered degrees of inferiority about the novelties appearing in their own community.

The revolutionary language heroes asserting the legitimacy of independence tend to become heroes after their death rather than during their lifetime. For the dispersed forms of English the great names are those of Noah Webster and H. L. Mencken for the United States, and E. E. Morris and S. J. Baker for Australia and New Zealand. Elsewhere the combined effect of many publications—specialized local dictionaries like C. Pettman's *Dictionary of Africanderisms* (1913) in South Africa and W. J. Avis's *Dictionary of Canadianisms* (1967) in Canada, with all the ancillary steps needed for their preparation—can be traced, but crusaders of the importance of Webster, Mencken, Morris, and Baker are less easy to find.

English has also become a lingua franca to the point that any literate, educated person on the face of the globe is in a very real sense deprived if he does not know English. Poverty, famine, and disease are instantly recognized as the cruellest and least excusable forms of deprivation. Linguistic deprivation is a less easily noticed condition, but one nevertheless of great significance. Shortcomings in the learning of English as a foreign language will be returned to later in the chapter, as will the recently introduced concept of 'Nuclear English'.

The earliest explorers and settlers immediately encountered geographical features, and flora and fauna, for which they had no names. If an aboriginal name existed it was normally adopted, sometimes, but not always, in a modified form. The earliest such loanword in the American colonies was *skunk*, a rationalization of a word used in an American Indian language of the Algonquin family called Abenaki. Similarly the early New Zealand settlers accepted the Maori word *weta* /ˈwɛtə/ as the name for the 'large wingless longhorned grasshopper that bores wood at the grub stage', an insect living luxuriantly in the forest-covered islands of New Zealand; and Australian settlers adopted the Aboriginal word *galah* /gəˈlɑː/ for the rose-breasted greybacked cockatoo that they found in *Terra australis* in such abundance.

Encounters with the aboriginal inhabitants, that is with the peoples already resident in these new territories, brought many terms across the social, political, and anthropological barriers dividing the competing cultures. From the Eskimos in Labrador, for example, Newfoundlanders adopted words like *adikey* (an outer garment like a parka), *oo-isht* (command to a dog-team to pull ahead), *sina* (the edge of a floating field of ice), and *tabanask* (sledge with a flat bottom rather than with runners);[1] and from African languages settlers in South Africa acquired words like *indaba* (a meeting for discussion, a conference) and *rondavel* (a round tribal hut, usually with a thatched conical roof). Australians took from the Aborigines words like *alcheringa*, the mythological golden age when the first ancestors were created, and *corroboree*, a festive or warlike dance of the Aborigines.

In all the colonized territories some British linguistic features were retained while the same features changed in Britain. In other cases the reverse happened, that is a particular feature remained unchanged in Britain but underwent some kind of change in the colonies. It is worth dwelling on this phenomenon for a moment in order to dislodge an important myth, namely that in some specified respects American (or Canadian, or West Indian, etc.) English has 'greater purity' than British English because it retains a number of seventeenth-century ('Shakespearian' or 'Elizabethan') or eighteenth-century features now lost in Britain.[2] A few examples:

In words like *port* and *more* the medial and final *r* is still fully pronounced in the United States as it was in Elizabethan England but is silent in British Received Standard.

Got and *gotten* were in free variation in seventeenth-century English but have changed in function since (see p. 29 above).

Circa 1770 the words *dormitory* and *voluntary* had two main stresses in Britain and in the US. This double stress remains in American English but not in Britain (/ˈdɔːmɪtrɪ/, /ˈvɒləntrɪ/).

I guess in the sense 'I think' is common in Shakespeare, and is found even in Chaucer. It is still usual in the US but is used in Britain only as a conscious Americanism.

It is not difficult to identify elements that point in the opposite direction.

In the seventeenth century medial *-t-* was pronounced /t/. This is still the case in Britain but not so in the US where it is pronounced /d/: *petal, satin, set-up*, etc., are all pronounced with /t/ in Britain and /d/ in US standard speech.

Shall and *will*, as indicators of the future tense, were carefully distinguished in English in the seventeenth century. They still are in educated Received Standard but not in the US.

In the eighteenth century in both countries the words *leisure, pleasure*, and *treasure* could be pronounced, equally acceptably, with a short or long stem vowel (/ˈlɛʒ-/ or /ˈliːʒ-/ etc.). Both countries have settled for a short vowel in *pleasure* and *treasure*; but for *leisure* British English has /lɛʒ-/ and American English /liːʒ-/.

Also in the eighteenth century, words like *fertile* were pronounced acceptably either as /aɪ/ or /ɪ/ in the second syllable. The first of these pronunciations has survived in Britain but only the second in the United States.

In other words both varieties of English have drifted substantially from Elizabethan and Augustan English but in different ways.

The same considerations apply to all the other forms of overseas English, in Canada, the West Indies, Australia, and so on. From the earliest period of colonization in North America and until about 1820 the movement of vocabulary was almost all westward to America. Some American words are recorded in the dictionaries of Nathan Bailey and Samuel Johnson (see p. 36), for example, but the impression one receives is that these were grudgingly-admitted exotic words. Throughout the nineteenth century and continuing to the present day 'many a piece of driftwood' (Sir William Craigie's expression) has come back to Britain from America. As often as not such vocabulary is regarded by British people not so much as driftwood but rather as oil from a stranded oil-tanker, in other words with resentment and with overt, or at best half-concealed, anger.

Barbara Strang[3] observed that 'on the whole it is the less noticeably American Americanisms that are most readily assimilated [in Britain]'. This is undoubtedly true. One has only to think of *to take a back seat, to belittle, boarding-house, to cave in, governmental, law-abiding,* and *lengthy,* all of American origin but not now retaining any distinctively American flavour.

More markedly American are three classes of words listed by Sir William Craigie in 1927:

1. 'There are naturally terms which owe their origin to the fresh conditions and experiences of the new country', e.g. *backwoods, blizzard, bluff, canyon, dug-out, Indian-file, prairie, squatter.*

2. 'There are terms of politics and public activity', e.g. *carpet-bagger, caucus, gerrymander, indignation-meeting, lynch-law.*

3. 'There are words and phrases connected with business pursuits, trades, and manufactures', e.g. *cross-cut saw, elevator, snow-plow, to corner, to strike oil.*

And there are many classes of American words that remain firmly unborrowed in British English, though they are encountered often enough in fiction and in magazines like *Time, Newsweek,* and the *New Yorker,* for example *faucet* (tap), *to honeyfuggle* (to obtain by cheating or deception), *nabe* (neighbourhood), *scam* (a fraudulent scheme), *schlemiel* (a bungling or unlucky person), *to schlepp* (to carry, to drag) and numerous other words of Yiddish origin beginning with *sch-,* and *sockdolager* (something sensational or exceptional). This area of seemingly unborrowable words is much more extensive than is generally realized. Without them one cannot hope to understand the novels of modern American novelists like Bernard Malamud and Saul Bellow, or, for that matter the daily speech of Americans.

Also unfamiliar to most British people is the distinctive vocabulary of ethnic minorities in the United States, and in particular that of the Blacks and that of people of Hispanic origin.

In this small book it is impossible to summarize the very elaborate work on these matters by American scholars, and in particular that of J. L. Dillard on Black English. It must suffice to say that Black English is a separable, differentiated, fully structured spoken variety of English, not easily tied down to particular regions in the US, potently political in its animosity towards the structured patterns of Received American, colourful, animated, fancy, and subversive. If it is possible to see a variety of English as a threat to the acceptability of the language handed down to white Americans from the seventeenth century onward, this is it. Its dislocation of normal syntax, its patterned formulas showing disregard for the traditional shape of sentences make it at once deeply impressive and overtly threatening to currently agreed standards.

It is simple enough to illustrate the holes it makes in the standard American syntactical cobweb:

All my black brother (uninflected plural)
A novel base on (loss of final consonant in *based*)
He a Black bitch (absence of the verb 'to be')
God didn't make no two people alike (double negation)

These are not the casualties of an imperfect learning of standard American but a creolized form of English, shaped from a need to disdain the language of those to whom Blacks are opposed, and, at whatever distance, shaped by some undemonstrable ancestral memory of patterns of speech brought from Africa several generations earlier by African slaves. If Black English is contrasted with any of the regional forms of English it can only be judged to be a disadvantaged, maddeningly inadequate, variety. Judged by Labovian standards,[5] and seen in extended form (not merely as grammatical paradigms) in journals like *Black World* and in the anthologies of B. A. Botkin,[6] but much more on the streets of the great cities of America, it constitutes a stridently alternative form of American speech, biding its time, a language that is richly imagistic, inventive, and combative.

The Spanish element in American English is equally important. At a very early stage English-speaking Americans made contact with Spanish explorers and settlers in the Caribbean and in Texas. American cowboys adopted the terminology of the ranch from Mexican Spaniards. In the days of the gold-rush, from 1849 onward, those seeking gold were as often as not Spanish rather than English. Spanish-speaking Puerto Ricans also flocked from the Caribbean in search of work in America. Many others came from South America. From the prolonged contact of the two languages—some 20 million people in the United States now speak Spanish as their first language—many Spanish words have made their way into the mainstream of American English. Some have gone further and become part of international English (for example *alligator, avocado, banana, bonanza, cafeteria, canyon, lasso, macho, marijuana, patio, potato, ranch, rodeo,* and *tornado*). It is not easy to classify the currency in American English of Spanish loanwords but it is soon evident to a visitor that such words are more likely to be encountered in western and south-western states than along the eastern seaboard, for example words like *arroyo* (deep gully), *burro* (small donkey), *mesquite* (tree with bean-like pods), *peon* (poor labourer in Mexico), *quirt* (riding-whip), and *taco* (folded or rolled and filled tortilla), all common-place in cities like Dallas and Houston but less familiar in other parts of the United States.[7]

It cannot be over-emphasized that American English is not merely the variety, mostly drawn from regions along the eastern seaboard of the USA, that one encounters in the speech of the better-known presidents, congressmen, and entertainers whose names become household words throughout the world. American English, as taught to foreigners, is Boston-based, classless, recognizably but not radically different from British English except in pronunciation, and capable of analysis into a reasonably learnable number of phonemes and morphemes. But this clinically analysed form of speech is not spoken by the majority of Americans, as visitors to Miami, Tuscaloosa, Raleigh (North Carolina), Madison (Wisconsin), Chicago, and so on, quickly discover. Social and political forces enable one variety or another of a language to attain and retain supremacy for a period. The interaction of these forces, most of them ungovernable in the end, will generate new sets and subsets of admired speech as the decades proceed, and these will not necessarily be those of the white inhabitants of the eastern seaboard.

The dispersal of the English language in other regions, the West Indies, Canada, New Zealand, South Africa, and elsewhere, has led to the emergence of further distinctive types of English in these regions. But with relatively minor exceptions these versions of English have become distinctive without any major feedback to the mother country, and without any particular effect on the kind of English taught to foreigners.

The English of the West Indies, influenced and invigorated by other local languages, has had a certain influence on British English because of the migration of substantial numbers of West Indians to Great Britain in the last thirty years or so. The *calypso* and *reggae* music, along with the life-style of the Jamaican Rastafarians, *ganja* and all, now form part of ordinary British life. So too do some of the West Indian foods and their names. For example, salted codfish has long been a favoured dish in the West Indies and it turns up as an ingredient of *stamp-and-go*, a Jamaican codfish fritter, and as *salt-fish cake* or *salt-fish fritters* in Antigua and elsewhere. West Indian immigrants have brought the dish, and the words, with them to many of the major cities of Great Britain. Doubtless many other words have made their way to Brixton, Leicester, Birmingham, and elsewhere, in the language of other West Indian immigrants. And more will follow as the links between these Caribbean islands—positioned neither on one side of the Atlantic nor the other but powerfully influenced by both American and British English—and Great Britain become more and more complex.

Space should be found, however, for a brief account of the most striking of the forms of English spoken south of the Equator, namely Australian English.[8]

In the 1950s one of my colleagues at Christ Church, Oxford, J. I. M. Stewart, when asked what he remembered most about Australia—where he had been a Professor of English in Adelaide—replied 'the all-pervading smell of gum-trees'. Abel Tasman in 1642–3, William Dampier in 1668, and James Cook a century later, had the same experience. The word *gumtree* is perhaps the earliest word formed in Australia from existing English words.[9] In the two centuries since the settlement of Australia began— a convict colony was established at Sydney Cove, a little north of Botany Bay, in 1788—pioneers, convicts, whalers, sealers, Aborigines, drovers, musterers, sailors, soldiers, missionaries, explorers, bushrangers, and a host of other small groups, gradually brought into being new varieties of speech and writing that are superficially very similar to those of the land they left but underneath teeming with differences.

Somewhere along the line a distinctive set of Australian accents became discernible (not just one, though they are often taken by people in Britain to be one), and Australian words and attitudes helped towards the formation of a stereotyped Australianness. The elements of this Australianness are very diverse, but they include a ragged-trousered informality, a laconically expressed desire for independence, an irremovable parochialism, a prolific power to create both euphemisms and also expressions that go beyond normal profanity, and a deeply embedded suspicion of Poms (more recently frequently called 'whingeing Poms').

In Britain the Australian language tends to be judged through doubtless unrepresentative forms of it carried abroad. Except for Patrick White's work, Australian English is most likely to be encountered in Britain in the amiable twitterings of popular entertainers like Rolf Harris or of Barry Humphries (whether as Sir Les Patterson, Australian Cultural Attaché, or as Dame Edna Everage); or in the dialogue of cinema or TV films like *Gallipoli*, *Tenko*, *My Brilliant Career*, and *The Club*. The last-named contained many expressions that Englishmen would regard as typical Australian English:

The Tasmanians are so in-bred that their planes have square wheels and hair under their wings.

He was giving her a Wellington boot [a euphemism for sexual intercourse].

Richard West, who set down these remarks in the *Spectator* in 1982, also reported that a few years before he had heard an Australian in Saigon say: 'It's six weeks now since I exercised the armadillo', another decently reticent euphemism for copulation.

Australian English abounds in such euphemisms and circumlocutions. But the main segments of distinctively Australian English lie in two broad areas: first, the triple-layered social types of pronunciation, now generally called Educated (or Cultivated), General (that used by the mass of Australians), and Broad (poorly educated Australians, people in the more menial jobs); secondly, in the vocabulary used to represent distinctive aspects of life in Australia. Distinctively Australian vocabulary perhaps occupies about 7 per cent of the speech of Australians in their everyday life. Such words include some that have made their way into international English—for example, *boomerang, budgerigar, cobber, corroboree, didgeridoo, dingo, dinkum, koala, kookaburra, sheila, tucker, walkabout,* and *wallaby*—but many that are virtually unknown outside Australia—for example, *bardy* (edible wood-boring grub), *bindi-eye* (small herb with burr-like fruit), *bombora* (dangerous water above a hidden roof of rocks), *boobyalla* (variety of wattle), *currawong* (crow-like bird), *funnel-web spider, furphy* (false report or rumour), *gibber* (boulder), *humpy* (Aboriginal hut), *mallee* (eucalyptus-type scrub), *mopoke* (nightjar, a type of owl), *mulga* (scrubby acacia), *pademelon* (small wallaby), *rosella* (kind of parakeet), *waddy* (Aboriginal war-club), *woomera* (Aboriginal 'throwing-stick' by means of which a dart or spear is propelled). Australians often use a questioning (rising) tone when answering a question. 'Where do you come from?' 'Wollongong?' (meaning usually 'have you heard of it?, is it a place you approve of?'). Distinctive Australian syntactic patterns have not been detected so far and would be difficult to isolate and identify. Nor have Australian scholars so far managed to pin down their regional variations of vocabulary except in unimportant matters like the local names for certain winds and for various sizes of drinking glasses. Doubtless regional variation is a reality. The identification of its main elements awaits the attention of Departments of Linguistics in Australia.

The varieties of English spoken in the USA, Canada, Australia, New Zealand, the West Indies, South Africa, and other areas where English is spoken by native speakers would require a monograph, or more, for a proper description of them. But English is also the second language of millions of people in the world. And this set of Englishes, that is English learnt as a foreign language in virtually every foreign country in the world, needs to be examined as a separate phenomenon, or set of phenomena.

English as a lingua franca

It is a commonplace that English has become a lingua franca 'rating a greater world spread than any other language in recorded history'.[10] In virtually every country in the world foreigners are learning English to enable them to speak across frontiers in a language most likely to be understood by others. In practice, however, such learners soon discover that the learning of English is in part a process of putting out of mind their own language. As this is virtually impossible, the varieties of English spoken by Indians, Nigerians, Japanese, Russians, Germans, and so on, tend to be markedly different one from the other, however closely they are based on the two main learning models, American English and British English. Foreign sounds and unfamiliar constructions abound in any of these internationalized varieties of English.

It is not difficult to collect examples of unidiomatic English used by foreigners. Thus:

1. You can throw the cow over the fence some hay. [Polish American speaker]
2. We went to the London Tower [= Tower of London] and the Westminster Abbey, and walked the whole of the royal wedding route from the Buckingham Palace to the St. Paul Cathedral and along the river. Tomorrow we are going to the British Museum and the National Gallery. [Chinese speaker]
3. We'll go for a walk with the car (*or* the feet/a bicycle/a motor bike). [Greek speaker]

Example 2 comes from an experienced and fluent speaker of English and represents a rare departure from an otherwise convincing command of the language. Examples 1 and 3 come from more demotic sources. One can only conclude from them that the rules governing English word order, the use of the definite article, and the idiomatic use of the noun *walk*, were inadequately mastered by the people concerned. Or, to put it another way, that the rules of the native languages concerned were not sufficiently laid aside in the process of speaking these sentences. These examples go some way to underlining the silent adjustments[11] that foreigners need to make to become fully proficient in the speaking of English.

The compilers of ELT (English Language Teaching) dictionaries for foreign learners[12] go a long way towards meeting the difficulties of foreigners. For example, they make a clear distinction between countable (*ship/ships, sea/seas*) and uncountable (*croquet, furniture*) nouns; they include as many collocations as possible, that is they indicate with what other words a given word is frequently or customarily used; they include construction patterns for verbs; and they use a restricted defining vocabulary. These features are in principle of undoubted value.

In practice, however, many difficulties arise. A foreigner can never artificially 'forget' his own language. A speaker of a tone language, for example, does his best to forget the tonal system of his own language and master the set of substitute arrangements (especially homonyms) in English. A foreigner accustomed to grammatical gender tries to accommodate himself to the flexionless forms of English adjectives, and also to the pitfalls of certain attributive and predicative restrictions in their use. Those for whom the phonemes /l/ and /r/ are perceived as one phoneme try to adjust their articulatory organs in a quite remarkable manner when learning English. The verbal patterns of foreign, especially non-Indo-European, languages contrast so sharply with those of English that the learner virtually has no basis on which to build except a vague concept of 'verbness'.

In two main areas the best intentions of the compilers of learners' dictionaries tend to be thwarted by the complications of English. In the *Longman Dictionary of Contemporary English* (*LDCE*), for example, there are some 39 'big letters' giving 'information about the way a word works in a sentence'. Thus [A] is appended to adjectives and nouns that come in 'position one', before a noun (the *main* difficulty, a *trouser* leg); [B] to adjectives that can come in 'position one' or in 'positions three or four' as complements (a *happy* man, the man became *happy*, she made him *happy*). These letters ascend a scale of difficulty until [V] is applied with a following numeral to verbs that are followed by various kinds of direct object (I saw *the man leave* [V2]; I helped *him to clean the windows* [V3]; we looked at *the man jumping* [V4a]). The most complicated of all, for example types like [Wv6; X (to be) 1, 7, 9], go far beyond anything that can be carried in the mind. The principle is sound, but in the end the learners are left breathless and unhelped.

The use of a restricted defining vocabulary, that is one which is more restricted than that conventionally used in dictionaries for native speakers, tends to place unnecessary and sometimes absurd constraints on both the compilers and the learners.

1. Definitions become festooned with cross-references, for example '*electric blanket*: a BLANKET with electric wires passing through'.

2. Since many familiar words like *volcano* are excluded from the defining list, related words often need to use somewhat amusing circumlocutions, for example '*lava*: rock in a very hot liquid state [even though *molten* was available], flowing from an exploding mountain [*volcano* unavailable]'.

3. The defining list is in fact much less restricted than it claims to be. For example, it contains no numerals and these are therefore printed as arabic numerals ('Those 2 are the brace of thieves!'). The list also contains only root forms (*bush* but not *bushy*, *control* but not *uncontrollable*). Nevertheless derivatives are repeatedly used in definitions: *Afro* 'a hair-style for men and women in which the hair is shaped into a large round *bushy* mass'; *kleptomania* 'a disease of the mind causing an *uncontrollable* desire to steal'.[13]

4. Incongruities abound because of the restrictive rules. Thus because *hinged, sliding*, and *barrier*, are unavailable, a *door* is defined as 'a movable flat surface . . .'; and because *trench* is unavailable, a *moat* is defined as 'a long deep hole . . .'

Foreigners are not helped by such hand-tying devices. Nor is their linguistic deficit likely to be made good by the barren and banal illustrative examples set before them in the standard ELT dictionaries and grammars, sentences like:

The cold weather kept us indoors.
The weather in early December was bleak and unpleasant.
He clapped his son on the back.
We heard with joy that he had escaped injury.

A dictionaryful and a grammarful of such examples will always leave learners with an uncrossable linguistic chasm when they come to read the works of Iris Murdoch or Virginia Woolf, let alone the poems of T. S. Eliot or W. H. Auden, or when they encounter the speech of the streets and the marketplace.

Professor Randolph Quirk, plainly recognizing the problems arising from the multiplication of types of learnt English, and from the inadequacy of the speech of nearly all foreigners who try to learn English, recently suggested a new approach. He wants lexicographers and grammarians to adapt English so that it may 'constitute a nuclear medium for international use'. This 'Nuclear English'[14] would have to possess certain general properties. It must be decidedly easier and faster to learn than any variety of natural, 'full' English; communicatively adequate, and hence a satisfactory end-product of an educational system; and amenable to extension in the course of further learning, if and as required.

He goes on to say that 'the lexical and grammatical properties of Nuclear English must be a subset of the properties of natural English', in other words that it must be a carpentered section of idiomatic English, with the more difficult features of the language set aside. 'Culture-free as calculus, with no literary, aesthetic, or emotional aspirations, Nuclear English is correspondingly more free than the "national Englishes" of any suspicion that it smacks of linguistic imperialism.' Specific examples are given of the way in which the carpentering would be done to find 'appropriate nuclei in grammar'. For example, sentences of the type *We offered the girl a drink* (called 'ditransitives') would be replaced by 'the prepositional alternative' *We offered a drink to the girl.* The 'English tag question (so often in the English of Wales and of Southeast Asia replaced by the invariant *isn't it?* or *is it?*)' might be thought to be 'disproportionately burdensome, with its requirement of reversed polarity, supply of tensed operator and congruent subject:

I'm late, *aren't I?/am I not?*
She used to work here, *didn't she?*
They oughtn't to go there, *ought they?*'

and could be abandoned in favour of *isn't that right?*, or *is that so?*, however unidiomatic these may sound to native English speakers to begin with.

Quirk gives numerous other examples, and remarks that 'in none of these instances . . . does the "solution" lie in going beyond the rules of ordinary acceptable English'.[15]

It is most unlikely that any such form of prescriptively reduced English will be regarded as acceptable either by the foreigners themselves (except the merest beginners) or by ELT teachers. Foreigners cannot be reduced to one amorphous mass labelled 'non-English-speaking', 'not a native speaker of English'. Far more to the point would be the acceptance by the compilers of ELT materials that specific allowance needs to be made for the requirements of particular areas. Ideally each dictionary, grammar, and course book should be prepared in at least eight different versions for learners of English in the following regions:

Europe and South America (Germanic, Slavonic, Romance, etc., languages)
Northern India (Indo-Iranian: Hindi, Gujarati, etc.)
Southern India (Dravidian: Telugu, Tamil, Malayalam, etc.)

Middle East and N. Africa (Semitic, Hamitic)
Africa (Bantu, etc.)
Far East (Japanese, Korean, etc.)
China   .
Oceania (Polynesian, Melanesian, etc.)

More sophisticated versions for groups within the main regions will be needed as time goes on. Provision will also need to be made, of course, for the various levels of learning, for children, for university students, and for older people.

English, when first recorded in the eighth century, was already a fissiparous language. It will continue to divide and subdivide, and to exhibit a thousand different faces in the centuries ahead. At present American English, or rather that variety of it spoken by White Anglo-Saxon Protestants, is the dominant form numerically, though the Received Standard of British English remains the form admired and sought after by most foreigners. The multifarious forms of English spoken within the British Isles and by native speakers abroad will continue to reshape and restyle themselves in the future. And they will become more and more at variance with the emerging Englishes of Europe and of the rest of the world. The English language is like a fleet of juggernaut trucks that goes on regardless. No form of linguistic engineering and no amount of linguistic legislation will prevent the cycles of change that lie ahead. But English as it is spoken and written by native speakers looks like remaining a communicative force, however slightly or severely beyond the grasp of foreigners, and changed in whatever agreeable or disagreeable manner, for many centuries to come.

Notes

Chapter 1: Some Preliminary Considerations

1. *The Listener*, 12 August 1982, pp. 13-14.
2. 'Cette étude . . . nous l'appellerons la *Sémantique* . . . c'est-à-dire la science des significations'. M. Bréal in *Études Grecques en France* (1883), XVII. 133.
3. In this book I have used the terms 'Old English' and 'Anglo-Saxon' as synonyms when referring to the English language before the Conquest. When referring to the people, their possessions, manuscripts, etc., I have normally used only 'Anglo-Saxon'.
4. Some distinguished modern linguistic scholars believe that such etymological distinctions are unimportant in any context of synchronic homonymy: see, for example, John Lyons, *Semantics* (1977), II. 551. The reason given is that 'the native speaker is generally unaware of the etymology of the words that he uses'. Professor Lyons perhaps underestimates the readiness of an educated speaker of English to believe that such distinctions exist even though he is only dimly aware of the etymological facts. Naturally no one could confidently claim to have a working knowledge of all homonymous distinctions; equally no educated person is totally unaware of such distinctions.
5. For example: 'Having lost the thread of syntax, Britain is becoming a linguistic desolation'. Brigid Brophy in *London Review of Books*, 4-18 February 1982, p. 17.
6. I discuss the matter at some length in *The Spoken Language as an Art Form: an Autobiographical Approach* (English-Speaking Union, New York, 1981).

Chapter 2: From Runes to Printing

1. Modern scholars conventionally print thorn as þ (capital Þ) and ash as æ (capital Æ), but print wynn as w (capital W) in order to avoid the confusion of wynn and the Roman letter p. The Anglo-Saxons also developed the symbol eth (ð)—the first example of which is found in a second and altered copy of a charter dating in its original form from 700 or 715 (Charter 5 in Henry Sweet's *Oldest English Texts*)—as a form of the Carolingian letter *d* (at this period written ð). In Old English manuscripts thorn and eth did not have different phonetic

values but were used positionally (thorn being more common initially, and ð more common medially and in final position). Of the two letters only thorn survived as a widespread and usual form in the Middle English period. The Norman scribes gradually replaced wynn by u, uu, vv, and w itself. In the other Germanic languages thorn and eth had a different history and both survive to this day in modern Icelandic.

Old English scribes occasionally used the runes to represent the words *wynn* 'joy', *ēþel* 'home', *mann* 'man', and *dæg* 'day' in their manuscripts.

2. Future time was normally expressed by the present tense: *Ic arise, and ic fare to minum fæder, and ic secge him* (I will arise, and I will go to my father, and I will say to him). The verb *sculan* (3rd person present singular *sceal*) normally meant 'must', and the verb *willan* (3rd person present singular *wille*) usually expressed volition ('wish to'). Only rarely, and for the most part only in late Old English, were they drawn on to express simple futurity, though in view of later developments the position in Vulgar OE. must have been very different.

3. 'In OE. the learned form *latin* occurs occas.; the pop. repr. was *lǣden* Latin, language, ME. *leden* speech, utterance (OE. *bōclǣden* 'book. language' was spec. Latin)', *The Oxford Dictionary of English Etymology*.

4. Wurdon feolagan and wed-broþra ('they became fellows and sworn brothers', of King Edmund and King Canute), *Anglo-Saxon Chronicle* 1016.

5. Replacing the native word *ǣ*, a word probably doomed in any case because of its brevity (it would have become modern English *ee*!).

6. Perhaps only *-broid* from *broiden* 'interwoven', the ME. reflex of OE. *brogden*, past participle of OE. *bregdan* 'to braid, interweave'. This form is now perpetuated in *embroider* (earlier *embro(u)der* crossed with the obsolete verb *broid*), drawn originally from Anglo-Norman.

7. Much later loanwords from French retain the French /ʃ/, for example *charade* (adopted in the eighteenth century) and *chauffeur* (twentieth century).

8. The *OED* provides ample evidence of currency of each of the five words used (and by no means only in literary sources) to mean the animal itself as well as the flesh of the animal.

9. I suppose it is not in itself surprising that the impact of printing on the language was not clearly perceived at the time nor for a considerable time afterwards. Thomas Hobbes, for example, in his *Leviathan* (1651) remarked: 'The Invention of Printing, though ingenious, compared with the invention of Letters, is no great matter' (Part I, chapter iv).

Chapter 3: From William Caxton to George Washington: 1476 to 1776

1. Christopher Hill, *Intellectual Origins of the English Revolution* (1965; paperback 1980), p. 9.
2. A letter of 16 July 1557 by Cheke to Sir Thomas Hoby (Everyman edition of Hoby's translation of Castiglione's *Book of the Courtier* (1948), p. 7).
3. Caxton's *The Book of the Knight of the Tower* (EETS, 1971), p. 31.
4. Ibid. I am not arguing that throughout his work Caxton always uses the spellings taken from this randomly chosen passage. But it is broadly true that his spelling system is more fixed than that of medieval scribes of a slightly earlier period, and more fluid than that of printers from about 1800 onward.
5. The unetymological or 'erroneous' spelling *delight*, from ME. *delit*, from OF. *delit* (L. *delectare*), became established in the sixteenth century by analogy with *fight*, *light*, etc. The spelling *delite*, which would have represented the normal development, is retained in some passages of the Authorized Version.
6. Surviving only in the falsely archaic word *ye*, as in 'ye olde Englishe tea shoppe'. It should properly be pronounced as 'the'.
7. Detailed histories of the letters *i, j, u*, and *v*, as well as of other letters of our modern alphabet, are provided in the *OED*, set down at the beginning of each letter of the alphabet.
8. Convenient tabulations of the main changes can be found in Barbara M. H. Strang's *A History of English* (1970), p. 174, and in C. L. Wrenn's *The English Language* (1949), p. 92.
9. This and the related phenomena of '*r*-insertion' (i.e. the insertion of such an *r* when the next word begins with a vowel, e.g. *near us*), and of the 'intrusive *r*' (e.g. *law(r)-abiding*), are treated in some detail in J. C. Wells' *Accents of English* (1982), I. 222 ff.
10. The best description of the system is provided by P. Clemoes, *Liturgical Influence on Punctuation in Late Old English and Early Middle English MSS.* (1952).
11. *The Arte of Rhetorique* (1560), ed. G. H. Mair (1909), p. 163.
12. *Life of Caesar* (1579) in *Plutarch's Lives*, ed. G. Wyndham (1896), V. 41.
13. *History of Britain* (1670) in *The Works of John Milton*, Columbia edition (1932), X. 34.
14. *Sermons* (1622), ed. G. R. Potter and E. M. Simpson (1959), IV. 53.
15. A more detailed treatment of the development of English prose style is available in I. A. Gordon's *The Movement of English Prose* (1966). I am much indebted to Professor Gordon, not only for what he says in this book, but because I was once his pupil and later his colleague.

16. Luke 14: 34 (Tyndale, 1534).
17. Ld. Berners, *Froissart's Chroniques* (1523), I. ccx. 251.
18. Joshua 15: 47 (Authorized Version, 1611).
19. Blythe, *The English Improver Improved* (1649, in 1653 edn.), p. 9.
20. Milton, *Paradise Lost* (1667), x. 652.
21. Caxton, *Charles the Grete* (1485), p. 193.
22. Spenser, *Faerie Queene* (1590), I. xi. 29.
23. Fuller, *A Pisgah-Sight of Palestine* (1650), I. xiii. 41.
24. 1 Cor. 15: 57 (Tyndale, 1526).
25. O. Walker, *Greek and Roman History* (1693), II. 310.
26. The *OED* s.v. *To* B lists 36 uses of *to* before an infinitive.

Chapter 4: The Disjunctive Period: 1776 to the Present Day

1. Mary Hyde, *The Thrales of Streatham Park* (1977), p. 112.
2. *Proposal for Correcting, Improving & Ascertaining the English Tongue* (1712), p. 15.
3. See also p. 141 for another statement about the superiority of the received standard in London and the need for regional speakers to conform with it as far as possible.
4. *Literary Review* (1756), I. VI. 294/1.
5. *Critical Review* (1785), LX. Oct., p. 300.
6. *A History of English* (1970), p. 78.
7. Ibid., pp. 78-9.
8. *A History of Modern Colloquial English* (3rd edn., 1936), p. 284.
9. Ibid., p. 285.
10. Ibid., pp. 285-6.
11. Dates of first recorded use of some of the words in the range *Se* to *Z* must await the publication of the fourth and final volume of the *Supplement to the OED*.
12. Further examples in Julian Franklyn's *Dictionary of Rhyming Slang* (1960).
13. For example, *harum-scarum* (1674), *helter-skelter* (1593), *hoity-toity* (1668), *hurry-scurry* (1732), and *roister-doister* (1553).
14. On the whole subject of such formations see G. V. Smithers, 'Some English Ideophones', *Archivum Linguisticum* VI (1954), pp. 73-111. Earlier examples include *fiddle-faddle* (1577), *tittle-tattle* (1529), and *sing-song* (1609).
15. It could of course be a portmanteau word from *scroll* and *lollop* (verb).
16. Though curiously *the half-asleep boy*, *the fast-asleep boy*, etc., are acceptably idiomatic.
17. *New English Grammar* (1892), I. 66.

18. There are numerous other uses of *one*, and of other words, as prop-words: see Barbara Strang, *A History of English* (1970), pp. 96-7, R. Quirk *et al.*, *A Grammar of Contemporary English* (1972), pp. 49-50.
19. Op. cit., p. 76.
20. The example is Professor Quirk's.
21. *Were* must be used (i.e. *was* would be incorrect) in *as it were* (= so to speak). There is much variation in *If I were/was you*, but *If I were you* is the more usual.
22. *Wh* is used as a convenient abbreviation of *what*, *where*, *which*, *who*, and other pronouns and conjunctions beginning with *wh*.

Chapter 5: Literature, Ritualistic Works, and Language

1. A case has been made out for the presence of one or two elements of fairly informal Old English in the annal for 755 (actually 757) in the *Anglo-Saxon Chronicle* (the extract concerning Cynewulf and Cyne-heard in MS. Corpus Christi College, Cambridge 173)—for example, a delayed superlative (*ond radost*), an informal use of *hie* 'they' to refer to both (unspecified in context) sets of adversaries, and a change in mid-text from indirect to direct speech. If true it is a sparse record to build a theory on. See C. L. Wrenn in *History* XXV (1940), pp. 208-15.
2. Preface 'On the State of Learning in England' to his translation of the *Cura Pastoralis* of Gregory the Great.
3. Postcard, signed C.S.L., in my possession.
4. Lines 243-6 in the text as printed in J. A. W. Bennett and G. V. Smithers, *Early Middle English Verse and Prose* (1966), p. 75.
5. From nos. 17 and 44 in Norman Davis's selection (Clarendon Medieval and Tudor Series, 1958).
6. *Sir Gawain and the Green Knight* 35.
7. Poem 27 (?1537), lines 9-10, ed. E. Jones (1964).
8. Examples from Volume 3 of *A Supplement to the OED* (1982).
9. *The Trimmer's Opinion of the Laws and Government* (1700), edited by Walter Raleigh (1912), p. 53.
10. T. Sprat, *The History of the Royal-Society of London* (1667), published in facsimile with critical apparatus by J. I. Cope and H. W. Jones (1959), ii. xx. 113.
11. Page 10 in the first edition. See James R. Sutherland, *Restoration and Augustan Prose* (William Andrews Clark lecture, University of California, Los Angeles, 1956), p. 10.
12. *The Life and Opinions of Tristram Shandy* (World's Classics, 1903), book 2, chapter 12, p. 103.
13. Ibid., book 6, chapter 11, p. 391.

14. Ibid., book 5, chapter 43, p. 372.
15. Ibid.
16. To go beyond this statement into the realms of literary criticism and of stylistics is, of course, beyond the scope of this book. For those who wish to explore such matters further there are many guides. Those which are primarily linguistic include R. Quirk, *The Use of English* (1962), M. A. K. Halliday, *Patterns of Language* (1966), and S. Ullmann, *Language and Style* (1964). More literary works include R. Wellek and A. Warren, *The Theory of Literature* (1949), I. A. Gordon, *The Movement of English Prose* (1966), and W. Nowottny, *The Language Poets Use* (1962). Also, the numerous volumes in André Deutsch's Language Library on the language of individual writers, Chaucer, Caxton, Shakespeare, Swift, Jane Austen, Tennyson, Trollope, Dickens, Joyce, etc.
17. 'The Father incomprehensible, the Son incomprehensible, and the Holy Ghost incomprehensible.' The Athanasian Creed.
18. Popularly known as the 'Breeches Bible' from its rendering of Gen. 3: 7 ('they . . . made themselves *breeches*'; AV 'aprons').
19. My own views, especially about the replacement of the Book of Common Prayer by the Alternative Service Book, have been set down in *Encounter*, August 1982, pp. 75-9.
20. *Sunday Telegraph*, 16 December 1962, p. 7.
21. Including Kingsley Amis, Christopher Fry, Richard Gombrich, Marghanita Laski, Iris Murdoch, Dame Freya Stark, and Dame Rebecca West.
22. *No Alternative: The Prayer Book Controversy*, edited by David Martin and Peter Mullen (1982), p. vii.
23. A useful set of such parallel passages can be found in *The English Language: A Historical Reader*, edited by A. G. Rigg (1968).
24. Julian Critchley, MP, in *The Listener*, 16 December 1982, p. 20.

Chapter 6: The Recording of English in Dictionaries and Grammars

1. Inevitably much of the substance of the first half of this chapter is drawn from a classic study of the subject, D. T. Starnes and G. E. Noyes, *The English Dictionary from Cawdrey to Johnson, 1604-1755* (1946). The relationship of the early dictionaries and the sources they drew on have been re-examined in a series of brilliant articles by a German scholar, Professor Jürgen Schäfer, but the full results of his work await presentation in a monograph now being prepared for press. It seems clear that Latin-English dictionaries were less important as sources than Starnes and Noyes believed, and that entries in works like Thomas Speght's *Works of our Antient and Lerned Poet*

Geffrey Chaucer (1598), both those that were accurate and some that were not, were carried forward mechanically into later general English dictionaries.

2. Edited by A. L. Mayhew for the Early English Text Society (Extra Series 102, 1908). The manuscript from which Mayhew prepared his edition also contained other works: *Liber Catonis, Liber Equivocorum, Parvum Doctrinale* or *Liber de Parabolis Philosophiae, Liber Theodoli,* and *Liber Anioni,* the last consisting of fables in verse.

3. Edited by S. J. H. Herrtage for the Early English Text Society (Original Series 75, 1881).

4. J. Bullokar, *An English Expositor* (1616), preface 'To the Courteous Reader'.

5. For example, he said that *druids* 'took their name from Δρυς, an *Oake*, because they held nothing more holy than an Oak . . . or because they were wont to exercise their superstition in Oaken groves'. For the true etymology (an ancient Celtic word that made its way into English via Gaulish and French) see the *Oxford Dictionary of English Etymology.*

6. It is worth remembering that Plato's etymologies in his *Cratylus* are equally undisciplined and risible by modern standards. 'So he called the lord of this power Poseidon, regarding him as a foot-bond (ποσί-δεσμον). The *e* is inserted perhaps for euphony. But possibly that may not be right; possibly two lambdas were originally pronounced instead of the sigma, because the god knew (εἰδότος) many (πολλά) things. Or it may be that from his shaking he was called the Shaker (ὁ σείων), and the pi and delta are additions.' (Loeb edition, English translation by H. N. Fowler (1927), p. 71.)

7. Thus Bailey's entry (1730). That in Chambers's *Cyclopædia* (1728) is virtually identical.

8. For further comments on Johnson's *Dictionary* the reader may wish to consult James H. Sledd and Gwin J. Kolb, *Dr. Johnson's Dictionary: Essays in the Biography of a Book* (Chicago, 1955); and W. K. Wimsatt Jr., 'Johnson's Dictionary' in *New Light on Dr. Johnson: Essays on the Occasion of his 250th Birthday,* edited by Frederick W. Hilles (New Haven, 1959). A facsimile edition, with a Preface written by myself, was published by Times Books Ltd. in 1979.

9. It is possible, no doubt, that these wrongly-attributed examples were inserted by one of Johnson's amanuenses and were simply overlooked by Johnson himself.

10. The most accessible account of the rise and development of the historical principle in lexicography is the Introduction (first published in 1933) to the *Oxford English Dictionary.*

11. In fact the published version was an amalgam of two papers read by

Trench at meetings of the Philological Society in London on 5 and 19 November 1857.

12. *Caught in the Web of Words* (1977). See also Hans Aarsleff, *The Study of Language in England, 1780–1860* (1967).

13. The best-known examples are: *Deutsches Wörterbuch*, edited by Jacob and Wilhelm Grimm *et al.* (1854–1960); *Woordenboek der Nederlandsche Taal*, edited by M. de Vries *et al.* (1864–   ); *Svenska Akademien Ordbok*, edited by C. W. K. Gleerup *et al.* (1898–   ).

14. H. Sweet, *A New English Grammar* (1891–8); O. Jespersen, *A Modern English Grammar on Historical Principles*, I–VII (1909–49); E. Kruisinga, *A Handbook of Present-Day English* (1931–2); H. Poutsma, *A Grammar of Late Modern English* (1926–9); F. Th. Visser, *An Historical Syntax of the English Language*, Parts I–III (4 volumes, 1963–73).

15. John Brinsley, *Lvdvs Literarivs: or, The Grammar Schoole* (1612).

16. *The English Grammar*. Made by Ben. Iohnson. 1640. (Scolar Press facsimile reprint, 1972.)

17. James Greenwood, *An Essay towards a Practical English Grammar* (3rd edn., 1729), Preface, p. 38.

18. Ibid., p. 39.

19. Preface, p. i.

20. Ibid., p. 26.

21. Ibid., pp. 127–8.

22. pp. vi–vii.

23. Ibid., p. viii.

24. Appendix, p. 239.

25. Especially in his *Syntactic Structures* (1957) and *Aspects of the Theory of Syntax* (1965).

Chapter 7: Vocabulary

1. See especially Hans Marchand, *The Categories and Types of Present-Day English Word-Formation* (1960; 2nd edn., 1969), the standard work on the subject.

2. The element *-ship*, denoting a state or condition, as in *friendship*, *scholarship*, *workmanship*, etc., is unconnected.

3. The arbitrariness of the connection of sound and meaning, except in onomatopoeic and symbolically expressive words, is regarded as axiomatic by linguistic scholars, but is less than obvious to most other people. The whole subject of phonaesthetic associations has been much discussed in recent years: see, for example, M. L. Samuels, *Linguistic Evolution* (1972), pp. 45–8.

4. Early variants include *cormogeon*, *curmuggion*, and *curre-megient*.

5. A Romany word. Variants include *didakai, -kei, diddekai, diddicoy, didekei, -ki, -kie,* and *-ky.*
6. See *OED* and Supplement s.v. *curfuffle, gefuffle, kerfuffle,* and *kurfuffle.*
7. Variants include *smitchin, smidgeon,* and *smidgin.*
8. Thus, for example, 'The word "homosexual" . . . is certainly a monster in the technical, mythological sense (the sense in which Wilde called hermaphrodites monsters) inasmuch as it consists of a Greek head on a Latin torso. It has, however, the merit not only of familiarity but of comprehensibility'. Brigid Brophy in *London Review of Books,* 21 April–4 May 1983, p. 8.
9. Ibid., p. 42. David Lodge wrote about the language of this book in an essay called 'Where It's At: California Language', in *The State of the Language,* edited by Leonard Michaels and Christopher Ricks (1980), pp. 503–13.
10. Since 1976 published monthly from September to May in Glassboro, New Jersey.
11. Penelope Gilliatt, interviewed in *Quarto,* Jan./Feb. 1982, p. 7.
12. Cr. L. *chelidonia,* OF. *messager,* OE. *nihtegale*; Anglo-Lat. *pagina,* L. *phāsiānus,* L. *tyrannus*; L. *sonus,* OF. *son*; late L. *asphodelus.*
13. *Letters,* ed. by M. Amory (1980), p. 228.
14. A comparison drawn from Virginia Woolf (*To the Lighthouse* (1927), Part I, chapter 9).
15. It is well known that colour words are difficult to render into other languages because, as John Lyons remarks (*Semantics* (1977), I. 246), 'the denotational boundaries between roughly equivalent colour terms in different languages are often incongruent'. Some languages have very few colour items, while English, and most European languages have up to eleven. Ancient European languages (Anglo-Saxon, Greek, etc.) are far less specific about colour than modern ones, but this is a different matter. Modern fashion colours (clothes, motor vehicles, etc.) form a virtually limitless class.
16. It is obvious, however, that *groupings* of numbers have not remained stable. The Anglo-Saxons counted in sixties rather than in hundreds; and binary digital systems (rather than decimal ones) are central to an understanding of computer programming. Ordinal numerals have also stepped out of line for special reasons, especially *second* (the Anglo-Saxons used the ancestor of *other*). And large numbers, for example, *billion,* and the names of SI units, have had an other than straightforward history.
17. Recommended books on the subject include Stephen Ullmann, *The Principles of Semantics* (1951), C. S. Lewis, *Studies in Words* (1968), and Geoffrey Leech, *Semantics* (1974).
18. A made-up example: none is given in Webster's Third.

19. 'The Structure of a Semantic Theory', *Language* XXXIX (1963), pp. 170-210.
20. The presentation of their views here is necessarily cryptic. Readers are urged to look out the original.
21. This sense was not treated by Katz and Fodor, as it first appeared (in Vol. I, 1972, of *A Supplement to the OED*) after the publication of their work.
22. Geoffrey Leech, op. cit., p. 20.
23. The collocations are mostly drawn from Webster's Third, not from Leech (whose list is unconvincing). John Lyons (*Semantics* (1977), I. 261-2) points out that adjectives like *good* and *bad* can be used in collocation with almost any noun. On the other hand an adjective like *rancid* may be used of butter and of virtually nothing else.
24. *On Certainty*, para. 61.
25. Among the most ambitious and authoritative textbooks of modern semantics is John Lyons's *Semantics* (1977, 2 volumes). Of the utmost value for professional linguists, it is not aimed at nor suitable for the general reader.
26. *The Listener*, 13 Jan. 1983, p. 10.
27. *Letters*, edited by Nigel Nicolson, VI (1980), p. 4.
28. The reluctance is far from total, of course. A fairly thorough survey of early comments on dialectal features, including those of Trevisa (1387), Caxton (1490), George Puttenham (1589), Edmund Coote (1597), and others, is provided by Martyn F. Wakelin, *English Dialects: An Introduction* (1972), pp. 34-63.
29. The examples are drawn from M. F. Wakelin's book, p. 53.
30. By W. Viereck, E. Sivertsen, and P. Trudgill respectively.
31. *The Times*, 23 Feb. 1983, p. 12.
32. This section is adapted from a broadcast talk that I gave on BBC Radio 3 in July 1982. The text was printed in *The Listener*, 29 July 1982, pp. 12-13, and in *The Third Dimension*, edited by Philip French (1983).
33. There are signs that public school slang is possibly a dying species. The older terms, once more or less rigidly restricted to particular schools, are no longer in use, and the present generation of public schoolboys seem to fall back more and more on the same-sex, same-age slang of their own generation in all parts of the country.
34. Letter to Lady Ottoline Morrell, 26 December 1936 (*Letters*, edited by Nigel Nicolson, VI (1980), p. 96).

Chapter 8: Pronunciation and Spelling

1. This chapter is adapted from a review-article that I wrote for the *Times Literary Supplement*, 20 August 1982, p. 900.

2. Numerous other examples of changes brought about by the Mitford factor (though not called that there) are provided in my book *The Spoken Word: a BBC Guide* (1981), pp. 9–16.

3. The concept of 'phonological space' was introduced by William G. Moulton in *Word* XVIII (1962), p. 23. It has far-reaching implications. It is obvious that any disturbance of the 'space' occupied by one phoneme is likely to have knock-on effects on related phonemes. Differentiation of the radical phonemes of a language is permanently necessary. Any crevice, gap, or hole in the phonetic system left by partial or total movement of any member of it will be instantly filled by a neighbouring phoneme. Any diminution of the space occupied by phoneme A because of the invasion of its zone by a neighbouring phoneme B will cause phoneme A to move into the space of phoneme C, and so on.

4. As a curious aspect of the problem of identifying words in a variety of speech not one's own, these three words in a dialect using a glottal stop for final /k/, /p/, or /t/ would be pronounced the same, /pɪʔ/. Expressed like that it would seem to introduce the risk of intolerable ambiguity, but the contextual meaning normally prevents misunderstanding even in such multiple cases of homophony.

5. Taken, for convenience, from the best book on the subject, D. G. Scragg's *History of English Spelling* (1974), p. 55. Another useful book is G. H. Vallins, *Spelling* (1954).

6. From D. G. Scragg, op. cit., p. 54.

7. It would not be a difficult exercise for British people to become accustomed to final *-or* in all the relevant words (*honour/honor, labour/labor*, etc.), or for Americans to become used to *-our*. Similarly it should be possible to come to an agreement about the spelling of such words as *marvellous/marvelous*, *travelling/traveling*, and *kidnapped/kidnaped* (the British forms given first in each case). More difficult (it seems to me) would be the resolution of *oe/e* in *oesophagus/esophagus*, etc., *ae/e* in *aesthetic/esthetic*, etc., and *ph/f* in *sulphur/sulfur*, etc. But a 'trade-off', if it could be achieved, in such relatively minor areas of spelling would help to bring the written forms of British and American English much closer together. In 1968 Dr Philip Gove (editor of *Webster's Third New International Dictionary*) and I lightheartedly discussed the possibility of making an approach along these lines to our respective governments but it came to nothing in the end.

Chapter 9: The Syntactical Arrangement of Words

1. In practice linguistic conservatives tend to restrict the apostrophe to names of persons only (*the edge of the water*, not *the water's edge*) but wide variation is permissible.

2. NP = Noun Phrase; VP = Verb Phrase.
3. T = the; N = noun.

Chapter 10: Dispersed Forms of English

1. See the *Dictionary of Newfoundland English*, ed. G. M. Story *et al.* (1982).
2. American English is treated in many standard works, among them R. I. McDavid's abridgement of H. L. Mencken's *American Language* (4th edn., and two Supplements), published in 1963 or, even better, in the three volumes of Mencken's work itself; A. H. Marckwardt's *American English*, revised by J. L. Dillard (1980); and *Language in the USA*, edited by Charles A. Ferguson and Shirley Brice Heath (1981).
3. *A History of English* (1970), p. 38.
4. Tract of the Society for Pure English 27, pp. 208–9.
5. William Labov, *The Social Stratification of English in New York City* (1965).
6. *A Treasury of American Folklore* (1944); *A Treasury of Mississippi Folklore* (1955); *A Treasury of Southern Folklore* (1964).
7. An account of the languages of the Hispanos in the United States is printed in a special number of *Word*, vol. 33, nos. 1–2 (Apr.–Aug. 1982).
8. For a proper understanding of Australian English it is essential to turn to standard books on the subject. General accounts of the Australian language include S. J. Baker, *The Australian Language* (1945; 2nd edn., 1966) and G. W. Turner, *The English Language in Australia and New Zealand* (1966). The best general account of Australian pronunciation is to be found in A. G. Mitchell, *The Pronunciation of English in Australia* (1946; rev. edn., 1965). Australian dictionaries include E. E. Morris, *Austral English* (1898), *The Australian Pocket Oxford Dictionary* (2nd edn., 1984), and, especially, *The Macquarie Dictionary* (1981).
9. G. W. Turner, op. cit., pp. 2–3.
10. Randolph Quirk, *Style and Communication in the English Language* (1982), p. 37.
11. Ludwig Wittgenstein spoke about such 'silent adjustments' in his *Tractatus Logico-Philosophicus* (1922), para. 4.002: 'Man possesses the capacity of constructing languages, in which every sense can be expressed, without having an idea how and what each word means— just as one speaks without knowing how the single sounds are produced. Colloquial language is a part of the human organism and is not less complicated than it . . . The silent adjustments to understand colloquial language are enormously complicated.'

12. The two most important are *The Oxford Advanced Learner's Dictionary of Current English*, edited by A. S. Hornby and others (first edition, called an *Idiomatic and Syntactic English Dictionary*, 1942; UK editions 1948 onward), and the *Longman Dictionary of Contemporary English* (1978).

13. Both examples from *LDCE*.

14. 'The Concept of Nuclear English', in his *Style and Communication in the English Language* (1982), p. 43.

15. Ibid., p. 45.

Bibliography

Many of the books mentioned below exist in later editions than the ones specified. The dates given are normally those of first publication.

Of earlier books on the history of the English language the most instructive are Henry Bradley, *The Making of English* (1904), O. Jespersen, *Growth and Structure of the English Language* (1905), and Logan Pearsall Smith, *The English Language* (1912). Each has been revised at intervals. More recent brief surveys of the language include C. L. Wrenn, *The English Language* (1949), S. Potter, *Our Language* (1950), and G. L. Brook, *A History of the English Language* (1958).

Of longer books, H. C. Wyld, *A Short History of English* (1914) and the same author's *A History of Modern Colloquial English* (3rd edn., 1936) are still standard works in most respects. But they have tended to be replaced by A. C. Baugh, *A History of the English Language* (1935), and especially by the best book of its kind, B. M. H. Strang, *A History of English* (1970).

For readers of German, K. Brunner, *Die englische Sprache* (2 vols., 1950) provides an immense amount of detail. M. Görlach's two smaller books, *Einführung in die englische Sprache* (1974) and *Einführung ins Frühneuenglische* (1978), are both valuable surveys.

There are numerous books on American English: a selection is given in note 2 for Chapter 10.

An excellent description of many aspects of English (Standard English, literary English, etc.) is available in R. Quirk, *The Use of English* (1962).

Grammar. Several European scholars, especially O. Jespersen, E. Kruisinga, H. Poutsma, and F. Th. Visser, have produced large historical grammars of English (see note 14 for Chapter 6 for details). H. Sweet, *A New English Grammar* (1891-8) is still valuable, as are three later, relatively small books, C. T. Onions, *An Advanced English Syntax* (6th edn., 1932), O. Jespersen, *Essentials of English Grammar* (1933), and R. W. Zandvoort, *A Handbook of English Grammar* (1957).

I. Michael, *English Grammatical Categories and the Tradition to 1800* (1970) is a detailed survey of the treatment of English grammar from Ben Jonson (1640) to 1800.

Of modern grammars the standard work, towering above all others, is R. Quirk *et al.*, *A Grammar of Contemporary English* (1972). An abridged form of the same book is entitled *A University Grammar of English* (1973). These are not easy books for the general reader, however, who may wish to turn to G. Leech and J. Svartvik, *A Communicative Grammar of English* (1975) or G. Leech *et al.*, *English Grammar for Today* (1982).

For points of usage H. W. Fowler, *A Dictionary of Modern English Usage* (2nd edn., revised by Sir Ernest Gowers, 1965) is still supreme. Smaller works include E. S. C. Weiner, *The Oxford Miniguide to English Usage* (1983) and the present writer's *The Spoken Word: A BBC Guide* (1981).

Pronunciation. The best pioneering books were by Daniel Jones: *The Pronunciation of English* (1909), *An English Pronouncing Dictionary* (1917), and *An Outline of English Phonetics* (1918). They have all been revised many times. The *English Pronouncing Dictionary* in its fourteenth edition (1977), revised by A. C. Gimson, is the standard dictionary of pronunciation in Britain. A. C. Gimson, *An Introduction to the Pronunciation of English* (3rd edn., 1980) is the standard short British work on the subject. It has been joined by a much larger scholarly work. J. C. Wells, *Accents of English* (3 vols., 1982), which deals with English in overseas countries as well as in Britain. Scholars will also find much of interest in N. Chomsky and M. Halle, *The Sound Pattern of English* (1968).

For the pronunciation of British place-names the standard work is the *BBC Pronouncing Dictionary of British Names* (2nd edn., 1983), edited by G. E. Pointon.

Dictionaries. All English dictionaries depend heavily on the twelve-volume *Oxford English Dictionary* (1884-1928) and *A Supplement to the Oxford English Dictionary* (Vol. 1, A-G, 1972; Vol. 2, H-N, 1976; Vol. 3, O-Scz, 1982; Vol. 4, Se-Z, forthcoming). Of smaller dictionaries in Britain, *The Concise Oxford Dictionary* (7th edn., 1982) is the standard work, though dictionaries of similar size published by Collins, Longmans, and Chambers are also very popular. For American English, *Webster's Third New International Dictionary* (1961) and its derivatives, especially *Webster's Collegiate Dictionary* (9th edn., 1983), are invaluable. Other widely-used American dictionaries include the *American Heritage Dictionary*, the *Random House Dictionary*, and *Webster's New World Dictionary*, all of which have also been published in smaller versions. A short description of English dictionaries published before 1955 is to be found in J. R. Hulbert, *Dictionaries British and American* (1955).

For etymology there are three widely-used works: C. T. Onions *et al.*, *The Oxford Dictionary of English Etymology* (1966), E. Klein, *Comprehensive Etymological Dictionary of the English Language* (2 vols., 1966), and E. Partridge, *Origins* (1958).

The standard English thesaurus (list of words arranged according to their meanings) is *Roget's Thesaurus* (1852, current edition 1982).

The standard dictionaries for foreigners learning English are *The Oxford Advanced Learner's Dictionary of Current English*, edited by A. S. Hornby *et al.* (3rd edn., 1974), and the *Longman Dictionary of*

Contemporary English, edited by P. Procter *et al.* (1978). Also useful for learners of English is A. P. Cowie *et al.*, *Oxford Dictionary of Current Idiomatic English* (2 vols., 1975, 1983).

General. Books routinely consulted by scholars include E. Sapir, *Language* (1921), O. Jespersen, *Language: its Nature, Development and Origin* (1922), L. Bloomfield, *Language* (1933), A. Martinet, *A Functional View of Language* (1962), and F. de Saussure, *Cours de Linguistique Générale* (5th edn., 1955). Details of several standard works on stylistics are provided in note 16 for Chapter 5. The volumes on the language of individual writers (Chaucer, Caxton, etc.) in the Language Library series published by André Deutsch are particularly useful.

On linguistic change, M. L. Samuels, *Linguistic Evolution with Special Reference to English* (1972) is recommended. A larger valuable, but difficult, book is J. Lyons, *Semantics* (2 vols., 1977). See also note 17 for Chapter 7.

Index